GOETHE'S FAUST

GOETHE'S FAUST

A LITERARY ANALYSIS

STUART ATKINS

HARVARD UNIVERSITY PRESS

Cambridge, Massachusetts

1958

Published in Great Britain by Oxford University Press, London

Printed in Great Britain

PREFACE

Information about an author often facilitates appreciation of his works, but sometimes there is so much of it that it cannot be effectively utilized in the critical interpretation of a single text. So, it seems to me, is the case with Goethe's *Faust*. Generous, if not indiscriminate, adduction of information about Goethe's life and world-outlook, about thematic correspondences between *Faust* and other works of his, and about the order of composition of the parts of *Faust*, has tended to prevent a sharp focusing of attention on the text itself. For this reason I here examine Goethe's best-known poetic work without adducing information of the sort just described.

Although *Faust* may properly be regarded as the work of a whole lifetime and can accordingly be read as the basis for a discussion of Goethe's moral and artistic development, it is also, I believe, a great dramatic poem, even a great poetic drama, in its own right. To say this is not to deny its incidental importance as a part of the total human achievement for which the name of Goethe has come to stand. Those who know that Goethe was something more than a great poet may consider it heresy to treat *Faust* for its own sake rather than for Goethe's. But if they remember that the reputation of Goethe's greatness is originally founded on his literary achievement, they will, it is certain, admit the justice of offering the mid-twentieth-century English reader an interpretative reading of that work of Goethe's which he is most likely to wish to read and most likely to find available in translation or bilingual edition. That intelligent discussion of Goethe's *Faust* is possible without extensive reference to the larger context of Goethe's life and works has been brilliantly demonstrated by such an excellent critic as G. A. Borgese, whose *Saggio sul "Faust"* (Milan, 1933) has unfortunately never been made available in English. C. Roos has also insisted on the necessity of evaluating *Faust* in strictly aesthetic terms, although his illuminating *Faustproblemer* (Copenhagen, 1941) represents an attempt to achieve that ideal indirectly rather than directly, inasmuch as a good part of this study is a cogent repudiation, based on evidence from a wide range of Goethe's writings, of various theories about the order of composition of parts of *Faust*—theories which have been used to explain away, rather than to explain, difficulties in the text. Most recently, in

Goethe's Faust: An Interpretation (Oxford, 1957), Alexander Gillies begins with the reasonable premise that *Faust* is indeed a tragedy; yet his allegorical reading of many episodes seems to me irreconcilable with this premise, with his own straightforward, almost realistic, analysis of much of the action of *Faust*—and with Goethe's known views on the proper place and function of Allegory.

It would be unwise to forget, however, that an escape from the Scylla of literary personalia might merely lead to the Charybdis of aesthetic subjectivism which Roos and Borgese actually avoid—to an emphasis on the self-sufficient uniqueness of *Faust* tantamount to a denial of the right to evaluate it by the standards also applicable to other great works of literature. It is, thus, surely still necessary to examine *Faust, A Tragedy* with reference to some larger context than itself (or even than that represented by the life and works of its author), if the vicious circle of self-definition is to be avoided. The most suitable frame of reference is, I think, the double context suggested, or even demanded, by the title of the play itself: the traditions of Western thought already definitely associated with the figure of Faust in the mind of Goethe and of the public for which he first wrote, and the larger group of traditions of European literature which relate to the concept of Tragedy. In my interpretation of *Faust* these two groups of traditions are, then, used for purposes of orientation. But since this is neither a study in the history of ideas nor an essay in comparative literature, they are not treated for their own sakes, but because they form the background against which Goethe's poem, given its legendary hero and its literary form, demands to be examined. What is said in *Faust*, and what the technique of its saying contributes to *Faust*'s effectiveness as a poetic statement, are the only themes of the following pages.

My reading of *Faust* has convinced me that it is basically a drama of character, and not, as has too long been assumed, an unhappy mixture of character drama and allegorical pageantry. In order to counter certain assumptions which underlie most criticism of *Faust*, I have found it necessary to analyze the dramatic action—to supply, as it were, an extended "argument of the play"—in terms of its dramatic characters. The result is an analysis which follows the order of events in the text more closely than it would have, had I been able to take for granted that the action of *Faust* (as opposed to what has been said to be its action) and certain other textual details were already clear to my readers. In treating the more familiar First Part of *Faust*, I have emphasized those aspects of it which have been most frequently neglected or misunderstood by previous critics, although

certain apparently obvious points and passages are dwelt upon at
some length because their full relevance is to be brought out in my
discussion, perforce more detailed, of Part II. If all quotations from
Faust are given in my own translation, it is because it seemed desirable
to avail myself of the greater accuracy which a translator not bound
by the necessity of avoiding infelicitous repetitions may often attain;
the line numbers in the margins permit the reader with the German
text to locate any quotation in its full context quickly and conveniently, and so verify both the translation and the propriety with which
the quotation is used. In translating, I have, when necessary, sacrificed
rhyme to rhythm—the rhythm of the German text—and both to
sense, so that I hope the reader of German will forgive the absence of
German quotations that would have required a much less economical
form of exposition than that actually represented by this literary
analysis of *Faust*.

My argumentation and documentation are, I believe, thus sufficiently complete to substantiate my interpretation of Goethe's text;
what might be deemed negative argumentation, my reasons for
differing with earlier critics, should be apparent from the textual
evidence adduced. I have, however, set forth my reasons for rejecting
certain traditional views on the scenes of *Faust* that precede Part II
of the Tragedy, scenes on the whole long satisfactorily interpreted, in
"A Reconsideration of Some Unappreciated Aspects of the Prologues and Early Scenes in Goethe's *Faust*," "The Prologues to
Goethe's *Faust*, and the Question of Unity: A Partial Reply," and
"A Reconsideration of Some Misunderstood Passages in the
'Gretchen Tragedy' of Goethe's *Faust*" (*Modern Language Review*,
XLVII, 362–373, XLVIII, 193–194 and 421–434). In my "Some
Lexicographical Notes on Goethe's *Faust*" (*Mod. Lang. Quarterly*,
XIV, 82–97) is brought the historical evidence for my readings of about
100 obscure or frequently misread passages. My reasons for rejecting
certain previous interpretations of details of *Faust II* or for empha-
sizing certain formal elements previously neglected, are offered in
"The Visions of Leda and the Swan in Goethe's *Faust*" (*Mod. Lang.
Notes*, LXVIII, 340–344), "The Mothers, the Phorcides and the
Cabiri in Goethe's *Faust*" (*Monatshefte*, LXV, 289–296), "Goethe,
Calderon, and *Faust: Der Tragödie zweiter Teil*" (*Germanic Rev.*,
XXVIII, 83–98), "Goethe, Aristophanes, and the Classical Walpur-
gisnight" (*Comparative Literature*, VI, 64–78), and "Irony and
Ambiguity in the Final Scene of Goethe's *Faust*" (in *On Romanticism
and the Art of Translation*, ed. G. F. Merkel, Princeton: Princeton
University Press, 1956, pp. 7–28). In several of these essays, and in

"The Evaluation of Romanticism in Goethe's *Faust*" (*Journal of English and Germanic Philology*, LIV, 9–38), I have offered evidence from Goethe's other writings that seems to confirm the rightness of my reading of *Faust*.[1]

Criticism of *Faust* is so extensive that it would be impossible for me to acknowledge here my indebtedness to predecessors; the notes and references in the above-mentioned articles must therefore suffice as my expression of gratitude to other Goethe scholars, to which I here add my thanks to Professor Victor Lange of Princeton University for the many helpful criticisms he made of the long manuscript I originally submitted to the Harvard University Press. In addition, I am much indebted to my colleague, Professor Howard Mumford Jones, for his reading of that manuscript; his general approval of it, no less than his concrete suggestions for shortening it, encouraged me greatly during the preparation of this book's present form, as did the comments of Dr. Thomas J. Wilson, Director of the Harvard University Press, during its final revision. Most of all, however, I am profoundly obligated to the severe but modest critic who has read and reread my manuscript a dozen times; to her is dedicated this latest, but surely not last, interpretation of Goethe's *Faust*.

S. P. A.

Cambridge, Massachusetts

[1] Some verbal echoes of the Bible to which I draw attention are no longer felt as such by modern German readers; that they were still "biblical allusions" in Goethe's day is clear, however, both from the Grimms' historical dictionary of the German language and from the notes in nineteenth-century *Faust* commentaries. Similarly, certain expressions now felt to be figurative, perhaps because of the currency they gained through *Faust*, still had their literal value when *Faust* was written.

CONTENTS

The Second Part of the Tragedy

GOETHE'S FAUST

CHAPTER I

The Fame of Goethe's Faust

Although completed in 1831, *Faust* had long before been acclaimed as Goethe's masterpiece and even as *the* representative work of German literature. By the middle of the 1770's private readings of scenes, parts of scenes, and series of scenes later incorporated into the First Part of the Tragedy had won the drama, often through hearsay, enthusiastic admirers. In 1790 Goethe published as *Faust, A Fragment*, the larger part of these scenes, variously revised, together with two new scenes written in the late 1780's. *Faust I*—"Dedication," "Prelude on the Stage," "Prologue in Heaven," and what was clearly labeled "The First Part of the Tragedy"—at last appeared in 1808, to be immediately acknowledged at home and abroad as a work of highest genius. Incorporating more than once again as much material as the *Fragment*, this definitive *Faust I* differs considerably in style and tone from the early manuscript, and radically from it and the *Fragment* in the function assigned to certain scenes and passages. Sections of *Faust II*—much of its first act and all of its third—were printed in 1827 and 1828; they appear, unchanged, in *Faust II* as published after Goethe's death in 1832.

Knowledge that *Faust* was gradually executed over the larger part of a long lifetime, and the independent success of *Faust I*, are the two factors which have militated most strongly against a convincing favorable critical interpretation of the play as a whole. Although the *Faust I* of 1808 announces that Faust is to obtain a broad view of human life after he leaves his scholar's study, and although it contains many passages that can only be considered irrelevant or, at best, tangential to its two main actions, Faust's repudiation of passive intellectualism and his disastrous relationship with Margarete were nevertheless sufficiently self-contained dramatic entities to permit its being read and performed as an independent drama. Generalizations about the meaning of *Faust* based primarily upon The First Part of the Tragedy became established critical commonplaces long before *Faust II* appeared, and since these proved to be irreconcilable with a coherent interpretation of *Faust* as a whole, many subsequent critics chose to regard its Second Part as a sort of arbitrary sequel to *Faust I*, as a work of slightly less or of much less poetic value according to the degree of respect they had for Goethe's name.

Faust I was composed over a longer period of time than *Faust II*, over a longer period than that between its completion and that of *Faust II*, and so there is no extrinsic reason for considering the latter a mere appendix to the former. Most of *Faust I* was written after Goethe's fortieth year, but because about a third of it goes back to his mid-twenties many a critic has implied that it is a product of youthful fire and the Second Part a work, though one of genius, of a flagging creative spirit. As the history of the text demonstrates, *Faust I* is primarily the compositional achievement of a writer well into his fifties, and *Faust II* was completed barely more than two decades later. Thus, *Faust* is the product of a period in its author's life when the rate of change of artistic and intellectual values is normally slightest. To regard it, as many interpreters have, as a sort of literary cathedral begun in the Romanesque style, continued in various forms of Gothic, and more or less completed in some subsequent architectural manner, is to forget that its sole architect is Goethe, whose whole maturity, artistic and personal, falls within one well-defined epoch in the history of European literary styles.

Though not in any narrow sense a German Romantic drama, *Faust* is a drama from the Age of Romanticism that with conscious catholicity of taste sought to perpetuate, revive, and disseminate simultaneously the poetic heritages of antiquity, the Middle Ages, the Renaissance, and the more recently discovered East. The mature Goethe's world outlook, however, was anything but typically romantic. Critics outside of Germany have frequently called him a romanticist, apparently considering the ruthlessness of the protagonist of *Faust* something represented as necessary or even desirable, perhaps simply misled by the external stylistic romanticism of the drama. German critics, on the other hand, aware of Goethe's unsympathetic attitude toward many of the manifestations of romanticism, have tended to disregard the frame of romantic

literary reference in which his *Faust* is best understood—and this despite the fact that many of them, imbued with ideas deriving ultimately from German Romanticism, have uncritically glorified Faust's ruthless vitality.

Unlike many of his famous romantic contemporaries, Goethe was openly hostile to metaphysical and theological speculation. "Germans," he declared to Eckermann, "are strange people. By their profound thoughts and ideas, which they look for everywhere and which they insert into everything, they burden their lives more than is proper . . . They come and ask what idea I have tried to embody in my *Faust*. As if I knew and could state it myself! . . . It would have been a fine thing indeed if I had wanted to string onto a single all-embracing idea a life so rich, so colorful, and so extremely diversified as that which I have represented in *Faust*." But the fame of *Faust* as a philosophical poem, firmly established by contemporary romantic interpretations of *Faust I*, has caused many readers of what was meant to be read as a play to seek in *Faust* only abstract speculative thought, to forget that in it ideas exist only insofar as they are part of the human experience of its only too human dramatic characters.

Faust is, of course, an expression of its author's world outlook, for life as represented poetically in it must ultimately be life as Goethe himself has seen, experienced, and interpreted it. This does not mean, however, that it preaches an explicit message. At the very time that Goethe was writing some of the passages in *Faust II* since frequently interpreted as quasi-didactic digressions, he also wrote a brief essay *On Didactic Poetry* in which he insisted that "all poetry should inform, though insensibly, and make man aware of what is important for him to inform himself of; the lesson has to be deduced as from life itself." It is in the sense of this statement, and in this sense only, that Goethe could make the often quoted claim that "poetry is a secular gospel." For two centuries critics have agreed that the greatness of a literary work must be determined without regard to the rightness or wrongness of the metaphysical or theo-logical system that it may embody. Convincing representation of man's emotional responses to the dilemmas and crises of life, and profundity of insight into the motives of human conduct, have won authors of earlier, less sophisticated civilizations the unqualified admiration of readers fully informed about depth psychology and archetypal myths. If *Faust* expresses what seem to be recognizable philosophical or religious truths, it is only because great poetry is a truthful reflection of human experience. Much of the philosophy discerned in *Faust* by Santayana and outlined in his study of *Three Philosophical Poets* is undoubtedly there. Some of it is Goethe's own, some is that of Goethe's age and of traditions then consciously or unconsciously accepted as valid; but some is surely little more than philosophic hindsight. Critics more sympathetic toward German idealism have managed to find a pleasanter world-view in *Faust*, although it remains doubtful whether their literary criticism has been better or worse than Santayana's by virtue of their less hostile ideological positions.

Almost as familiar as the legend of a philosophic *Faust* is the legend that Faust himself is the embodiment of a particular civilization, or of the typical man of that civilization. Oswald Spengler's formulation of this thesis in *The Decline of the West* has been widely disseminated, although it has lost much of its original clarity with the passage of time and so is felt to be a poetic figure of speech rather than a statement about the meaning of *Faust*. Nevertheless, to read *Faust* with the preconception that Faust is a sort of animated and articulated historical generalization may well leave a reader with the impression that Goethe's drama is a poor substitute for a pseudo-philosophy of history.

The practice of excerpting bits of wisdom from works of literature is no more modern than are some of the forms of wisdom which have been extrapolated from *Faust*. In his own youth Goethe read with enthusiasm Dodd's *The Beauties of Shakespear*, but in later years he insisted, as in the essay *Shakespeare and No End*, that no dramatist can be properly appreciated on the basis of the evidence afforded by even the most elegant extracts. If most poets have something to say, and important ones usually say it about something important, to assume that it will be said in specific places within a poetic work is still to confuse the part with the whole. The wise reader of *Faust* will therefore acknowledge that it may contain some Goethean wisdom, the wisdom of a man whose life was certainly rich in human experience, but he will hardly expect to find explicit in it the whole of its author's philosophy of life. Faust is not Goethe, and the drama bearing his name is only one of Goethe's many works.

The legend of the difficulty of satisfactorily understanding *Faust* is clearly associated both with its reputation as a philosophical poem—being a German one, it must be as difficult to read as most German philosophic works notoriously are—and with Goethe's reputation for profundity as disseminated by Carlyle, Emerson, and other eminent Victorians. That *Faust II* is particularly difficult is a critical commonplace which some recent critics attempt to refute by simply asserting the opposite. The truth is, rather, that *Faust I* is easier to read because the reader is already familiar with many details of plot and situation. He knows something about Marlowe's play and can easily accept the idea of a pact with a devil; he has probably heard Gounod's opera and is prepared for the romantic love of Margarete and Faust; he may have ready Shelley's translations from Prologue in Heaven and the Walpurgisnight, or know Boito's *Mefistofele*, and so be unsurprised by the cosmic framework of the drama or by other innovations of Goethe's. Most of *Faust II* will be unfamiliar at first reading, however, and many a reader who has perused a synopsis of it beforehand is disturbed to find that a summary of the dramatic action, in the sense of Faust's adventures, does not properly prepare him to accept with good grace the long digressions which this part apparently contains—especially if he has been inoculated with the idea that it is an afterthought of senile genius. Actually, the first part of *Faust* is as novel as the second for one who knows only earlier treatments of the Faust story; but unless he is somewhat alert he will ignore the implications of what is unfamiliar and see in it only a dramatic potpourri about several different Fausts who, with Berlioz's musical figure, share in common the fate of damnation.[1]

In the pages that follow, the analysis of even the "familiar" *Faust I* is occasionally detailed, simply because it is of utmost importance to establish the uniqueness of those parts of it too often unconsciously confused with other "Fausts." But to approach *Faust* with an unprejudiced mind will not obviate all the difficulties which it presents to today's reader. The reader of German will find the language of the text archaic in places—sometimes it was intentionally so when written—although it is always far closer to contemporary German than is that of Shakespeare to modern English. The non-German reader will probably be repelled by a text so long that it can be performed in its entirety only under circumstances far more favorable than those required for an uncut *Hamlet*. English critics have, indeed, often regarded *Faust* as a work of epic proportions and discussed it with cosmic poems like *The Aeneid*, *The Divine Comedy*, and *Paradise Lost*, and the English reader, despite such an example as Hardy's *The Dynasts*, is likely to recoil from trying to assimilate *Faust* as a theatrical work even though he accepts as drama one of

---

[1] Since the last words of Mephistopheles in *Faust I* are "With me! This way!" (addressed to Faust), it is easy to assume that the moment of damnation has come and that the play is over.

Shakespeare's rarely performed plays.[2] Because of the relative insignificance for English literature of monumental drama, many find it difficult to appreciate that in the great age of romanticism various European literatures were successfully enriched by works superficially analogous in form to Goethe's *Faust*. Theoretical considerations alone make it evident that poetic drama on the scale of *Faust* cannot be intended to be read or seen only as a sort of colossal tragedy of the type of *Macbeth* or *King Lear*. It takes over twenty hours to perform *Faust* in its entirety, much too long a time to sustain continuous dramatic suspense or even unbroken interest in the fate of a single dramatic figure. *Faust* falls into parts which naturally present the ear, the eye, and the inward eye with psychologically necessary contrasts of style and idea, and yet it can be said to form a theatrical whole also, as its full title, *Faust, A Tragedy*, laconically insists.

Faust is probably no more and no less difficult to understand than, let us say, *Hamlet*. Both works have the quality of resisting facile simplification. Both have been interpreted in a highly subjective fashion by generations of readers and critics, so that it is hard to imagine how either work actually seemed to its first public. If Shakespeare's audience could understand allusions—historical, heraldic, emblematic, or legendary—which now require detailed notes, Goethe's more literate one still possessed a familiarity with biblical and classical matters that the demands of a modern education have made uncommon today. A full third of the text of *Faust* presupposes a fair knowledge of Greek and Latin mythology; however, this knowledge probably does not need to be so detailed as that which most commentators on *Faust* display. Goethe's text often provides all the commentary that a classical allusion requires, although it is occasionally helpful to know that a certain reference was perhaps meant to be stranger than other allusions now almost equally mysterious. The reader of Goethe's day was hardly expected

---

[2] In *Antony and Cleopatra* there are forty-two scenes or changes of tableau; despite its much greater length, *Faust* has only three more. Although it is often asserted that one reason why *Faust II* is more difficult than *Faust I* is that it has more scenes, it has seven less. Each part of *Faust* requires nineteen stage sets, of which three in each part are multiple (Outside the City Gates, Walpurgisnight—Walpurgis Night's Dream, Prison; Pharsalian Fields, High Mountains—Lower Mountains—On a Foothill, Palace; Formal Park with Great Rectilinear Canal—In the Palace—Great Courtyard); in *Faust II* the setting of the scene High-vaulted Narrow Gothic Room is repeated from *Faust I*, and so also is perhaps that of Pleasant Landscape. (Whether Goethe ever expected *Faust* to be performed uncut, as it sometimes is, may well be doubted; he himself made drastic cuts in *Faust I* when a performance was planned for the Weimar theater.)

to accede to an author's footnote request to turn aside from a text for a few days to read a work of the size of *The Golden Bough* in order better to understand what he was reading. If, remembering that *Faust* is a dramatic poem, potentially a theatrical representation, a reader does not succumb to the lure of learned digression, he will find that he can assimilate it in units of some size and so gain simultaneously a feeling of both its dramatic and monumental qualities.[3] If he thinks of *Faust* as a series of evenings in a theater possessing magnificent actors and the best of technical equipment, he will have an incalculable advantage over readers who atomistically concede over-importance to details or who attempt to read it as one grandiose Shakespearean tragedy, and he will perceive the compositional principles that make Goethe's poem aesthetically commensurable.

"There are three kinds of readers," Goethe once wrote. "Those who enjoy without any judgment, those who sit in judgment without any enjoyment, and, between these, a minority which judges while it enjoys and enjoys while it judges." It may be supposed that Goethe liked the last kind of reader best and wrote *Faust* for him. For such a reader the following chapters are intended. And it is my hope that he will be persuaded that I am right in holding the unconventional view that *Faust* is primarily drama; that, as drama, it is action; and that the action of *Faust* is neither more nor less than the development of its protagonist's dramatic character.

[3] Each of the following chapters is a discussion centering about one such unit or group of units in the text of *Faust*.

REALMS OF THE SPIRIT

CHAPTER II

Poetry and Life

Faust is prefaced by a verse Dedication which, despite its forbidding name, is largely a prologue in a European theatrical tradition universally honored until the advent of social and naturalistic drama; accordingly, Goethe let it be scheduled to open a performance of *Faust I* planned in the 1810's for the Weimar stage. The convention that a prologue of the author's own composition must be as disarmingly modest as possible is strictly observed, and only with the most timorous diffidence does Goethe allude to the applause or approval which custom demands be mentioned. Yet unbecoming servility is avoided, since Dedication is simultaneously the elegiac expression of its author's humble acceptance of life's vicissitudes and the lyric expression of his humility in the presence of the mystery which is artistic creation. As such it avoids the other common fault of prologues, that of being merely witty even when mere wit will establish the wrong mood for the proper reception of the play to follow.

For all its sentimental elements, however, Dedication is not a romantic lyric but an occasional ode in the tradition of poetry of wit. The opening contrast between youthful poetic enthusiasm and the mature poet's awareness that not every vision can be artistically realized is nicely paralleled in the second stanza by the contrast between the joys of youth and the painful losses brought by the passing of years. In the third, the friends of youth who constituted the first audience for parts of *Faust* are opposed to the great impersonal public that, hearing the poet's song (*Lied*), will catch glimpses of private suffering (*Leid*) as it has been transmuted into tragedy. For most of the final stanza, therefore, the world of poetic creation is a place of refuge from harsh reality. But then the epigrammatic potentialities of the elegiac stanza's couplet are exploited for the first time, to express the paradox that the spirit realm of poetry may be more real than the immediate, tangible present.[1]

What I possess seems something far away,
And what has vanished is as real as day.

The poet's symbolic world, one of many real worlds and a reflection of parts of them, is a primary reality so long as we choose to remain in it. "As imagination bodies forth / The form of things unknown," Theseus declares in *A Midsummer Night's Dream*, "the poet's pen / Turns them to shapes, and gives to airy nothing / A local habitation and a name." The poet of Dedication, however, holds a mirror up to Nature wherein essence and phenomenon, the ideal and the real, are seen as he sees them. If he emphasizes the seemingly independent existence of his dramatic characters, the "wavering shapes" first apostrophized, he also insists that in recollection the figures of life blend with those of myth and legend (*Sage*). And if he associates the substance of elegy (*Klage*), "Life's labyrinthine-errant course," with that of "cantos"[2] whose fundamental truthfulness to nature is symbolized by the equation of his song with the impersonal music of the wind-played Aeolian harp, it is because what follows is to be a basically objective dramatization, on an epic scale, of the epic of human life. But Dedication is not simply an announcement of the theme of *Faust* or of themes to be developed in *Faust*; it is also an integral part of *Faust* and establishes at the outset of the drama the value of various motifs and images that are to have central significance in it; *Wahn* as illusion rather than mere delusion, labyrinth as a symbol of life, "the spirit realm" as the symbol of creative power, and the tones of the Aeolian harp as the audible voice of Nature are among the more immediately obvious of these.

33–58   Implicit in Dedication is the premise that poetry mirrors the world. The corollary of this, that all the world's a stage, and the closely related question of whether artistic truth and theatrical artifice can be reconciled, are central themes of the next prologue,

[1] In the German, *Wirklichkeiten* (realities) is the emphatic final word, bearing two strong stresses in the context of a stanza marked by complete metrical regularity.

[2] Since Dedication is the first preface of *Faust I*, the term cantos, recalling epics read to their authors' patrons or otherwise published as each book was completed, simultaneously implies that the First Part is neither one play nor one part only of the whole *Faust*.

Prelude on the Stage. For although, after one prologue, an audience is ready for the curtain to rise on a stage set and for the dramatic action proper to begin, Goethe lets a second prologue, a dramatic scene unconnected with the action of *Faust* and performed on a bare stage, follow the first. Since, moreover, it does not contain the direct allusions to the play it precedes which are customary in comic or apologetic curtain raisers, so that it is superficially a mere theatrical divertissement like Casti's *Prima la musica e poi le parole* (1786); and since at least two of its three actors are not in historical costume, although by Goethe's day older dramas, and modern historical ones like *Faust*, were regularly done as costume pieces; Prelude on the Stage may be said to represent the irony of quadruply disappointed expectation. Its bare stage and costumeless players indicate that the actors of *Faust* represent human beings first and foremost, and historical figures only secondarily; that *Faust*, although it is a costume piece whose proscenium stage is also to be the stages of Attic drama, medieval mysteries, and Renaissance theatrical art, is a play whose sets are, above all, those that poetry can project more vividly than the most inspired stage designer. The absence of any immediate connection with the Faust theme, like a second prologue when one alone is customary, or the transparent fiction that a foreign troupe is about to present the play which follows, is again a warning to be prepared for a work of unusual features, and marks a first introduction to dramatic techniques and conventions which, though not entirely unfamiliar, were not standard theatrical practice on the German and European stage of the early nineteenth century. And so, by its very example, Prelude on the Stage proclaims that *Faust* is to demand, not unlimited suspension of disbelief, but simultaneous awareness of the worlds mirrored, the mirrored images, and the holder of the mirror.

The Director's opening speech abruptly introduces a world of practical realities. The vague "many" (*Menge*) of Dedication becomes a theater public which must be entertained, and the operational entity "popular taste" (*Geist des Volks*) replaces the "spirit realm" (*Geisterreich*) of high art. The measured regularity and insistent rhymes of elegiac stanza give way to an almost conversational freedom of versification as rhymes are now indifferently masculine or feminine, couplets are interspersed among quatrains, and lines, even ones that rhyme together, have a varying number of stresses. The Director's somewhat heartless comparison of the demand for theater tickets with that for bread in time of famine alludes to a form of economic crisis still all too common in early nineteenth-century

Europe. If he is properly cynical about the use that has been made of the increase in literacy, a yet recent achievement of the Enlightenment, his equation of theater entrance and the strait gate leading unto life eternal only exemplifies the new "realistic" secular humanism in one of its more negative forms. It is therefore not surprising that he should casually enjoin his Poet to perform the "miracle" of providing a play which will satisfy the heterogeneous audience usually found in a theater.

59–88   In his reply, couched in the stanzaic form of Dedication, the Poet opposes to the Director's utilitarianism an exalted, "romantic" view of his art.[3] For him, poetry is primarily the expression of an inwardness fostered by favorable circumstances, and, like the poet of Dedication, he uses "spirit" in the sense of creative power, although with the new connotations "soul" and "mood" also. As a perfectionist he is consistent in asserting that time alone is the ultimate test of worth, but his incidental depreciation of the Moment, of time here and now, is at once vigorously and effectively repudiated by the Player. For it is a premise of *Faust* that the Moment is a symbol of positive value, that the value of existence can be determined without reference to any afterworld, whether that—as here—of posterity or that of another life. The Player speaks as one whose only audience is contemporary; but as on the stage of drama all moments are contemporary in their turn, so on the stage of life each moment of a worthwhile human existence should contain its own significance. "A fine young fellow here and now," he declares, "Is something worthwhile too, I think," and he urges the Poet to communicate without diffidence his vision of life in a work reflecting the totality of human experience as represented by "all the choirs of Phantasy"— Reason, Common Sense, Feeling, Passion, and Folly.

89–165   Any persuasive power of the Player's moderate words is counteracted by the Director's injunction to give the undemanding public as much mere spectacle as possible, and the Poet finally repudiates further artistic peonage in a magnificent lyric-rhetorical outburst affirming all poets' subjective independence.

No doubt you think that for your sake a poet
Should desecrate and waste the highest gift—
His right of man—that Nature's granted him.

---

[3] There is a comic-pathetic contrast between the Poet's dreams of poetic grandeur and his actual position, since he is not today's author but an eighteenth-century *Theaterdichter* whose humble task it was to adapt the work of others to the requirements of a specific theatrical troupe.

Less by the substance of his hyperboles, than by the intensity of personal feeling which they succeed in conveying, he demonstrates the limited validity of the Director's pessimistic view that it is almost hopeless to expect effective poetic communication in the theater. "Properly" understood or not, poetry can be felt to be an impressive revelation of man's creative powers and a fundamentally truthful interpretation of the world in which men have their being. Basic both to this world and to that of art are the concepts of harmony and rhythm which the Poet chooses to see revealed in poetry alone. He may not actually be the universal poet of his impassioned speech, but, for all his failure to appreciate life's natural complexity—his personified Nature has only the monotonous task of spinning the thread of life which the poet-weaver then changes into living patterns —he shares some measure of that vital force which can alter the texture of life's fabric. This is the conciliatory view of the Player, who at once attempts to mediate between the Director's pragmatic view of poetry and the Poet's vision of it as a supreme human revelation. If he urges, "Why not make use then of these splendid powers / And in your literary business hours / Conduct affairs the way that lovers do!", it is only to insist the more forcibly that art is both expression of experience and technique of communication, and that the work of art—for example, a novel—corresponds to a form of human experiencing or, in romantic terms, comes into being through a process of organic growth.

From the novel, the epitome of a complex literary action, the 166–213 Player immediately turns again to drama. "Let's have a play of this kind too! / Just pick some bit of all that we call life!" For *Faust* is to be a drama of the epic of life, picturing its errors and truth for the young—and young in spirit—who can appreciate verve (*Schwung*) and meaningful illusion (*Schein*). "Who thinks himself complete is never to be pleased; / One who is still becoming will always thankful be." The Poet acknowledges the justice of the Player's observations by objecting only that he no longer possesses the enthusiasms and intense emotions on which he drew for poetry in earlier years. And so the Player, after a reassuring depreciation of mere physical youthfulness, is able to make unchallenged the clinching point that poetic youth is above all mastery of the artistic medium.

Yet gentlemen who're old, like you,
Are duty-bound to strike familiar chords
With easy grace and courage true,
May pleasantly meander towards
A goal which they themselves have chosen.

214–42   The Prelude ends with the Director's demand for action, and we are left with the impression that the romantic view of poetry as the expression of mood (*Stimmung*) is to be reconciled with an almost classicistic "make poetry obey." The technique of a play within a play—here within *Faust* but before The Tragedy of Faust—exemplified and, as it were, made familiar by the Prelude will be exploited with many variations in the drama to follow, and so also will that of shifting occasionally from highly flexible verse into set lyric forms, a technique becoming familiar to audiences of Goethe's day from verse translations of Calderón's then popular plays and from the romantic dramas they inspired. The high values here attached to human achievement, to *Werden*, and to clarity and truth, even when commingled with error and deception, will hold for all the rest of *Faust*. Exploiting all the machinery of the theater, the cosmic included, *Faust* will move with the "prudent speed" demanded by the Director from Heaven through the World to Hell—or at least to the hell-mouth of old morality plays. At times reminiscent of later, eighteenth-century farces with music on secularized redemption themes still most notably represented by *The Magic Flute*, *Faust* is only incidentally morality or spectacle and remains first and foremost a poetic drama of human life in all its significance.

CHAPTER III

The Nature of Man

Only the final prologue, Prologue in Heaven, is explicitly connected with the action of the play to follow; but it too is no more an integral part of that action than are its two predecessors. Although many of its external features patently derive from the opening heaven scenes of the Book of Job and of medieval and later morality plays, it is as untraditional theologically as it is in its dramatic function. During his dramatic life the hero of The Tragedy of Faust will have no occasion to turn or return to the Judaeo-Christian personal God and will consistently deny that man can ever have certain knowledge of any afterlife. By its unorthodox features, then, this prologue establishes, not the absolute rightness of Faust's religious position, but the irrelevance to the poetic structure that follows of issues of orthodoxy traditionally associated with earlier Fausts. By restating and developing themes and symbols already introduced in Dedication and Prelude on the Stage, and by introducing cosmic machinery that adumbrates the use of magic and the supernatural in the tragedy now about to begin, it completes the frame of reference in which alone the characters and action of that drama can be fully understood.

Uninsistently placing the heaven of the prologue in post-Copernican space, the Archangels' descriptive hymn of praise equates God and Nature as coexistent mysteries by stating that no one can "fathom," can understand completely, either God or the realm of physical causality. While it establishes sun and light as the supreme symbols both of an ordered cosmos and of impenetrable cosmic mysteries, it presents the earth—to which, significantly, two of its

243-70

three stanzas are almost entirely devoted—as rapidly alternating between light and awesome darkness and as a setting for the interplay of violent forces. The evident relief with which at the end of their hymn the Archangels again praise the measured motion of the sun hints strongly that, from any vantage point less favorable than that of a transcendental Being's faithful retainers (*Gesinde*, Mephistopheles' term for all the Lord's attendants), it must be quite difficult to discern a reassuring cosmic design in the working of terrestrial forces.

271–99   Inability to see any total cosmic order is represented by Mephistopheles, who at this point adduces man, "the little god of earth," as the most obvious example of an irrational element in the substantial world. Although his role is superficially that of Satan, the Adversary who tempts and afflicts Job, Mephistopheles is more aggressive and impudent than his biblical counterpart. He comes uninvited, and, without his presence having been acknowledged, makes the insulting assertion that human misery, even human bestiality, are consequences of men's partaking in the divine essence, in their having been granted "that gleam of heavenly light," *radius divini luminis*, which they call Reason. As an omnipotent Being, the Lord may properly disregard the challenging implications of what Mephistopheles has said and, insinuating that it is simply the expression of querulous discontent, prefer to catch his dialectic opponent in the lie that there are no men whom he would care to torment. For, asked about Faust, Mephistopheles is suspiciously quick to identify him as "The Doctor."

300–22   Of the traditional Faust it had never been said, as of God's servant Job, that there was "none like him in the earth, a perfect and an upright man, one that feareth God, and escheweth evil." But in an enlightened eighteenth century, when reason and knowledge were so highly esteemed that a Faust motivated by passion for truth could conceivably be redeemed—witness the plan of a *Faust* by Lessing—Faust had ceased to be a name to conjure with for those who wanted to warn good Christian men against the fatal consequences of evil ways. Nevertheless it was, and still is, somewhat startling to have Faust introduced as a prototype of human goodness at this point. For although it may at first seem that Faust is offered as an exception to Mephistopheles' generalizations about mankind, it soon becomes evident that the Lord is not justifying His ways with one exceptional example, but is speaking about Man as well as about Faust. Accordingly, when He authorizes Mephistopheles to lead Faust—"As long as he's on earth, alive"—gently along his road, He adds, "Men err as long as they do strive."

This generalization, as sweeping as any that Mephistopheles has made, is the Lord's first specific statement about the nature of man. As it were underlined by the dramatic irony of Mephistopheles' failure to heed its implications—he only thanks the Lord for being allowed to play cat-and-mouse with Faust while Faust lives—it is a statement of key importance for any interpretation of *Faust*. That finite men cannot achieve perfection by their own effort, that their striving to realize their aspirations can only implicate them in error, is a truism of Judaeo-Christian theology. Not to strive, however; to succumb to apathy, the deadliest of mortal sins; to lose the will to live—by the time of Rousseau and Kant it was widely acknowledged that the rational component of human personality, Mephistopheles' "ray of divine light," was at best barely the master of the voluntaristic one—this is to cease to exist on earth at all. The permission which is granted Mephistopheles and which so delights the sadist in him is, therefore, nothing more than the authorization of Faust's continued existence; for, as the Lord's final speech will make clear, Mephistopheles' function is simply to keep man active. "Our nature," Pascal wrote, "is in movement; complete repose"—the *unbedingte Ruh*' of that speech—"is death." To be led gently along Mephistopheles' road is thus simply to be a living human being.

"The Ways of Heav'n are dark and intricate, / Puzzled in Mazes 323-34 and perplext with Errors; / Our Understanding traces 'em in vain, / Lost and bewilder'd with the fruitless Search; / Nor sees with how much Art the Windings run, / Nor where the regular Confusion ends." In this pious expression of human humility from Addison's *Cato*, "error" is used with the Latin value "winding," also present in the German *irr*, "astray," and its derivatives. The Lord's "Es irrt der Mensch, so lang er strebt" is thus ambiguous verbally as well as dramatically; from His highest vantage point, life is seen as an intricate maze the pattern of which only Divine Understanding can fathom, and what in Dedication was subjectively lamented, "Life's labyrinthine-errant course," becomes the divinely ordained lot of finite man and the source of man's tragic dignity. Even more important for any interpretation of *Faust* than the Lord's first statement about the nature of man, however, is His second, more optimistic one, which recalls Helvétius' "It is by Error that Man can advance to Truth." For He warns Mephistopheles that at the end of all his efforts he will be compelled to admit that "A good man, in his groping intuition, / is well aware of what's his proper path." Not Faust only, the "spirit" Mephistopheles is to "divert from its primal source" if he can "seize"—both understand and, with a play on another meaning of *erfassen*, lay hold of—it, but any good man possesses the innate power to discern a meaningful pattern in life's "regular Confusion."

The Lord does not indicate, however, with what degree of success the good man will pursue the proper course that his sharing of divine attributes like Reason permits him to discover. For if *Faust* is not to represent a struggle between God and a minor devil—Mephistopheles' "bet" is a meaningless challenge—neither is it to be a paradigmatic demonstration of divinely revealed truths. It is to answer, rather, the question "How is a man 'good'?" by showing that the traditionally unworthy figure of Faust can be paradoxically used to demonstrate man's ability, at once human and divine, to discover that his life is part of a great, meaningful order. Goodness itself, however, is not defined—perhaps because, by the eighteenth century, it was already notoriously relative. Thus, when he first appears to Faust, his role that of Spirit of Negation and Annihilation, Mephistopheles will explain that he is "Of that force a part / Which, willing evil always, always good produces. / . . . Since all that people call creation / Deserves to end in ruination." For he does not regard himself, as the Lord regards him, as an unwitting stimulus to good, but simply considers good and evil interchangeable terms. And even the Lord asserts hardly more than that this is a world not completely bad, inhabited by men whose imperfection is their strength. He may imply that the totality of what is, is meaningful, but He never rashly asserts that whatever is, is good; and He leaves the goodness of a good man vaguely general, the only thing certain being that it may be unconventional if it is to be exemplified by Faust, who could never plausibly be transmuted into Cicero's *vir bonus*, a Christian gentleman, or an eighteenth-century paragon of sentimental middle-class virtue, let alone into a saintly man of God. Yet with such men as these, and with countless ordinary varieties of good men, Faust must nevertheless be presumed to share a god-given power of aspiration, and if his labyrinthine course ultimately leads him to something which human-divine reason can consider insight into right values and a sense of life's right direction, it will prove to have been one viable way of life.

335–49   While there is no systematically developed theology or philosophy in Prologue in Heaven, there is nothing in it that cannot be interpreted as harmonizing with the tenets of the larger Christian churches, however ambiguous some of the Lord's statements may be. In it God is the source of all being, omniscient and omnipotent; Mephistopheles is no Manichean Anti-God, but the positive stimulus which negative criticism can provide; and man has the power to choose between right and wrong, although it is not stated whether it lies in his own power to make this choice an effective one, as the Pelagians believed, or whether he must be specially granted some form of grace. From the "fountainhead" that is the source of Faust's spiritual strength there emanates a force which permeates all creation, and this is defined in the Lord's benediction as Love made visible in Beauty and in physical and biological Process (*Werden*).

May you take joy in beauty's living richness!
May that which ever causes change and life
Encompass you in love's propitious bonds,
And may you give the permanence of thought
To things you see in transitory form!

In *Faust*, then, God is Being and Becoming as revealed in the realm of observable phenomena, and He can be immediately experienced as Love, the only power other than Reason that is explicitly attributed by Prologue in Heaven to both God and godlike creatures.

For all its superficial Judaeo-Christian theological convention-ality, the impression of which is helpfully strengthened by its morality play setting and by deliberate echoes of the Book of Job, Prologue in Heaven contains no references to such central Christian doctrines as revelation, the Trinity, the resurrection of the flesh, original sin, grace, or the communion of saints. These omissions, and the absence of any allusion to the Son of God, are surely conscious, although they may pass unnoticed because of Goethe's Mephistophelean insistence on Old Testament parallels,[1] for the religious problem of *Faust* is one older than Christianity, one which has concerned men everywhere. Faust may be a historical-legendary figure of the European Renaissance, but this is merely incidental to his universal human significance. Certain only is that he, like Job, is a finite man, ignorant of God's true nature, although we may surmise that his traditional rebellion against God is, like Job's, a venial sin.

That Prologue in Heaven can express the "theological" pre-suppositions of *Faust* in less than half the space needed to set forth its aesthetic premises would seem to indicate that only in the sphere of art and drama did Goethe consider his innovations sufficiently radical to demand full statement. Indeed, this final prologue would

350–53

[1] Thus, when Mephistopheles challenges the Lord's guarantee of Faust's ultimate illumination, which must be based on divine foreknowledge, he introduces his challenge with the words "What will you wager?" This phrase is an echo of Luther's "Was gilt's" (Job 1, 11: What's at stake?), a colloquial phrase to emphasize the certainty of a statement and hence without any counterpart in English translations of the biblical verse.

come dangerously close to being an unimportant exercise if its primary function were to state explicitly what must also be implicit in the text of the tragedy proper. But it has a more important function than simply to insist on the more-than-individual significance of the dramatic action to follow. For it definitively establishes the value of symbols which are to reappear again and again in The Tragedy of Faust. God, sun, light, day, clarity; spirit, reason, thought; causality, being, becoming, blossoms and fruit, striving—these are some of the symbols of what is to be regarded as good. Evil is represented by Mephistopheles, negation, dust, the bestial, the serpent and, by implication, darkness, willful irrationality, lifelessness, apathy, the static, and so forth. Man's sphere is the earth, and for man, the Lord's budding tree, stands the undaunted grasshopper of Mephistopheles' opening speech, in which words of Job's comforters are pervertedly combined with those of the Voice out of the whirlwind to provide the vivid simile,

Men seem to me—I trust Your Grace won't mind—
To be like crickets of the long-legged kind
That fly by leaping from the grass
And then fall back to sing the same old song.
Would *they* were but content with that! Alas,
They grub in any filth that comes along.

"The little god of earth" is a creature "of its folly half aware," compelled to seek unachievable satisfactions and yet intuitively knowing that the way of apparent error is its necessary labyrinthine course. For to be human, as Mephistopheles himself concedes at the end of the scene, is a virtue even in a god.

I like to see the Old Man now and then,
And take good care to keep relations civil.
It is quite decent of a mighty Lord
To be so human, talking with the Devil.

Prologue in Heaven is, above all else, an extension of Dedication and Prelude on the Stage, and the three prologues together constitute the frame of reference in which the data of existence presented in The Tragedy of Faust may be objectively evaluated. After the stylistic variety of its multiple prologue, the multiplicity of styles in the multiple drama to follow can be felt to symbolize not sudden thematic changes but the complexity of life itself. And, as this final prologue has made clear, the theme of the Tragedy is to be man's power to discern, without the aid of revelation, a rational or cosmic order in the complex phenomenal world in which he lives.

CHAPTER IV

Solitude

When Faust is revealed sitting uneasily at the desk of his narrow Gothic study, the stage ceases to be only a timeless realm of general truths about art and life, about man and God. Historical reality also is represented, the realm of human finiteness in which the tragic component of existence may reveal itself as action and as drama—hence the subheading "The First Part of the Tragedy." After celestial luminosity comes the darkness of human night, and the room which Faust describes is the prison of partial knowledge, the solitude of thought and egotism, the poverty of a sterile intellectuality that deprives man of harmony with nature. The Renaissance scholar has gone beyond the limits of medieval knowledge and wishes to go still further, but his physical environment remains that of earlier men of learning whose very titles he despises. Hoping against hope and aspiring despite despair, Faust is rebelling against the horizontal confinement of an architectural style whose strong vertical lines had, in the time of Goethe, become generally recognized as the symbol par excellence of spiritual aspiration.

After the polished elegance of Dedication and the Archangels' 354–85 hymn, after the flexible verse dialogue of Prelude on the Stage and Prologue in Heaven, Faust's opening lines must strike the ear as primitive doggerel. In language archaic, they insistently recall, despite their basically modern tetrametric regularity, a kind of versification that had begun to disappear from serious German poetry as early as the sixteenth century.[1] In that century lived the best known Faust of

---

[1] Archaic is the frequent omission of pronoun subject, the avoidance of long clauses, the paratactic ordering of ideas, and the use of words like *schier* (the adverb

history—the name Faustus, "the lucky," had long been a favorite of magicians—an astrologer, conjuror, physician, alchemist, and adventurer. Many stories of magic, some as old as the ancient pagan world, were attached to his name both during his lifetime—they were valuable publicity for a man never averse from self-advertisement— and afterward, when he came to be regarded as a wizard who had defied God and indentured himself to the devil. Several versions of his story had been printed as chapbooks by the end of the sixteenth century, when fears of heresy made witchcraft a matter of serious concern to Christians everywhere; subsequently it was never forgotten that Faust had been a contemporary of Martin Luther.

In Goethe's day the most admired German poet of the age of the Reformation was Hans Sachs, whose ingenuous tales and plays, all in rhymed verse similar to that of Faust's first lines, were considered examples of a sound indigenous tradition never developed because of the triumph of literary neoclassicism. Their stiffness is as much due to a circumscribed view of the nature of art as it is to the use of primitive techniques, and the persons in Sachs's plays suggest puppet figures. But, although the first section of Faust's monologue offers a repudiation of conventional knowledge on much the same grounds as those given by Faustus in the opening scene of Marlowe's *Tragical History*, the ultimate source of the various German popular dramas and puppet plays on the damnation of Dr. Faust in which similar monologues are regularly found, Faust is not to remain for long the uncomplex and even mechanically implausible heretic of tradition.

Many Renaissance thinkers regarded magic as nothing less than "the utter perfection of natural philosophy," believed that magic could give knowledge of ultimate truths and the power which such knowledge brings. And so to Faust it is a potential avenue of escape from academic futility and a possible means of achieving worldly advantage. The Church Fathers had conceded that magic could be either white or black, good or evil, but Faust clearly inclines to the view that utter perfection is never properly man's, that recourse to magic of any kind is in some measure evil, for he is constrained to declare that no scruples or doubts afflict him, that he fears neither

---

"sore"), *tun* (the auxiliary verb) and *die Mund* ("guarding force"). Since much sixteenth-century German verse was syllabic rather than accentual, an effect of metrical archaism is created by establishing a dominant pattern of octosyllabic lines, irregularly stressed—"Stúdied have Í Philósophy"—and then assimilating lines with extra un- stressed syllables to that pattern. Thus, a couplet which would elsewhere be an iambic pentameter line followed by a trochaic one—"Dafür ist mír auch álle Fréud' entríssen, / Bílde mir nicht eín, was Réchts zu wíssen"—must here be read as marked.

Hell nor Devil. Thus Faust, "poor fool," is not the primitive egoist with whom he at first seems to be identified, for he is half aware— as Mephistopheles told the Lord he was—of his folly.

With Faust's lyric apostrophe to the moon, the archaic manner 386-97 is abandoned.[2] Nothing could be more fashionably modern in Goethe's earlier years than the construction "moonlight that I have waked and seen arrive," nicely exemplifying a neologistic usage made popular by Klopstock's then famous *Messias* and Odes. There is still an occasional metrical irregularity, but it is, as in the rest of *Faust*, subordinated to the sense of the lines, not forcibly super-imposed upon them.[3] Although the abandoning of his first puppet-like stiffness of speech gives to Faust's invocation of the melancholy light of the moon modern-romantic overtones, his wish to commune with nature is not Rousseauist but magical. He envisions himself as a disembodied spirit, "disburdened of all learned obfuscation," at one with the elemental forces of nature, and this is almost to wish for death. The Faust who has lamented that a professor can know nothing, who has turned to magic so that he may perfect his under-standing of Nature, is in his heart of hearts aware that what he seeks is either impossible or, if possible, incapable of satisfying the insatiable essence of his personality. He has not perhaps contradicted himself literally, but he has expressed sentiments irreconcilable, if only because of their lyric aura, with his original intellectual self-assurance and rigidity. Faust, then, is the contradictory creature whom Mephistopheles described to the Lord, a complex human individual.

Although his first scene includes a brief exchange with the Earth

[2] The transition is prepared for by the introduction of greater metrical regularity and more complicated syntax during the lines immediately preceding, and it is partially concealed by Faust's continued use, until the lines "Where colored window panes obscure / What should be sunlight sweet and pure," of the monotonous rhymed-couplet pattern that began with "So here I am, poor idiot me, / No wiser now than with no degree!"

[3] Only three lines between "O didst thou, light of the full moon" and "That is your world—if world it can be called!," inclusive, are not regular iambic-tetrameter: the last line and the couplet "With spirits floating a mountain cave discover, / Above green fields in thy twilight hover." Goethe's handling of the rhymed tetrameters and penta-meters of *Faust* is more flexible than English translations usually reveal. The German text of *Faust* has fewer couplets, greater variations in line length, and more variety of rhyme—and more feminine rhyme—than even the best of these translations. Indeed, it would not be too much to say that Goethe handles rhymed verse with a freedom comparable to that Elizabethan writers allowed themselves in using blank verse; accordingly, two unaccented syllables may replace one unaccented one, although three never do so (except in the archaic lines already commented upon), and lines may begin, especially after a line with feminine rhyme, with a stressed syllable.

Spirit, a dialogue with his assistant Wagner, and the choral singing of an Easter oratorio, Faust is alone on the stage for at least three-quarters of its acting time. Inasmuch as an apparent expository soliloquy turns into a long dramatic monologue with brief interruptions, the scene Night exemplifies eighteenth-century monodrama, a lyric-dramatic theatrical form which, winning favor through Rousseau's *Pygmalion*, was highly fashionable for some years, and its musical climax may be said to stand stylistically three centuries removed from its archaic beginnings.[4] The aesthetic principle of stylistic variation announced in Prelude on the Stage is applied so unobtrusively, however, that what is really a multiplicity of styles merges with logically contradictory first impressions of Faust's dramatic character to leave a final impression of unifiable complexity.

There has always been a tendency to think of literary figures as human beings who enjoy autonomous existence; with the rise of the study of psychology this tendency, originally a mark of the naïve mind, came to be shared by many critical readers. That authors can succumb to the illusion that characters whom they have created are real people is an attested fact, and that literary figures may act exactly as do personalities with the same traits of character in real life has been acknowledged by the exponents of widely differing psychological schools. Although it would be unwarranted to assume that verisimilitude was one and the same thing in literature and in life, a plausible psychological analysis of Faust's character is doubtless possible—it would presumably have to subsume his contradictory personality traits under some large pathological categories—but it is aesthetically irrelevant to the final impression of Faust left by the whole of *Faust* or by any one of its larger units. To anticipate, this impression is one of a man of deep feeling, rich intellect, inexhaustible vitality; of a man courageously avid for truth, intolerant of error, hostile to baseness; of a man who, seeking truth, on occasion succumbs to error and baseness because he cannot curb his strong will; of a man whose terrible egotism is redeemed less by his visible virtues than by a faith in himself which ultimately equals faith in the innate worth of Man; and, above all, of a man so likable that sympathetic self-identification with him in moments of passionate triumph or of bitter despair is always possible. The Faust of the scene Night is this man at the height of his distinguished academic

---

4 Even as opera was originally intended to re-create classical Greek drama (actors, singing chorus, musical accompaniment), so monodrama, its exponents could claim, had its prototype in pre-Aeschylean drama, which knew but one actor. Two "archaic" styles are thus amalgamated in the present scene.

career; only for a fleeting moment does he resemble, puppet-like, the unsympathetic figure of history and legend.

Faust's aloneness is the theme which explains the scene's formal   398–417
affinity with monodrama. Faust is alone because, although a professor for but ten years, he has already left the last outpost of charted knowledge and so has lost all intimate contact with his students, his colleagues, his fellow men. If, like the traditional Faust, he complains of material poverty, of lack of worldly honor, it is only because these conditions are often the mark of social failure; for, unlike him, he has acquired the highest professional dignities and, presumably, the corresponding emoluments, is esteemed both by his ambitious colleague-assistant Wagner and, as the following scene will make clear, by a great lay public. But, in his desperately negative mood, Faust subjectively exaggerates his isolation, seeing his immediate environment as the symbol of a dead past, as a prison which cuts him off from life and light, even as a burial crypt in which he feels the hopeless, poignant loneliness of death. His depression is extreme but not complete, and so he can turn to magic as the avenue that promises an escape from the dead end of finite knowledge.

No pact with the devil is necessary, for Faust is a magus rather   418–59
than a necromancer. His aspiration is to know first causes, to achieve a feeling of oneness with the cosmos that will release him from the prison of his isolation. The first process which he tries is one of prayer—invocation of spirits—and mystic contemplation. The sign of the macrocosm inspires an inner vision of the harmonious interplay of those forces, natural ("forces of Nature") and at the same time divine ("forces of Heaven"), that make up the total scale of being, but by its very scope it is a vision that surpasses human understanding. Faust's mystic self-apotheosis, his "Am I a God?," is an illusion far more fugitive than the Poet's analogous deification of his visionary function in Prelude on the Stage. The vision of the golden chain implies a source from which its buckets must be filled, and so Faust is constrained to admit that the "sources of all being" remain inaccessible to him, that he is the passive spectator of a great spectacle. His obscure compulsion, his "groping intuition," is toward active participation in an existence larger than that which he can achieve through his own isolated efforts; his thirst for knowledge is merely the form into which this compulsion to escape the limits of self—of self-awareness and even egotism—has been sublimated by the circumstances of his professional career.

Accordingly, it is with visible annoyance that Faust turns the   460–513

pages of Nostradamus' book. Hope revives as he catches sight of the
sign of the Earth Spirit, and he expresses a heroically human *amor
fati*:

My heart has strength to face the world again,
To bear all earthly joy, all earthly pain,
To battle with the hurricane
And not to flinch, though found'ring on the main.

For a moment Faust ceases to speak in rhyme, the audible
symbol of normal waking reality in the text of *Faust*, and then he
"sees," so intense is his will to project it, the spirit whose sign he
has been magically contemplating. The "Vision terrifying" upon
which he cannot bear to look expresses Faust's own awareness that
he is no "superhuman" creature, but only "a worm that writhes
away in fright"—the imagery is that of the German version of the
Book of Job—because he feels the unbridgeable gulf between himself
and God. Yet knowing intuitively that he shares divine attributes,
he counters this feeling with the words,

Shall I retreat before thee, shape of flame?
I am Faust, and we are both the same!

The Earth Spirit then defines itself as both being and creative force:

In floods of life, in action's storm,
I rise and fall,
Weave to and fro!
Cradle and grave,
An eternal sea,
A weaving varied,
A life that glows—
As such do I toil at time's whirring loom,
Creating the living garment of God.

Faust, however, is still sufficiently transported by his mystic experience to cry, "Thou who movest everywhere, / Spirit creative, how
near I feel to thee!" He has demonstrated a fuller understanding of
Nature than did the Poet of Prelude on the Stage—the Earth Spirit's
weaving symbolism is as it were a correction of the Poet's depreciation
of the workings of Nature as mechanical spinning—but he succumbs
to his sense of finiteness, of immediate physical limitations from
which there seems to be no escape, and the vision vanishes with the
oracular words, "You're like the spirit that you comprehend, / Not
me!"

As Faust collapses, asking whom he, "image of the Godhead," 514–601 does resemble, his question is audibly answered by the knocking at the door which announces the arrival of his assistant. But it is only one answer. For "The plodding, arid pedant" who has destroyed Faust's "fairest happiness" by intruding upon "this wealth of visions" clearly shares far fewer of the essential attributes of Faust's Earth Spirit than does Faust himself, although he might also claim on Scriptural authority to resemble God, and so the interlude with him serves to demonstrate that Faust's sense of worthlessness is subjective only. At the same time, however, the scene relieves the formal monotony of monodrama and the dramatic tension created by Faust's physical collapse, which by no means represents a complete psychic breakdown, as his—pardonably blunt—contributions to the conversation make clear. Even though no longer the sole figure on the stage, Faust remains spiritually as isolated as ever, for there is no effective communication between himself and Wagner, whose remarks he regards only as platitudes. Wagner, on the other hand, however attentively he listens to the words of his admired superior, remains the living confutation of Faust's principle, so often fatal for the heretics Faust will soon mention, that effective persuasion must speak from the heart. Indeed, Wagner's zealous but unimaginative pursuit of all knowledge as naïvely professed in his exit line, and his naïve faith that technical skills like declamation, textual criticism, and historical analysis suffice for coping successfully with all practical and theoretical problems, are traits that mark him as Faust's inferior and insist that, if Faust is in error, his errors are the relatively noble ones of a man who has just demonstrated a high degree of insight into the manifest complexity of the phenomenal world.

The interlude with Wagner occupies the time needed for Faust's sense of elation to disappear. In monodrama this passage of time might have been indicated by a musical section which incidentally recapitulated themes already heard, but Goethe's method is more solidly dramatic, for it allows the establishing of thematic connections with the preceding sections of *Faust*—its prologues—as well as with the first part of the present scene. Thus the "sources of all being" for which Faust languished are recalled by Wagner's allusion to the "sources" made accessible by the textual critic's diligence, and both suggest that "primal source" from which, according to the Lord, Faust is never to be diverted. The theme of art and life, of world and stage, is reintroduced as that of drama and history when Faust warns that Wagner's dream of an imaginative reconstruction of "the spirit of past ages" is likely to be "at most a grand theatrical display /

With excellent pragmatic Buts and Yets / That suit the mouths of puppet actors best." And the antithesis—considerably reconciled by the end of Prelude on the Stage—between poetry as self-expression and as effective communication reappears in Faust's unqualified scorn of the rhetorical skills to which Wagner attaches such great importance.

602-33   From the words with which Wagner accepts his dismissal we learn that the scene Night is taking place on Easter Eve, a fact of considerable importance for the motivation of its musical climax. An even more important technical-dramatic reason for the interview with him appears only after Faust is again alone:

How could the voice of such a man intrude
Where spirit-fullness compassed me about?
But, ah! this once I owe you gratitude.
Of mortal men the saddest, without doubt,
You snatched me from that desperation
Which then did threaten to destroy my mind.

A scene of temporary madness or of complete physical collapse so early in the action of The Tragedy of Faust could only have seriously diminished the stature of its protagonist by making him even more a pathetic figure, and less a heroic one, than he already is. Therefore, Faust's recognition that it is insanity to seek a literal escape from human finiteness is represented as a moment of complete self-abasement, of almost fatal depression. "By rights, beside that giant apparition / I should have felt like one of pigmykind," he continues, and then grudgingly—hence his "I, image of the Godhead" and "I, more than contemplative Cherub"—admits to himself that it was *hubris* to believe that he could achieve complete identification with divine creativity. For a while still his feelings are characterized by ambivalence—"I felt myself so small and yet so great"—but finally he accepts the fact that his must be "man's uncertain fate," and asks whether he, a finite creature, is at all capable of effective activity.

Who is to teach me? What am I to shun?
Am I to heed one impulse or another?
Alas, the things we do, no less than those we suffer,
Restrict the ways our lives can run.

634-55   No longer speaking as a frustrated scholar, but for all men who feel their human insufficiency, Faust declares,

Unto the highest concepts of the mind,
Of alien substance ever more and more adheres;

When we acquire what man as good reveres,
We call what's better an illusion blind.
Life-giving feelings of unrivaled worth
Are stilled amid the tumult of this earth.

The mere thought that his spiritual hopes and aspirations may be
crushed against his will by material considerations—the sense of
responsibility which Care symbolizes—now reduces him to complete
despair.

When Care once settles deep within your heart,
She causes you many a secret smart
And, in that cradle restless, of joy and ease deprives you.
The masks she wears are always new—
She can as house and home, as wife and child appear,
As fire, water, poison, steel.
You wince at blows you never feel
And are compelled to mourn for losses you but fear.

His initial evaluation of himself now completely reversed, Faust cries,
"I am not like the gods—this I too deeply feel! / My counterpart's
the worm that grubs its way through dirt, / That, as in dust it eats
and lives, / A passer-by destroys and buries with his heel." In his
hypochondria he has swung from the infantile naïveté of believing
that all questions can be answered, that man is unconditionally free,
to the other extreme, to the primitive, fatalistic passivity of Job's
comforters.

The image of man as a creature of the dust, a helpless animal, 656–736
reminds Faust both of his own immediate, hated environment and
of that mortality which dust also symbolizes. With his apostrophe to
the hollow skull that he sees among the many things crowding the
shelves of his room, he makes his first direct admission that other
men than himself have vainly desired truth, although this admission
is only incidental to his personal feeling of the vanity of partial
knowledge and of possessing instruments that can only furnish
partial knowledge. Surrounded by useless and even unused possessions, Faust himself now recalls two pragmatic maxims.

If you would own the things your fathers left you,
You have to merit their possession.
What is not used becomes heavy burden;
No moment can use aught save that which it brings forth.

And at this moment he espies a vial of poison and realizes its potential
use. Like Job, Faust is in a state of spiritual torpor from which death
seems the only escape. Unlike Job, however, he is able to justify

suicide to himself, poetically and sentimentally, as a possible escape—from a world in which he sees paralyzing Care ever triumphant—"Into new spheres of pure activity" and as a heroic demonstration "That in their courage men can rival highest gods." Intoxicated with his own rhetoric, he fails to answer the question whether one "but now a worm" deserves the bliss he envisions, and he considers only fleetingly the possibility that death may be a dissolution into nothingness. Filling a ceremonial goblet, he remembers earlier, happier occasions on which it had been used, thus emphasizing that he has never been so isolated from other men as now—"Since all alone," Keble was soon to write, "so Heaven has willed, we die." Finally, raising it to his lips, he toasts the new day.

737–807   At this quintessentially monodramatic moment, the words of an Easter cantata are heard. The dawn which Faust has toasted is no unknowable morrow, but life made bearable on this earth. With its "Christ is arisen! / Joy to that Mortal who / Man's imperfection knew, / Care and annoyance too— / All that's our prison," the first Angels' Chorus proclaims man's godlike power to resist triumphantly the forces seeking to annihilate him. Although Faust remains unable to believe the message of the Resurrection literally, in the dust which is the verge of death he has been reminded of an example of suffering far more genuinely heroic than his own (second Angels' Chorus). With Christian ceremonial are associated recollections of other forms of religious experience—notably sentimental-pietistic and sentimental-pantheistic—and these memories unite to destroy Faust's sense of utter aloneness. The urge to be superhuman is completely subdued, and tension finds release in tears even as it did when, at the end of Dedication, the poet surrendered himself to the creative instinct. With Faust's ego in sufficient measure restored—"Earth claims me once again"—the scene closes as the Angels' Chorus recapitulates in a Christianized variation the larger *Faust* theme that all creative activity, human or divine, is of one essence.

When your deeds worship Him,
When love you demonstrate
Feeding your fellow men,
Teaching them lessons great,
Giving them joy's omen—
Then is your Master near,
Then is He here!

CHAPTER V

Faust's View of Man

The creating of a Faust of far greater complexity and psychological depth than the Fausts of older tradition has been achieved only by postponing the usual early introduction of his traditional antagonist, Mephistopheles. Dramatically the sacrifice is not great, since the scene Night builds up steadily and convincingly to a brilliant theatrical climax of its own. And since its theme is one of universal human significance, it is clearly relevant to the larger design of *Faust*. Nonetheless, the practical exigencies of dramatic form and the limitations imposed by the choice of a well-defined legend demand that Mephistopheles and Faust be brought together as soon as possible. Unfortunately, a man just reduced to tears by sentimental religious memories cannot plausibly invoke the minions of Hell, at least until he has had time to become his normal self again. This is one reason for the scene Outside the City Gates.

There are, however, other more important reasons for it. After a "religious" Prologue in Heaven, the songs of worship heard at the end of Night can too easily be mistaken for supernatural voices, especially since the normal associations of Easter music tend to obscure the primarily secular quality of Faust's quasi-religious experience. The Faust of that scene is a man evidently worthy of admiration and pity, but it is still uncertain whether he is a sentimental monster—Byronically romantic and human only by virtue of his faults—or whether he is more capable of common humanity than his treatment of Wagner, under unusual conditions to be sure, has indicated. And although the strengthening of a climax by the introduction of musical accompaniment is still familiar theatrical practice, especially in films, difficult is the ascent from the operatic back to the strictly dramatic. Outside the City Gates is a return to familiar Faust traditions and to familiar dramatic style; at the same time it confirms and clarifies statements already made by indicating their larger context, and it introduces new dramatic data and elaborates on themes yet undeveloped.

808–902   The broad daylight in which the scene begins is the world of life and light that Faust had been on the verge of renouncing. Ordinary people, representative of different outlooks according to their age, temperament, or social status, move across a stage which has suddenly been transformed into a crowded tableau reminiscent of a Dutch genre painting, and the pulsing life of gregarious humanity throws into high relief the abnormal deathliness of Faust's awful night of solitude. An old woman who crystal gazes and otherwise serves the amorous and matrimonial propensities of the fair sex represents the first introduction of the theme of vulgar magic and witchcraft—the mercenary profanation of an art which Faust has been seen to cultivate from religious or philosophical motives. Immediately before Faust and Wagner enter, soldiers pass by singing cantata-like lines; after each has spoken once there is a peasant dance to the accompaniment of a folksong-like chorus, so that the first half of the scene is technically *vaudeville* (spoken drama with musical interludes). As such, the "polydramatic" equivalent to monodrama, it furnishes the needed transition to the straight dramatic style of its latter half.

903–1021   Faust's paean to spring paints the setting of the scene in words more eloquent than any theatrical realism, and his own animation is reflected in the dactylic lilt of lines which make clear that he has not regarded his recent rescue from death as a form of Christian religious experience, for he sees in the Resurrection the symbol of man's annual rebirth—"The Lord's resurrection they celebrate, / For they themselves have been resurrected"—and refers disparagingly to "the churches' venerable night." Indeed, the whole tenor of his speech, with its somewhat sentimental personification of Winter, Spring, and Sun, with its facile equation of Man and Nature (of people and flowers), is almost glibly anthropocentric, and its logical culmination is Faust's unqualified and uncritical identification of himself with all humanity. "Now great and small cry with delight, / 'I'm human here, and that's my right!'" It is now the humanist Wagner who feels isolated, who scorns as evil the spirit of joy and song which has taken possession of the many. Faust can accept graciously and without condescension the tributes which the Old Peasant offers him, although they are inspired by a medical career which he would rather forget, and for all the eccentricity of his personal religious views, he is not so romantically immature and iconoclastic as to be unable to reply in kind to the dignified Peasant's "Our helper was helped by the Helper above."[1]

Despite any momentary self-identification with the mass of humanity, Faust is so much an individual that he no more merges with his environment than does the Wagner who is so conscious of being out of place. A few steps upward are enough to separate Faust and Wagner from the throng, to bring *Faust* itself back to the higher plane of drama dealing with the destiny of an individual, though representative, man. Faust's account of his and his father's medical alchemy is a passage of exposition recalling the inauspicious and presumably typical beginnings of the distinguished career which has brought Faust to the limits of formal knowledge. Its primary dramatic function, however, is to fill out the picture of Faust's early religious experiences and make clear his complete alienation from all the commoner religious traditions of the civilization in which he lives. For the stone on which Faust rests with Wagner has brought back the memory of pietistic tears and fasting which failed to wrest from God the miracle of divinely cured plague. Not only is the motive for Faust's repudiation of the religion of his fathers here suggested; Faust's youthful faith in the magical power of prayer appears as the germ from which has developed the unrealistic reliance upon magic that has already been almost fatally disastrous for him. To degrade God to a creature magically subservient to man's will is to deny with Mephistopheles the independent dignity of either man or God: in *Faust* magic and transcendental religion are one potentially dangerous mode of experience. If man confuses the symbolic with the literally real, he willfully exposes himself to the forms of paralyzing frustration which Faust has experienced and is, as Faust declares, fortunate if he "still can hope / From this great sea of error to emerge." The simple peasants who gratefully revere Faust have not confused their "helper" with "the Helper above," and Wagner was perhaps wrong in saying that in their respect for Faust they might with a little encouragement have knelt before him as before the host, although his remark helps explain why Faust's thoughts follow the train they do at this point. As for the basically accurate picture which Faust gives of alchemical medical practice, it is luridly colored by the repugnance which he feels toward the whole period in his past of which it is but one part; for that practice surely represented an

1022-55

---

[1] Faust's appropriate answer is, "Revere the One who sends us succor / And teaches us to help each other."

advance in the history of medicine—Wagner's philistine observations at least make this point clear. The sense of guilt which Faust associates with the knowledge of being a poisoner whose crimes have gained him shameful praise is thus ultimately due to an awareness that his way then had not been the right one, perhaps to an obscure awareness that his way of magic now is not a better one.

1056–1117   The idea of material progress, on which all of Wagner's hopes and faith are centered, is a theme of no great interest to Faust in his present mood—"What we don't know is just what we might need, / And what we know fulfills no need at all"—and as evening falls he attempts to turn the conversation back to the more congenial one of what he called God-Nature. But even as theistic and magical religious experiences can assume egoistical and wish-fulfilling forms, so also can pantheistic ones. Not content to be aware of the life-giving force of which the Sun is a symbol, Faust momentarily wishes, Icarus-like, for wings to bear him along a godlike aerial path so that he may forever see the beauty of departing day. As a mature personality he is able to interpret the fleeting dream with its mystical elements as a special form of an apparently universal human response to beauty and sublimity, but what he regards only as an innate psychic quality is clearly one manifestation of the larger obscure compulsion which makes men aware of life's proper course. From Wagner's narrower viewpoint Faust's vision is an immaterial fancy, and Wagner ironically fails to realize that the sense of expansion which his own intellectual pleasures afford him is merely another form of the basic urge which inspires Faust's joy in natural beauty and his dream of eternal flight. Although Faust knows more of the labyrinthine complexity of the human soul than does Wagner, his knowledge is but finite too. Although he has achieved insight into the harmony of the macrocosm and into the harmony that can exist between man and nature, he still cannot reconcile the material and spiritual aspirations of man, the "two souls" that dwell within his breast.

1118–77   Even when Faust confesses a despairing view of the contradictory nature of man, a view superficially similar to Mephistopheles' cynical remarks in Prologue in Heaven about the human grasshopper, the power of aspiration still asserts itself in him, and he cries,

Oh, if in the air there spirits be
That hold dominion twixt the earth and sky,
Descend, ye powers, from the golden haze
And let me know a life no longer drab!
Indeed, did I a magic cloak possess

To carry me to lands exotic,
I would not barter it for costliest raiment,
Not even for the mantle of a king.

With this magical wish twilight comes, and Wagner, after warning Faust with pedantic thoroughness against the danger of invoking aerial spirits, urges a return to the comforts of home. The scene ends as the two scholars go back into the city accompanied by a black dog which Faust, perhaps worked upon by Wagner's demonological observations, suspects of coming from the realm of magic until, ironically, Wagner's pragmatic remarks restore an atmosphere of prosaic reality.

CHAPTER VI

The Gamble of Life

Outside the City Gates virtually completes the exposition of Faust's character, but it still remains to be seen whether his view of man is merely a subtle manifestation of the egocentric impulse that could once find its outlet in magical religion, or whether it represents also a true insight—true meaning consonant with the values posited in the prologues to *Faust*—into the divinity of man. Echoes of Prologue in Heaven have favored the last alternative, but it cannot be confirmed within the self-contained system of natural religion expounded by Faust. Confirmation is provided, however, at the very beginning of Study (I), the first of two successive scenes in Faust's college chambers.

1178–93   As he enters with the dog that attached itself to him and Wagner at the end of their Easter walk, Faust is heard speaking to himself.

The fields and meadows I've forsaken
Are covered now by deepest night,
Which does our better soul awaken
To feel an awesome, holy might.
Departed now's all wild desiring
Along with doing's stress and strain;
The Love of Man at last is stirring,
The Love of God revives again.

The theme of his soliloquy—monologue as a conventional revelation of a dramatic character's state of mind, and not as monodramatic exposition—is religious awakening, and his emphasis on brotherly love and love of God is very close to Jesus' teaching that on the commandments enjoining these two loves "hang all the law and the prophets." Although there is nothing explicitly Christian in the theological framework of *Faust*, the similarity between the Christian view and Faust's suggests that, despite his humanistic ideas, Faust has some insight into what is conventionally regarded as religious truth. This impression is strengthened by the form of the verse in which he speaks, the hymn stanza used by the Archangels of Prologue in Heaven. But when it has transpired that the poodle who disturbs his train of thought is Mephistopheles, there will be no doubt that Faust's religious views represent positive values, since it is a devil important in Christian tradition and the emissary of hell in the Faust legend who is made uneasy by them.

The objection might be raised that Mephistopheles is not the traditional devil, so that it means nothing even if he reacts as devils traditionally do to the mention of Christian themes; it may even be argued that, since his function has been defined by the Lord as serving as a creative stimulus, his interruptions are proof that Faust is momentarily in danger of succumbing to the error of religious passivity. The first objection might be valid were it not evident that throughout this scene Mephistopheles is primarily, in his own words, "the spirit that always denies," a self-definition which insistently recalls the Lord's remark about spirits of negation; the opposite of what he says, that which he contradicts, should therefore be relative truth. Furthermore, his behavior and stratagems are now those traditionally ascribed to devils; the relatively close adherence to traditional supernaturalism, and especially Faust's elaborate conjury with Christian words and symbols, must be regarded as deliberately emphatic in a work which has deviated so freely from tradition and whose theological frame of reference has so far avoided being unambiguously Christian. In its special context Mephistopheles' disapproval implies that what Faust says is to be taken at its traditional face value and that Faust's religion is essentially a noble and worthy one. The objection that Mephistopheles' primary function is to stimulate creativity is thus not relevant to the evaluation of Faust's ideas, although Mephistopheles may be serving unconsciously to keep Faust from seeing religious contemplation as an end in itself.

After his first aside to the poodle, Faust returns to his meditations. 1194–1209 The sense of inner light and self-understanding which he expresses is to be regarded as the fruit of a personal awareness that is in the best sense religious.

Again we hear the voice of Reason speaking,
And Hope begins to flower again;

The streams of life we would be seeking,
And to life's source we would attain.

These lines, spoken to the accompaniment of growlings which Faust considers discordant with "the sacred harmonies / That now my soul completely do encompass," recall Mephistopheles' assertion that reason is a gleam of celestial light which man bestially misuses, and they echo Faust's formulation on Easter Eve of magico-religious aspirations that could lead only to hopeless frustration. Yet Faust's personal religion, un-Christian though not anti-Christian, is able to give him the power to hope, to live looking forward, whereas the hope-filled message of the Easter chorale was to him only a memory of experiences long since outlived, a memory that could conserve his life without providing the impetus to carry it further along a "proper course."

1210-1321   Mephistopheles' second interruption leaves temporarily uncertain what turn Faust's thoughts on "the good and the beautiful" might next have taken. But since Faust describes as "contentment" the mood which the poodle has destroyed, the fruit of his religious reflections would presumably have been, not superhuman yearnings like those of the night before, but recognition of the importance of wisely directed activity. For his translation from the Gospel according to St. John, undertaken as a sort of magical aid to reestablishing his lost sense of immediate revelation—*John* was regularly used for white magic and exorcization—seems to be leading him to this insight into the importance of Doing as the visible demonstration of man's godlike powers, when Mephistopheles finally puts an end to speculations clearly inimical to his own designs. In writing—"with confidence"— the words "In the beginning was the Deed," Faust shows considerable understanding of the dynamic nature of God as posited in Prologue in Heaven, and it is but a step to appreciation that the universal principle of *Werden*, of process and change, may well furnish him a touchstone for evaluating human action. It must be emphasized, however, that in turning to the New Testament for inspiration Faust shows no interest in the person of Christ, no concern with the Christian-theological implications of *Logos*. It is only during the subsequent hocus-pocus with Mephistopheles in behemoth form that he introduces traditional Christian symbols and alludes directly to Christ. Although traditional religious elements confirm the rightness of Faust's insights, and although a dozen lines of "archaic" tetrameter—those beginning "But, alas, though I summon all my spirit's forces, / Contentment no longer within me courses"—immediately precede the freer ones that concern the translation and so suggest a return to the legend of a Faust fated to choose between God and Devil, Faust's religious experience is formulated in such general terms that he remains a representative of good men everywhere and does not even now incongruously become the exponent of one particular creed.

With the emergence of Mephistopheles in the dress of a wandering 1322-58 scholar, Faust for the first time is confronted by an antagonist intellectually comparable with himself—one who may pretend that he is subject to conjury and to laws that govern the creatures of Hell, but who we know has plenary powers in all matters affecting the physical Faust. The taunting irony with which Mephistopheles regularly addresses his intended victim is well matched by the ironic sophistication of Faust's replies, although Faust, unlike his opponent, occasionally lapses into blunt and even impassioned directness. And if Faust is a man half aware of his folly, Mephistopheles is a devil with no realization of the insufficiency of his own tactics. Over-confidence alone can explain Mephistopheles' answer to the question "What is your name?"

> The question is absurd
> From one who, far aloof from all appearance,
> Shows such great scorn for the mere word
> And only strives to reach the depths of essence.

To revive Faust's thirst for knowledge of ultimate truth is to pave the way for the traditional offer of magical powers in exchange for a human soul; but a gratuitous reminder that Faust has been very free in his interpretation of the Word—both Gospel and *Logos*, as well as the professorial words which Faust declared the night before he would "no longer peddle" and which Mephistopheles is tauntingly alluding to—risks reawakening his impulse to seek in traditional religious thought the resolution of his spiritual discontent.

If Faust's antagonist, Mephistopheles, is, either in the Lord's sense or in his own, "the spirit that ever denies," he is also the spirit of negation within Faust himself, and, with his introduction, full dramatic externalization of Faust's negative thoughts and feelings has become possible. His dramatic function is thus highly complex and will vary from scene to scene as he variously represents Faust's baser impulses, Faust's awareness of his own follies or Faust's sense of his finite helplessness, and as he variously symbolizes evil and destruction, man's finite limitations or, as the agent of the cosmic machinery of *Faust*, magical wish-fulfillment and human irresponsibility. At this point, however, his role is a traditionally diabolic one, and his first, enigmatic definition of himself as "Of that force a part / Which,

willing evil always, always good produces" is so elaborated as to
identify him with those Fallen Angels who vainly seek to undo what
God has wrought. If *Logos* is the power to achieve presence or, in
Faust's humanistic terms, the power to act creatively, Mephistopheles
is here the dialectically necessary counterforce of destruction. And if
Prologue in Heaven has established Light as the symbol of God,
Mephistopheles' cosmic myth gives eternal priority to Darkness and
represents Light as dependent upon the presence of inert matter, of
impermanent physical bodies, for its manifestation.

1359–87   Faust, however, has demonstrated his awareness that the living
garment of God is eternally rewoven, that birth and grave are
interdependent phenomena (vision of the Earth Spirit), and so he may
rightly taunt Mephistopheles with the fact that his destructivity
affects only parts of creation, never its enduring totality. Pretending
frankness, Mephistopheles at once concedes that he can hinder
neither the continued existence of land and sea nor the constant
self-reproduction of living things—the doctrine of the ineradicability
of life, based upon the apparent phenomenon of spontaneous
generation, was regularly adduced by eighteenth-century exponents of
theism—but his rage against whatever is, is in the best Satanic
tradition. His special reservation of the element of fire to himself
subtly emphasizes his role as emissary of Hell, and his arrogating
to himself of "waves and tempests, quakes and fire" nicely accords
with popular demonology. Since his myth is, however, irreconcilable
with the divinity of force posited in Prologue in Heaven and already
recognized quite clearly by Faust, he recognizes the futility of his
present tactics when Faust, mocking his admitted impotence to
oppose successfully "the ever-moving, / Beneficially creating Force"
that works in the creation, ironically calls him "Chaos' strangely
inconsistent son," and so he requests permission to withdraw.

1388–1529   Mephistopheles' over-zealous protestations that the laws of Hell
oblige him to obtain this permission suggest to Faust—the maneuver
is traditional—the corollary of a binding contract with the devil.
But Mephistopheles evades discussion of any pact at a moment when
Faust is impervious to devilish sophistry. Faust's skepticism about
the validity of a devil's word is especially evident when he counters
a second request for dismissal with an invitation that Mephistopheles
tell him "good tidings," for the biblical phrase can only be ironic
when applied to a message brought by the Spirit of the Everlasting
No. When Faust definitely refuses to play his little game, Mephistopheles undertakes to provide magical entertainment—and so
further demonstrate his supernatural powers. Assisted by the spirit

creatures already heard during Faust's exorcization of the poodle-hippopotamus, he hypnotizes Faust with a dream cantata of song and picture, of smell and taste and touch, that describes erotic, Bacchic, and other physical pleasures in language sensually mystic. The "sea of illusion" in which he wants Faust immersed is the realm that, as in Dedication and Prelude on the Stage, mediates between the real and the ideal, between the sensual and the spiritual; if Faust remains in a quasi-visionary state, he may soon be impelled in a direction more congenial to Mephistopheles' purposes. And the old dramatic convention, familiar to the public of Goethe's day because of the great interest then taken in Calderón, that characters in a trance or even asleep may remember what they hear while unconscious, permits Faust to hear Mephistopheles' avowal of indebtedness to his spirit and rodent assistants. For he must be somewhat persuaded that Mephistopheles is not an entirely free agent if he is ever to enter into any sort of permanent relationship with him. When he awakens— Mephistopheles' parting words are "Dream on, friend Faustus, till we meet again"—he is already unable to distinguish clearly between reality and dream, is again aware of a sense of frustration and ready to fall back into a state of despairing incertitude that, by its very negativeness, will make him more amenable to Mephistophelean suggestion.

When Mephistopheles again visits Faust's study, the poison of 1530-43 doubt has done its work. The arrival of a student seeking academic counsel will soon make clear that the Easter holidays are past; a new university term is beginning, and Faust once more faces the familiar professorial routine from which he had so confidently hoped to escape through magical experience. Mephistopheles' choice of cavalier dress, to which he so carefully draws Faust's attention, is thus meant to reawaken the feeling of imprisonment in a narrow academic world. If Mephistopheles still insists that he is bound by magical limitations—hence the traditional demand that Faust thrice invite him in—it is only to persuade Faust that the laws of Hell guarantee far greater freedom than those by which men usually live, while his courtly clothes, subtly recalling the traditionalized role of the devil on the Spanish and Austrian stages, are a reminder especially valid for the eighteenth century that the life of a German commoner is a circumscribed one.

Faust knows that the negative freedom offered by Mephistopheles 1544-71 cannot satisfy his own sense of boundless aspiration, that it is in fact irreconcilable with any finite human existence. "Renounce!

Renounce!" he asserts, is a law of life from which there is no magic escape, a remark consonant with his Easter Eve observation that "our very acts, no less than what we suffer, / Restrict the ways our lives can run." Now, as then, his mood is one of hopeless frustration, but this time there is not even the rebellious gesture of suicide. Restless, his creative powers inhibited, Faust is unable to act upon the external world—"The god that dwells within my breast / Can deeply stir my inmost being, / But though it reign o'er all my faculties, / It can produce no outward action"—and can only wish, Job-like, for death.

1572–1648   To Faust's passionately sentimental visions of sudden death, Mephistopheles opposes deliberate reminders of his conduct on Easter Eve, taunts intended both to aggravate Faust's pathological mood and to keep him aware of a devil's supernatural powers. The unrest with which Mephistopheles has infected him reaches its climax as Faust repudiates the instinctive, childlike feeling which restrained him from suicide and curses the illusions which make physical life tolerable. The spirit and its self-esteem; the delusory splendor of the phenomenal world; glory now or fame hereafter; possession of family, servants, or implements; the power of wealth to incite venturesomeness or to encourage slothfulness; the pleasures of narcosis; the supreme favor of love; hope; faith; and, above all other things, patience—these Faust curses as delusions, and in cursing them he seemingly repudiates any claim to normal human existence. Yet he has not cursed life itself, has repudiated neither activity nor exertion of will. His outburst is satanic pose and is so recognized by Mephistopheles, who sensibly enjoins, with a taunting allusion to Faust's Easter promenade,

What like a vulture at your vitals gnaws,
Your grief—leave games with it behind;
The lowest company gives you cause
To feel that you are one with all mankind.

But Mephistopheles has not caught up Faust's words immediately. A sycophantic Spirit Chorus first compliments Faust on his world-destroying powers, flatters him with the appellations "demigod" and "Powerful / Scion of man's earth"—echoes of his own earlier "I, image of the Godhead" and "I, more than Cherub"—and urges him to reconstruct within himself a finer world. This injunction echoes Faust's view, expounded to Mephistopheles but a few moments earlier, that there are godlike creative powers within his breast, while the latter's allusion to a vulture of vexation—a quasi-acknowledgment of the Promethean nature of Faust's sentiments—harmonizes with both the tone of the Spirit Chorus and his own pose of helpful sobriety. Pointing out only that Faust is being exhorted again to desire and to act, to leave solitude for the world outside—the words of the Chorus seem to be simply a Mephistophelean projection of Faust's uncrushed vitality—Mephistopheles at last makes the traditional direct offer of his services which Faust's great curse has warranted.

Faust has no need to ask what Mephistopheles' offer means, for 1649-91 his curse was a willful invitation to his visitor to offer what emissaries of Hell always do—a magical escape from the frustrations and inhibitions of finite existence. He at once asks Mephistopheles' terms. As a humanist, or philosophical naturalist, he refuses to consider seriously the usual condition of serving Mephistopheles in the next life, although it is possible that as a theologian he ironically makes his profession of indifference contingent upon the devil's destruction of what God has wrought: "When you've reduced this world to rubble, / The other can then have its turn." Since Mephistopheles is only authorized to corrupt Faust "as long as he's on earth, alive," and has expressly declared that he has no interest in corpses, his insistence that Faust's skeptical attitude justifies taking the risk which would be to bargain away one's soul simply means that he is playing his traditional role properly. But Faust is perfectly aware that devils traditionally purvey nothing but baser material satisfactions or empty illusions.

And what, poor devil, can you offer?
Was any human spirit in its high endeavor
E'er understood by like of you? . . .
Show me a fruit that rots before it's plucked
And trees that bring forth leaves each day anew!

It is only when Mephistopheles tauntingly insinuates that divine dissatisfaction is merely a symptom of impermanent physical youth—"And yet, good friend, there also comes a time / When one enjoys a bit of quiet feasting"—that Faust makes any compact with him.

But Faust's agreement with Mephistopheles is not that made by 1692-1711 the traditional Faust. Like Mephistopheles' challenge to the Lord of Prologue in Heaven, it is couched in the from of a wager. Unlike that challenge, it is accepted as a valid bet by the party challenged and emphatically restated by the challenger in such a way as to emphasize that it is not the traditional agreement by which the party of the first part agrees, if certain conditions are fulfilled, to serve the party of the second part in an afterlife. For Faust, having already declared "May my last day be that on which / You make me think I'm satisfied," goes on to declare,

If ever I to some moment say,
"Linger a while, thou art so fair!"
Clap me in irons that very day,
I'll gladly perish then and there!
Then can the death-bell loudly toll,
You of your servitude be free at last;
The clock can stop, no hour be told,
And time for me be something past.

What Faust has magniloquently promised to demonstrate is that life has meaning only in terms of motivation, of aspiration. He is willing to gamble his very identity, his existence as a conscious personality, on the validity of the principle that no moment of satisfaction can be an end in itself. And when Mephistopheles warns him that his words will not be forgotten, he formulates his challenge for a third time, now not with rhetorical pathos, but in plain, objective, even scientific, language. "If I am static, I'm a slave— / Yours or another's, it's all the same." This expression of Faust's full recognition of the truth implicit in Prologue in Heaven, that the nature of man is in movement, demonstrates that he is far more aware of man's proper course than the bombastic tones of his great curse may have led Mephistopheles to believe.[1]

1712–40   That Faust's irritation with life's frustrations and his passionate expression of this irritation constituted no final repudiation of all generally accepted values is confirmed by his reaction to Mephistopheles' request that he bind himself in writing. What Mephistopheles calls the "oratorical exaggeration" of Faust's bitterly ironic comments on the need of anything but his word of honor emphasizes that Faust's rejection of "the spirit's self-esteem" was not so absolute as it sounded in his curse. For now Faust replaces the term "delusion" by the more positive "illusion" (*Wahn*)—the word used in Dedication for the poet's creative dream and by himself in Night as a limited synonym for highest spiritual values. Despite his protests, however, he gives Mephistopheles a written confirmation of his challenge; the actual writing of it in blood, which Faust regards as

---

[1] Although Mephistopheles' "This very day, at the Doctoral Banquet, / I will perform my servant's duties" (11.1712–13) alludes to an undeveloped motif, it also serves to recall that the long Easter holiday is over and so again emphasizes that Faust has resolved to invite Mephistopheles' offer of magical services only after some weeks of careful consideration.

nonsense, is done hastily, for to emphasize too much this bit of stage business (upon which the devil of a "Faust" must insist) might easily produce the impression that the contents of the document were as traditional as its form.

In earlier versions of the legend of a pact with the devil, and indeed in almost all treatments of the theme to appear since Goethe's *Faust*, we know *why* the pact is entered into before it is signed. Calderón's Prodigious Magician expects to obtain possession of the beautiful Justina; Theophilus of Cilicia hopes to obtain advancement within the Church; the chapbook Faust and the Faustus of Marlowe's tragical history want knowledge and power; Peter Schlemihl sells his shadow for money; Thomas Mann's Adrian Leverkühn is willing to sacrifice all else if he may achieve artistic greatness. This Faust, however, enters into an agreement with Mephistopheles without having said why he does so; *how* he has happened to do so and *that* he has done so are all that is so far clear. He does not want sensual satisfactions; he already enjoys his world's esteem; he has learned, almost at the cost of his life, the lesson that he cannot hope for absolute knowledge through magical means. Is, then, Faust's compact with Mephistopheles unmotivated, a bit of literary sleight of hand, or is it motivated unconsciously, being a sort of reflex action the reason for which is understood only after the moment of action is past? If Goethe's Faust were a historical person, not a literary figure, it would only be possible to surmise his hidden motives. But since he is the hero of a drama, of a work of art—one, indeed, which purports more explicitly than most works of art to be an interpretation of life—the *why* of the gambling of his life against Mephistopheles' confident cynicism must be satisfactorily explained. Too scrupulous an artist to let Faust be trapped by his own rhetoric (which would contradict the principle of human freedom posited both in Prologue in Heaven and in every legend of a pact with the devil) and too experienced a writer to hope to delude the intelligent and critical reader with the pseudo-motivation of rhetorical lyricism (pseudo-motivation from the point of view of stage drama, though perhaps honest enough motivation for lyrical narrative or closet drama), Goethe, through Mephistopheles, frankly draws attention to Faust's rhetorical "oratory" and so as it were demands that we expect the true explanation of what is otherwise, aesthetically as well as rationally, the nonsense of a blood pact.

Having signed the agreement, Faust for the first time specifically 1741-84 refers to it as a compact (*Bündnis*) rather than as a wager, a promise or, with deliberate indefiniteness, "something in writing." And for the first time he gives reasons for his having dared to gamble his dynamic vitality against the inertia-producing forces which Mephistopheles represents. "I puffed myself up far too much," he tells Mephistopheles somewhat unflatteringly, "In your class only do I belong." Pride goeth before a fall, pride is the commonest explanation of neurotic behavior, and his pride, Faust now admits, suffered enduring hurt when he recognized on Easter Eve that Nature must in the last analysis always remain a closed book to him. The result has been a disruption of his powers of sustained thought, a nausea with knowledge, and so he now hopes to find surcease in what he regards as the joyless "depths of sensuality" and by experiencing distractions to which, aware that true mysteries are ever impenetrable, he can only refer disparagingly as "magical externals." His desire to alternate and commingle pain and pleasure, chagrin and success, to know perpetual unrest, is the expression of a need to atone for the *hubris* of his intellectual aspirations (*Wissensdrang*), all of which he now with neurotic irrationality regards as a disease of which he has somehow been cured. Awakened to what might be called the tragic implications of human finiteness, he obscurely feels that he can atone his guilt by taking upon himself the experiences of all mankind, experiences surely the humanistic counterpart to the sins of man which the religious scapegoat is said to assume as his sacrificial burden.

There is, however, more to Faust's wish to share the lot of all mankind than a somewhat childish desire to seek one's own deliberate hurt because one cannot have the pleasures one wants. An urge to achieve total self-realization in the sphere of things intellectual has been frustrated, but Faust now voices the hope that he may "expand his self to the self of everyman." There thus lies behind both his original intention and the one that has determined him to avail himself of Mephistopheles' services a single impulse, the compulsion to achieve full development of his personality, to discover, either on a rational plane or an emotional one, an integrating totality of experience. In the light of cold reason, his change of intention promises nothing but new frustrations on new planes, for totality, as Mephistopheles warns him, is not for man—here as in Prologue in Heaven the creature of day and night, of imperfect insights—but for supernatural beings only.

1785–1805   If man cannot achieve the totality which Faust irrationally desires—"But this is what I want!"—one reason is that, given a creation of infinite possibilities, totality represents an infinity, a concept of which eighteenth-century man had become highly conscious because of its frequent adduction in popular expositions of modern secular metaphysics. Man can, however, perhaps achieve a wholeness, a spiritual harmony, a psychological integration analogous on a finite level with totality on an absolute one—this is the message of the Lord's benediction at the end of Prologue in Heaven (a scene just recalled by Mephistopheles' assertion that God alone enjoys eternal light), the doctrine that the whole can be grasped by created beings through symbolic understanding alone. That Faust should want the impossible is not displeasing to Mephistopheles (hence his "A good reply!"), for the basis of his actions is a belief that Faust will at some point discover that he wants something possible after all, that he will renounce the whole for one of its non-integrated parts. On the other hand, a Faust under the illusion that Mephistophelean services can achieve the impossible may become seriously disillusioned, want nothing more, and so through apathy escape Mephistopheles' clutches. The latter, accordingly, ventures some sobering observations designed to counteract his first incautious approval. "Yet," he adds, echoing one of Wagner's sententious remarks during the Easter Eve discussion of rhetoric, "there's one point that seems a trifle wrong: / While time is short, that art"—he refers to Faust's wish to share the lot of all mankind—"is long." In other words, we must not seek the infinite within finite time. And so he goes on to make the apparently comic proposal that Faust can best be all things if he take a poetic short cut, if he hire a poetaster to teach him how to combine irreconcilables simultaneously in one entity.

Since this proposed escape from time is obviously ironic, Faust will rightly heed only its crushing implication that he wants the impossible.

What am I then, if there is no attaining
Those crowning heights of humanness
Toward which my every fiber's straining?

He fails to notice that, with his ironic "A good reply!," Mephistopheles had suddenly shifted from the intimate "thou" customary between spirit creatures and mortals to a more formal "ye." What for him and Mephistopheles is simply ironic politeness, is for the spectator a distorted echo of the passage in Prelude on the Stage when the Player (the role is often assigned the actor who plays Mephistopheles), speaking with friendly formality, urged that its Poet in his "literary business hours / Conduct affairs the way that lovers do," the Mephistophelean counterpart of which advice is to let a poet "have you fall in love, with youthful ardor, / According to a plan that you will order." The positions of these two exponents of the function of art are diametrically opposed; the Player wanted the very process of artistic creation to resemble some pattern of human living, whereas Mephistopheles proposes that a form of art shall deliberately violate the laws which govern life. As a spirit of negation Mephistopheles holds poetry in low esteem, sees only its artificial conventions—hence his use of the term *Poet* instead of the more natural German word *Dichter*—and ignores the fact that conventional symbols may express truths as well as falsehoods. The supreme irony of the situation, then, its romantic irony in the full sense of that misused term, is that Mephistopheles, remaining strictly in character, has served to recall that one valid means of achieving an integrated view of life may be through the experience of a work of art.

1806–50   Although Faust can never be what Mephistopheles sneeringly calls "Sir Microcosm," *Faust* itself still may be a valid symbolical representation of the apparently irreconcilable phenomena which are man's life. Indeed, as creative activity, artistic creation is by definition one form of the workings of the *Logos* as defined by Faust in his interpretation of the Gospel according to St. John, and thanks to the successful popularization in eighteenth-century Germany of the idea that a poet is a second maker after the Great Maker God, the larger perspective opened up by Mephistopheles' strikingly stylized exhortation can hardly have been missed by Goethe's cultivated contemporaries. That the echoing of Prelude on the Stage has been deliberate seems to be confirmed by the answer which Mephistopheles gives to Faust's despairing "What then am I?" For, instead of citing the appropriate "Which of you by taking thought can add one cubit unto his stature," he insists that Faust is and will remain what he is even if he wear a tremendously high wig or stand on cubit-high socks, examples which taken together recall French classical tragedy and the Attic tragic stage.

With his false analogy Mephistopheles momentarily crushes Faust's hope of achieving a microcosmic totality of experience, and Faust confesses that his sources of inner strength have nothing more to offer him, that he is as remote from the infinite as ever. He is at last ready to follow Mephistopheles and seek new experiences, but his "How do we go about it?" represents a lapse into laconic, unrhetorical speech implying that he hopes for little from what is now to come. By reminding him that the university is for him a "place of torture," Mephistopheles effectively associates his preparations for departure with his long-desired escape from the prison of imperfect knowledge, and further discussion is prevented by the approach of a student.

Before the entrance of the Student whom he has undertaken to 1851-67 interview in Faust's stead, Mephistopheles allows himself a moment of anticipatory triumph. His villain's monologue, delivered in Faust's academic costume (*Maske*), briefly recapitulates the most immediate themes of *Faust*. He is pleased with Faust's readiness to scorn Reason and Knowledge, and he counts on illusory and magical distractions to establish a taste for the false that will permanently alienate Faust from speculative search for truth and deprive him of that dignity which is the divine in man. For Mephistopheles, Faust's impulse to aspire is simply evidence of a spirit so immoderate, so unrealistically exalted, that it "o'erleaps all earthly joys," those pleasures which he himself regards as the goal of all human striving. Thus man is again represented as an insect whose upward leaping is futile, and Mephistopheles pictures an insatiable Faust, corrupted by riotousness and meaningless inanity, who shall at last writhe helplessly in the tantalizing presence of earthly food and drink. So pleased is Mephistopheles with his imaginary and traditional diabolic triumph that he confidently asserts, "And even though he were no convert to the devil, / Destruction still would be his fate." Only after this last reminder of the untraditional penalty of annihilation which Faust is committed to pay if he loses the gamble of life does the Student enter and Mephistopheles again become the polished devil who knows so well how to fit his manner to his mask.

A comic interlude, the first extensive "light" passage since Prelude on the Stage, brings to an end the opening section of *Faust*. During the two scenes with Mephistopheles Faust's study has been the setting for discussions of universal spiritual issues; now it is again a college chamber, and the absent Faust is once more the scholar and teacher hero of a specific body of legends and traditions, not only a representative man seeking to discover life's meaning. The loose introduction of a new character and of burlesque elements demonstrates that the Tragedy of Faust is not to be closet drama, for the interlude is farce in a late medieval manner, a satirical Dialogue between Devil and Student on traditional themes. And as a parody of the Dialogue between Faust and the Devil it casts new light on issues and themes of both the larger unit and the total work into which it is integrated.

Like Faust, the young Student finds the academic environment 1868-1907 depressing, although his knowledge of it hardly extends beyond physical externals, and his observation "Nothing green, not a tree can be seen" indicates that his immoderate thirst for learning does not exclude a genuine Faustian impulse to maintain contact with the whole order of nature. Mephistopheles, by almost at once preaching earnest diligence, reveals that his first offer to Faust of hedonistic delights was motivated by the traditional role he then played. What he says about philosophy, law, and theology might have been said in Faust's opening monologue had it followed the pattern established by earlier Faust plays, in which a critical survey of the four faculties explains why the Fausts of Marlowe and others turn to magic. Medicine escapes the devastating analysis applied to logic—the general education course of its day—Philosophy, Law, and Theology, not because Mephistopheles has had his fill "of the dry tone" of his first remarks and feels he must again "really play the Devil," but simply because Faust himself has already treated the theme of medicine with passionate seriousness in Outside the City Gates.

1908–63   For the unsophisticated Student, Mephistopheles can mix truth and falsehood with an impunity impossible in Faust's presence. Contrasting its artificial analyses of human reasoning with the loom-like complex simultaneity of actual thinking, he condemns school logic for never producing creative thinkers, "weavers of thoughts." Because weaving has been a symbol of meaningful complexity since Faust contemplated the sign of the macrocosm and since the Earth Spirit defined itself for him, its mention recalls a central theme of *Faust*. Then Mephistopheles' use of the eighteenth-century chemical term *encheiresis naturae* to illustrate the principle of an inexplicable all-uniting force leads to a discussion of Philosophy (Metaphysics) and an attack on empty verbalism which will become more virulent when Theology is reached. Although he never mentions the Word which was in the beginning, he does refer disparagingly to the Holy Ghost, so that his iterated expression of hatred of the word reaffirms the value Faust has attached to *Logos*.

1964–2000   With regard to Law, Mephistopheles is superficially a revisionist anxious to obviate anachronism and inconsistency; but behind his appeal to Reason and Natural Law—his "The law that is innate in us" is the Poet's "right of man that Nature's granted" in Prelude on the Stage—lies the great Anarch's awareness that without tradition there can be only the legalized anarchy of countless subjectivisms. His discussion of Theology, emphasizing only the bitter antagonisms that textual interpretation has produced, ends with an allusion to the schism between Homoousians and Homoiousians that suggests the long-standing difficulty of finding Christian symbols with universally accepted values and so implicitly justifies the use of a special eclectic theological frame of reference in *Faust*. And his preceding assertion, that only by accepting uncritically the doctrines of one teacher can one "enter through the Gate of Safety / Into the Temple of Certitude," faintly echoes the Director's reference to a theater entrance as a strait gate—which, as Prelude on the Stage made clear, was the Gate to the Temple of Art the Interpretress of Life.

How little the Student grasps what his interviewer has said 2001–50 becomes evident when he now immediately asks for a "little word" on Medicine. This Mephistopheles defines as the science of the macrocosm of natural laws applied to the microcosm of human physiology, only to elaborate on the art of its practice with generous *double-entendre* and with clearly anti-Faustian insistence that the Moment is simply something to use or misuse at will. Completely confused by the motley dictum, "Gray, dear friend, all theory is, / And green the golden tree of life," but tentatively promised a later interview, the green Student leaves after Mephistopheles has inscribed in his keepsake the serpent's words to Eve, *Eritis sicut Deus* [Genesis has *dii*] *scientes bonum et malum*.

With both Faust's fateful sense of his godlike qualities and the 2051–72 greater *Faust* theme of the divinity of man appropriately recalled, Faust returns. For all his intellectual maturity and professional eminence no more an experienced man of the world than the young freshman—he even feels ill at ease about his scholar's beard—he tacitly accepts Mephistopheles' proposal first to see the "little" world of everyday life and then the "great" world of the leaders of state and society. Only a few lines earlier "the great and little world" meant "macrocosm and microcosm," but these terms suddenly lose all cosmic significance as the dramatic action shifts rapidly from the plane of intellectual and spiritual issues—of art and aesthetics, of religion and theodicy, of conflicting philosophies of life, of theoretical problems of value—to one of multifarious human experiences in a world of social relationships. The general exposition of *Faust* is completed. Like the section now terminating, which has been primarily closet drama despite contrasting elements included in it, each new unit of the Tragedy will still have its own dramatic exposition on an appropriately smaller scale; the large themes of the drama have been set forth with such emphasis and clarity that they will need no further elaboration. Faust and Mephistopheles can well sail away lightly on the latter's magical balloon-cloak when they quit the study which has symbolized both man's eternal aspiration and his eternal self-frustration.

THE REALM OF
COMMON HUMANITY

CHAPTER VII

Song, Wine—and Woman

The Tabard of *The Canterbury Tales* is the common meeting place of representatives of all strata of society, and, in the Boar's Head of *Henry IV*, prince and rogue, knight and commoner, meet almost as equals. For if all the world's a stage, it is also what Fitzgerald's Omar calls "this batter'd Caravansarai / Whose Portals are alternate Night and Day," the great room in which all men dwell together. Faust's initiation into the common life of mankind begins with a visit to a Leipzig tavern associated in later legend with feats of magic attributed to the sixteenth-century Faust, and the scene of the action becomes the realm of universal human interests and experiences which he professed the wish to share at any cost.

To introduce or reintroduce an introverted scholar to the outside world by first bringing him face to face with the complete extroverts conjoined in Auerbach's Cellar is no tactical error of Mephistopheles, who promised himself in his villain's monologue to drag Faust "through life's disorder, / Through meaningless inanity." Faust's striking taciturnity confirms the impression already established that he will not be easily seduced by vulgar pleasures, and the banality from which he now remains aloof is what Mephistopheles confidently declared his squirming victim would, when finally corrupted, "plead for in vain." As a tavern of the kind frequented by students to whom he has lectured, Auerbach's Cellar can only confirm the pedagogical skepticism to which he gave such bitter expression in his opening soliloquy. And, although he is no aged scholar, the youthful or would-be youthful exuberance of its guests recalls by contrast the years with which Mephistopheles has already taunted him and prepares for our soon seeing him persuaded that he needs to be rejuvenated.

In a play of normal length, the farcical scene Auerbach's Cellar would be overlong for what it contributes to the dramatic action. If we momentarily ignore the fact that *Faust* is not simply a colossal five-act tragedy and measure this scene against the drunken porter's speech in *Macbeth* or the gravediggers' dialogue in *Hamlet*, it will be found to be proportionally much longer than either of these bits of comic Shakespearean digression, which in any case come at moments of much greater dramatic tension. In itself an Interlude of the Conjuror and the Drinkers, Auerbach's Cellar is also a genre painting, an indoor counterpart of Outside the City Gates, like which it exhibits a wealth of popular motifs. If, as has been suggested, the last scene in Faust's study marks the end of a full evening in the theater, then Auerbach's Cellar may be regarded as an amusing curtain-raiser for the second large section of *Faust*. Although Dedication, Prelude on the Stage, and, in some respects, even Prologue in Heaven have no explicit connection with the dramatic action of *Faust*, they constitute an indispensable introduction to the play, particularly to its aesthetic and ethical premises. Similarly, Auerbach's Cellar is highly significant as a general preface to Faust's next adventures, although his part in it is completely passive.

2073–2157   The opening stage direction, "Drinking Society of Merry Companions," and the uninhibited behavior of the students who have speaking parts, suggest that Auerbach's Cellar is not uncomfortably empty. Four students who never use names to address or identify one another represent a cross section of student social life. Frosch is The Freshman; Brander, The Sophomore; Altmayer is Oldfellow, the upperclassman who has somewhat developed his intellectual powers; and Siebel is Fathead, the man unfit for university life who cannot bear to separate himself from fraternal sociability. But since the bulk of seventeenth- and eighteenth-century German students came from lower middle-class backgrounds, these merry companions also represent the lesser orders of society to which Mephistopheles has proposed first to introduce Faust.

Until the entrance of Faust and Mephistopheles, the atmosphere is one of forced gaiety. The lull on which the curtain rises is broken by Frosch's appeal for drinking and laughter, then immediately followed by his pouring of wine over Brander's head when accused of failing to contribute "Some foolish prank or swinish ribaldry." Siebel's demand for roaring song is not at once satisfied, since Brander objects to the political theme of Frosch's first vocal effort—

he expresses the German common man's gratitude that he need assume no political responsibility—and Siebel himself interrupts Frosch's next two folksongs because their amatory themes remind him that Frosch has been his successful rival and successor in love. In malevolently wishing his former mistress a supernatural lover (*Kobold*—hobgoblin and, also, incubus), Siebel equates sensuality and bestiality, and both of these with witchcraft; the goat that is to bleat "Good Night" to her is to come from the Blocksberg, setting of the witches' Sabbath, while she herself is a vampire for whom "a good fellow of real flesh and blood" is "much too good." The theme of Siebel's jealous tirade against animalistic eroticism is then given final formulation in Brander's "In cellar nest once lived a rat," explicitly announced as "a song of the newest cut."[1] Its theme is the mortal agony of a poisoned animal, and its *pointe* the equation of physical suffering with love for three reasons—that of frustration in the first stanza, that of satiety in the second, and in the last that of a similarity between death spasm and sexual orgasm. Fable may endow animals with human characteristics, but it is also possible, as Mephistopheles asserted in Prologue in Heaven, for man to degrade himself to the level of beasts—and here Altmayer accuses the sentimental Siebel of seeing in the song's rat "the spitting image of himself."

These words are the cue for Mephistopheles to enter with the 2158–2244 companion who twice on Easter Eve referred to himself as the "image of the Godhead." His introductory remarks to Faust imply that the habitués of Auerbach's Cellar are typical of those met in any tavern frequented by German students. But, although he professes to wish that Faust may see "how easy 'tis to live," his cynical observation about the "little wit and much enjoyment" with which the frequenters of taverns perpetually dance the round of their confining circle like young cats chasing their own tails indicates that he is not really seeking to persuade Faust that tavern life is the perfect answer to all man's hedonistic desires. Challenged by the students' hostile reaction to the presence of strangers, he deliberately plays the limping devil in obvious disguise and, having successfully countered Frosch's allusion to Jack Ass of Rippach, is permitted to sing a "brand new piece," the Song of the Flea, which treats the tragicomic fate of an animal even lower in the life scale than Brander's rat. In view of Brander's earlier objection to political song, the omniscient Mephistopheles can felicitate himself on his adroit

---

[1] Since *Nest* may mean not only "nest" but "filthy hole," *Kellernest* also suggests "a dump of a (wine-) cellar"; if the ambiguity is intentional, the habitués of Auerbach's Cellar are being equated with cellar rats.

insinuation of political satire into the evening's entertainment, although the allusion to Spanish and other court life seems to be appreciated only by Altmayer, who cries "Long live freedom, long live wine!"

2245-95 Seizing upon this correlation of freedom and wine—is not Bacchus god of license?—Mephistopheles offers to provide drinks and so prepares to reveal his supernatural powers. What follows is superficially like one of the scenes of magic which in Marlowe's *Tragical History* and in German Faust plays afford comic relief and incidentally emphasize their supernatural frameworks. In *Faust*, now that its hero has left a world of intellectual and spiritual interests for more profane and vulgar milieus, magic has ceased to be a noble aberration and becomes vulgar entertainment—"Error" as apostrophized in Mephistopheles' parting words at the end of this episode. It is now at best only a necessary aesthetic evil, the poet's instrument for creating atmosphere, for syncopating his dramatic action, for transparently disguising ideas and symbols, and so he can let Mephistopheles' theatrical illusions be labeled "jugglery" and "hocus-pocus." Like Prelude on the Stage, Auerbach's Cellar openly concedes the ambivalence of the artistic statement, and although its dramatic climax, the students' complete confusion of the imaginary and the real, is the triumphant creation by "Illusory image and word" of an atmosphere simultaneously comic and grotesque, Siebel will afterwards rightly insist that "All was deception, lie and semblance."

Although Prologue in Heaven is an affirmation of the innate power of man to achieve spiritual dignity, to partake imperfectly of the perfection of God, it offers no scale of values by which the relative worth of imperfect men may be established. In Auerbach's Cellar, on the other hand, in this Prologue in the Tavern of Life, a working scale of values is introduced. Man is not, as Mephistopheles asserted in his first speech to the Lord, "more bestial than any beast," but may take his place at differing points on the great scale of being which ranges from the most highly complex living organism down to the simplest forms of vegetable life. Man has the power of metamorphosis—he is the grasshopper which, although Mephistopheles chose to ignore the fact, moved up the scale of life when it ceased to be a worm-like larva. Thus, in the scene Night, the dispirited Faust could accept the epithet "worm" as properly applicable to himself and only repudiate it when he experienced anticipatory exaltation at the thought of new spheres of pure activity in a next life. The grasshopper is a symbol of man's perfectibility, of his power to aspire to participation in the divine, and Mephistopheles, by his own admission unable to destroy life or matter, must content himself with denigrating the value of what God has created and with seeking to degrade living forms—man particularly—within the order of creation.

On man's finite plane, animalization or brutalization is the counterpart of annihilation or negation in the hypothetical realm of eternal absolutes. Below the lowest beast comes the lowest plant, and below these, though still created, there is only lifeless matter, whose lowest form is the dust to the devouring of which Mephistopheles told the Lord he would reduce Faust. In Auerbach's Cellar the dominant theme is the brutality and brutishness of man pervertedly using his freedom so that he may become unlike man-God and like man-beast. If the atmosphere is demonic, it is less because of Mephistopheles' harmless display of theatrically supernatural powers than because the tavern's habitués are moved by an all-destroying spirit of negation which does not even wear the Mephistophelean mask of intellectual roguishness. Indifference to the commonwealth, jealous hatreds, sadistic cruelty, inhospitableness, and base suspicion have all been given vent before Mephistopheles begins to launch the barbed shafts of his own cruel sarcasm at "the merry company." Here none will object to Brander's francophobia, for this world is a place of beasts devouring one another, and the "swinishness" felt to be unfortunately lacking at the opening of the scene is shared by all the "merrymakers" in its climactic moment of greedy drunkenness. "Like swine that wallow in the mire," they sing, "We feel as fit as cannibals!" The "insight into Nature's depth" evoked in Mephistopheles' conjuring formula—itself significant for its quasi-equation of animal ("he-goat") and vegetable life ("grape-vine") with dead matter ("the wooden table")—has proved to be a look into the depths of human nature.

The moment of "superb well-being" is too literally cannibal- [2296–2336] istic for the taste of Faust, who diffidently expresses his desire to leave. Mephistopheles, however, insists on first completing his apologue, and tells his titular master, "First see how Bestiality / Reveals herself in all her glory." When he turns the wine into purgatorial fire, there is an outburst of physical violence which he nicely directs against itself. If Frosch, in his opening appeal for merriment, compared his companions with wet straw (dampers), if Mephistopheles has called Siebel an old wine-tun and been in turn called a broomstick, these were but figurative epithets. Below the animal world of self-destructive bestiality comes the vineyard kingdom of which each of Mephistopheles' victims is, in the consensus of all the others, but a passive part. Only after the full demonstration of his powers, which is simultaneously the demonstration of his only realizable aims, does Mephistopheles vanish with Faust.

While Auerbach's Cellar as a whole elaborates the Mephistophelean view of man only adumbrated in Prologue in Heaven and, unlike that prologue, shows man in a notably non-cosmic perspective, its latter part forcibly recalls the framework of magic which is essential to the Faust legend. Since this framework alone makes possible the wide range of experience which Faust will share, the almost gratuitous introduction of the supernatural into the dramatic action of this scene establishes the precedent for equal dramatic license at later points when plot development rather than theme or symbol can most economically be stated by a free use of theatrical magic. And the passive role of Faust throughout the scene sets for the first time, under circumstances completely plausible from a psychological point of view, a dramatic precedent within the Tragedy of Faust proper—the pattern of a symbolic dramatic action independent of Faust's direct personal participation but highly relevant to the understanding of his fate.

In contrast to Auerbach's Cellar, the next scene, Witch's Kitchen, introduces elements of the fantastic for which there are no important analogues in earlier treatments of the Faust legend. Many of its details are transparently symbolic—not the least its apes, medieval emblems of lust and incontinence—for it is impossible to forget that talking apes must be actors and that a witch's kitchen, however magnificently realized by the stage designer, belongs to the realm of make-believe. The careful stage directions suggest the realistic grotesqueries of the younger Teniers, and thus Witch's Kitchen is the supernatural companion piece of the stylized naturalism of Auerbach's Cellar, many of whose motifs it elaborates satirically. Of these, the most important is the motif of erotic desire, for although wine, woman, and song proverbially go together, the Leipzig inn lacked its Mistress Quickly or Doll Tearsheet.

2337-2427   Faust has consented to "be cured" magically of a feeling of being thirty years too old, but he enters the Witch's Kitchen with expressions of repugnance iterated then and later which insist again that magic is no longer to be regarded in *Faust* as the symbol of spiritual aspiration, but as the symbol of man's powers of self-degradation and self-dehumanization. As man-like creatures who lack or repudiate reason—they speak in fragmentary sentences and regularly confuse cause with effect—the Apes represent the motif of dehumanization and bestialization in a more extreme, more obvious form than it was given in Auerbach's Cellar. As cooks of "watery charity soups" they are adulterators of the pure and genuine, yet to judge from the Buck Ape's passion for gambling and Mephistopheles' ironic allusion to lotteries they would also be the easy dupes of others. Theirs is a world where the ignorant sneer at the ignorance of others, where rudeness and disorder reign triumphant.

While Mephistopheles has directed his attention to the Apes' activities, Faust has been silently preoccupied with viewing what transpires to be a vision in a magic mirror. The nervous staccato of the preceding dialogue, to the choppy doggerel of which Mephistopheles' utterances were finally assimilated, suddenly gives way to the lyric legato in which Faust expresses his awakening to the magic of woman's beauty. Thanks to their special setting, lines in themselves no more elevated in tone than many of his earlier speeches convey the effect of noblest lyricism, and Faust reveals once again that he is capable of all-embracing passion. The very wholeness and intensity with which he loses himself in his vision of perfect womanly beauty—he seems not to hear the cynical observations of Mephistopheles the willing procurer—lend a cloak of genuine dignity to his sensual desire. In a world of demi-men Faust can still remain the hero or demigod. If it was *hubris* for him to aspire to all knowledge or to want to share the lot of all mankind, it is no less *hubris* for him to beg of wingèd Love to conduct him to the "essence of all paradises." [2428–40]

At this critical juncture Faust does not merely succumb to the spell of eroticism; he also acknowledges the force of Love, which he had cursed in a cynical moment at the beginning of his second interview with Mephistopheles, for it is consonant with his character for him honestly to acknowledge any ultimate reality of which he achieves awareness. He may be transported by what is offered him as a supernatural vision and be speaking almost unconsciously, but that his comprehensive curse was not the expression of a purely negative skepticism is now a certainty. His reluctance to resort to base magic showed that he had not permanently renounced intellectual and spiritual self-respect, even as his unqualified approval of the perfection of the recumbent beauty in the mirror has just been an acknowledgment that seemingly delusory appearances may have intrinsic value simply as expressions of an ideal. Dramatically, Faust's innate nobility is emphasized by the fact that this section of the scene is a playlet with parallel actions. One culminates on the [2441–64] imaginative plane to which Faust has been transported; the other reaches its simultaneous climax as the Apes break the crown of misgovernment and folly which they ask Mephistopheles, with his hearth-fan scepter the mock monarch of this simian world of sub-human madness, to dress "with sweat and with blood." And when the Apes proclaim the triumph of the uncreating word and assert the fabrication of nonsense rhyme to be the creation of thought, Faust, still engrossed in the mirror, cries, "Alas, to madness I'm transported!" To a crescendo of noise which even Mephistopheles finds dizzying, erotic vision is succeeded by burning passion, and the questioning hope of Faust's dazed awakening is transformed into strong-willed desire that will brook no let or hindrance—hence his command "Let us but quickly get away!"

2465–2576   With the low comedy of the singed Witch's entrance the dramatic action is again on one plane only, and the atmosphere of the rest of the scene is not frenetic, but urbane and satiric. If Faust has been erotically awakened *before* he has imbibed any potion, it is because erotic desire is a magical force, at once natural and divine, over whose existence Mephistopheles and his helpers have no control, although they may hope to exploit it for destructive ends. The magic mirror has been the theatrically convenient occasion of a sexual awakening which is the birthright of all mankind. And so, after Mephistopheles with nice irony has written off the traditional devil as allegory, the Witch becomes a businesslike hostess only too ready to serve "safe" customers. When informed that "you-know-what" is wanted for Faust, she insists on Satanic-sacramental preparation before he may take the drink. With the musical use of glasses and kettles—in Goethe's day the parody of spiritualistic ritual would suggest the methods of the great Cagliostro—the stage becomes the setting for a charlatan's séance, as Faust bluntly and Mephistopheles tolerantly observe. Now Faust becomes the visible though reluctant center of the stage so that there will be no doubt that his physical rejuvenation is meaningless hocus-pocus—the word applied by Mephistopheles to the Witch's preparations. Accordingly, he gives her bombastic reading of a numerological text, one even less reasonable than most such rhymes, an attention which he did not and could not give the more meaningful nonsense of the earlier part of the scene. Mephistopheles, with a cynical allusion to trinitarianism, frankly labels her utterances antilogous, and Faust correctly recognizes that in her claims of a hidden "science" there speaks "A chorus of a hundred thousand fools."

2577–2604   Faust's ordeal ends with two motifs from Auerbach's Cellar:

student drinking ritual—"a man of many degrees" is no novice in drinking rites—and flame from liquid. When he steps out of the magic circle of senseless inanity, having drunk the philter which is to rejuvenate him, the Witch's kitchen again becomes a stage set which, for all its strangeness, is no less naturalistically "real" than the most fashionable spa. Hence Mephistopheles, after having told the Witch that she may tell him on St. Walpurgis' Eve what favor she wants in return for her services, prescribes for Faust vigorous exercise as the necessary concomitant of the medicinal waters just imbibed. "I'll teach you later on to value lordly leisure, / When very soon you'll feel with the intensest pleasure / How Cupid can awake and nimbly leap about," he declares, and then he leads his too easily contemplative companion away without letting him look again into the magic mirror, assuring him that he will "in the flesh soon see / The paragon of womankind."

Neither Faust's rejuvenation nor a visit to a witch's kitchen—let alone one to a witches' Sabbath—is a traditional element of the Faust legend. The discursiveness and digressiveness of this scene, its patently theatrical virtuosity, thus serve to recall that *Faust* is no mere reworking of older materials only. Its true *raison d'être* is not to rejuvenate a man whose extraordinary intellectual powers have brought him academic glory in early years, but rather to insist again that universal aspects of human experience, and not the unique adventures of a particular magician, are the great theme of *Faust*. All womankind can be represented by any woman, all love by any beloved. The Faust of tradition lusted for a supernatural Helen. This Faust may, as Mephistopheles says in the aside that closes the scene, "Soon see in every woman Helen," but in her whom he truly loves he will discover not—as he will believe—the paragon of women, but the very essence of womankind.

CHAPTER VIII

The Sentiment of Love

Like Witch's Kitchen, the scenes which represent Faust's love for Margarete develop motifs not traditionally associated with the Faust of legend, but without them *Faust* would not be a drama of truly universal significance. For all the affective complications of newly awakened sensuality are subsumed in *Faust* under the complex manifestations of love that characterize the course of Faust's connection with Margarete. In a class-conscious society familiar with examples of the lifelong fidelity of aristocratic personages to mistresses of unexceptionable probity, a love affair such as that between Faust and Margarete could easily seem indistinguishable from the beginnings of a stable relationship. If their love is from the start felt to be ill-fated, however, it is partly because Faust's compulsion to experience man's lot in its totality cannot be reconciled with his remaining within or close to the little world of the much less complex Margarete; but it is also because he has tragically committed himself to know both pain and pleasure—the price of present happiness can only be suffering later.

2605–77   The Faust who accosts Margarete on her way home from confession is no uncomfortably sedate scholar, but a man who has acquired a certain superficial proficiency in the art of forcing his attentions upon unescorted women. Regarding himself as a connoisseur of seducibility, he is visibly delighted with the prospective conquest of a beauty whose charms are spiced with both innocence and impertinence. His taste in women is that of countless seducers or would-be seducers in literary works from classical times down to Goethe's day and beyond, but his bragging assertion that he could seduce a girl like Margarete in seven hours reveals an ignorance of the complexities of seduction which would strike even the most dull-witted reader of the virtuous Pamela's entertaining adventures. Mephistopheles can calmly disregard Faust's threat to part company with him if he does not immediately procure him Margarete, for Faust is still dependent upon the tutelage of one who understands the more advanced lessons to be learned from the Italian novella. And so Faust can boldly assert his brutal rakishness in one moment, and in the next beg, like any eighteenth-century sentimental lover of Marivaux, Madame Riccoboni, or the Abbé Prévost, for a fetish from his beloved's possessions.

Only familiarity with the long-windedness of eighteenth-century treatments of the themes of seduction and desertion—themes already anticipated in the Soldiers' and Peasants' songs of Outside the City Gates, and in Auerbach's Cellar—makes it possible to appreciate fully the virtuosity with which, by means of an unconventional and almost impressionistic dramatic technique, the story of Faust and Margarete is told with all relevant detail in the equivalent of about fourteen-hundred iambic tetrameter lines. Less than two-thirds of the second large section of *Faust* are devoted to this story, which nevertheless seems to develop without nervously disturbing syncopation. The fleeting introduction of the heroine, the summary exposition of the hero's unsubtle designs, and the brusque formulation of the conventional plan of action by the latter's confidant in the opening scene, Street, are assimilated to the amorous impatience of Faust for which we have been prepared. The next scene, however, in Margarete's room, is noticeably longer, and the contemplative and lyric soliloquies of psychological exposition which dominate it mark a retarding of the tempo of the love story. Then will come another outdoor scene, primarily a concise exposition of plot developments, which in turn is followed by the dramatic exposition, with generous farcical digressions, of the maneuvers by which Mephistopheles prepares Faust's formal introduction to Margarete. So many different varieties of scene succeed each other in this part of *Faust* that extensive understatement and abbreviation, counterbalanced by full statement only at critical moments and by the sparing use of gratuitous elaboration at a few uncritical ones, leave a final impression not of skeletal bareness—so disturbing in older, brief treatments of the theme of seduced innocence—but of a "modern," highly varied complexity. And, because formal variety is an already well-established structural feature of *Faust*, stylistic variation can be accepted as a valid substitute for the complexities of plot and emotional analysis which were and are standard features of novels and dramas whose main theme is the sentiment of love.

Mephistopheles' pretended ignorance of the object of Faust's desires is hardly consistent with the preliminary interest he had taken in her religious exercises. His voluntary proposal to introduce Faust into Margarete's room during her imminent visit to a neighbor is incidental evidence of an omniscience scarcely reconcilable with unconvincing protestations of non-omnipotence of the sort that brought Faust into the Witch's kitchen. If Faust can be involved in a deep emotional entanglement whose unsatisfactory outcome will leave him cynical about love, the first important step toward his total degradation will have been taken. For it was long a truism of moralists that it is the first step which counts; in the eighteenth century the Rake's Progress was a rapid descent from almost innocent pleasures pursued from motives both good and bad to profligacy willfully cultivated because of a habitual thirst for evil. Hence it is most important that Faust be represented as acting from mixed motives, since emotional confusion is one possible intermediate stage in a transition from relative moral integrity to a complete repudiation of moral values. Parodistic impudence alone does not motivate Mephistopheles' comic-moralizing tone after Margarete's first rebuff of Faust and in such later scenes as Neighbor's House or Garden, nor does it explain why his language is more richly interlarded in this part of *Faust* than elsewhere in the drama with moral sentences and biblical quotations of proverbial character. His ironic "moral lessons" are not only jibes at Faust; they are also ironic underscoring of the fundamental theme of a dramatic action in which the motif of seduced innocence is the paramount symbol of the ambivalence of all human conduct.

2678–83   From her competence in warding off Faust's advances it is evident that Margarete knows an unchaperoned young woman dare not let courteous flattery involve her in a course of conduct which might innocently tarnish her reputation or perhaps weaken the defenses of what the eighteenth century called a woman's virtue. Although Mephistopheles has assured Faust that she is "completely innocent," this is an assertion designed to whet Faust's sexual appetite rather than a verified or verifiable statement; certainly her priestly absolution is morally meaningless in a drama whose a-Christian frame of reference has been iteratedly established. It is therefore no surprise to discover that the young woman doing her hair at the opening of the scene Evening is preoccupied with favorable thoughts of the attractive though "jaunty" gentleman who spoke to her earlier in the day. Six lines suffice to expose her sympathetic reaction to Faust's first advances because hers is probably the commonest standard response of sentimental heroines, whether these are to be tragically seduced or whether they are to make a permanent conquest. Margarete is dreaming the eternal romantic dream, but for her the sometimes harmless confusion of the archetypal dream of womanly self-fulfillment with the traditional sentimental formulation is fraught with danger and the widest tragic implications.

With his entrance into Margarete's small, tidy room Faust has 2684–86 suddenly penetrated to the very heart of the realm of common humanity. The symbolic importance of the moment is underscored by his initial silence; this is neither the silence of momentary moral scruples, nor of a seducer's calculated plannings, nor yet of the sentimentalist's erotic fantasies. In the plainest, if not most humble, of environments, Faust becomes momentarily aware of the primal forces in human life and senses, to be sure only obscurely, the mysterious complexity of their interworkings. In the context of sentimental drama his long soliloquy is a passage of full psychological statement of a lover's feelings in his beloved's room—an old enough literary motif—that balances out the laconic style in which the action is being developed. In *Faust*, it is his first, unconventional expression of the idea, hitherto expressed only in the concluding lines of the Easter Morning chorale, that true religious experience is inevitably accompanied by a compulsion to shape one's life in accordance with some broader principle than personal will. Yet it is entirely consonant with the theological and philosophical premises of *Faust* that its hero should not be studying magico-mystical symbols of cosmic forces, should not be engrossed in the interpretation of the Old or New Testament, and that he should in fact intend the unscrupulous seduction of a respectable young woman at the moment when he undergoes this experience. For in his love for Margarete, however profane it may be, there is implicit some measure of that sacred love which is the Lord of Prologue in Heaven.

In a lyric of *Thus Spake Zarathustra*, Nietzsche asserts that "All joy desires eternity, / Profound, profound eternity!" Although Nietzsche's concept of eternity cannot perhaps properly be equated with time without end, he is surely correct in asserting that true joy is always accompanied by the instinctive wish that it might be eternalized. The crumbling ruins of temples to primitive gods and of monuments to grandiose ancient conquerors testify to this no less vividly than does Horace's more sophisticated view that poetic fame may endure longer than the most solid brass. The heroes of Greek legend, like the heroes of less illustrious cultures, were granted a shadowy afterlife and occasionally even deification, and in Christian culture there is ultimately an eternity to be enjoyed or suffered by every individual. In the literature of eighteenth-century Europe the desire to eternalize the sense of life's meaningfulness which accompanies being in love is most commonly expressed with the use of symbols borrowed from Christian thought. Countless lovers confusedly envisaged heavenly bliss as the eternal fulfillment of their mortal loves, and the poetry of that age of ever more secularized Christianity is replete with ineptly used religious symbolism. Faust's soliloquy in Margarete's room conserves the religious overtones once almost obligatory, yet it does not introduce explicit Christian elements inconsistent with his character or with the humanistic tenor of *Faust*, for its religious vocabulary is limited to words with pre-Christian or extra-Christian connotations.[1] It thus develops the theme of moral concern negatively introduced by Mephistopheles, and at the same time gives depth to the syncopated dramatic representation of Faust's relationship with Margarete; while further establishing the sentimental setting in which this section of *Faust* must be understood, it reintroduces the larger *Faust* theme of the potential timeless significance of the transitory moment.

2687-2716   The sanctuarial twilight apostrophized by Faust is that of the chapel or the sacred grove, and the "sweet torment of love" which he invokes draws its sustenance from that Hope which in a more irreligious moment he so bitterly cursed. His exclamatory approval of the sense of quiet, order, and contentment emanated by Margarete's room is no objective description, but the revelation of an affirmation, under the influence of love, that the values of experience may have more than momentary significance. Poverty—complained of in his opening monologue—he can now regard as a minor circumstance, and can at last appreciate that a confining room, a "prison," need not be a symbol of unhappiness, discontent, and frustration. As he seats himself by Margarete's bed his reflections become more concrete, but even domestic realities now represent only the eternal constants in human relationships—the love which binds the family together, the ties of piety existing between members of different generations,

---

[1] Examples are *Heiligtum*, "sanctuary"; *Tau der Hoffnung*, "Hope's dew," recalling the commoner *Himmelstau*, "manna"; *Seligkeit*, "bliss"; *Himmelreich*, any "heaven"; *Engel*, "angel" as a being which represents goodness; *Frevel*, the term in the Lutheran Bible for "violence," "error," "oppression," "cruel hatred," *etc.*, in Old Testament contexts—it is rare in the New Testament—and in eighteenth-century German literature with classical Greek themes the regular word for "impiety," "a most criminal offense against divine law."

and love which makes "the cottage" of routine duties "a heaven."
In the context of these elaborations on idyllic and patriarchal themes
almost religiously sacred in moral-sentimental literature of the later
eighteenth century, the "ecstatic awe" by which Faust is seized on
raising the curtain of the bed is a form of religious feeling, an
acknowledgment in some sense not simply intellectual or rational of
the meaningfulness of human existence. His subsequent apostrophe
to Nature, generalizing a momentarily regained faith in the goodness
of existence, suggests that the natural, life-giving forces which work
within the child "weave"—the symbol's pregnant value has been
established in Prelude on the Stage and in Faust's vision of the
Earth Spirit—a human being who develops divine attributes.
Incidentally the divine shape of the sentimental lover's beloved,
"godlike image" as Faust uses the term marks his first unqualified
assertion of the divine dignity of man since his Easter Eve repudiation
of faith in his own godlikeness as mere illusion.

When Faust becomes aware of the incongruity between his 2717-52
musings and the motives which have created the occasion of them,
he can only explain his disturbed psychic state in terms of an
irreconcilable opposition between sensual impulse and *Liebestraum*—
a word of Goethe's coinage in which "dream," given this context,
can only be synonymous with "illusion" as used in Dedication and
Prelude on the Stage. Margarete is again for Faust, though now
more idealized, the desired beloved, but her dramatic significance
as a symbol of timeless human experience has been permanently
established. Faust may momentarily renounce his designs on
Margarete, but Mephistopheles' comic cynicism weakens his good
resolutions—or, since Mephistopheles is the externalization of
Faust's worser self, allows them time to weaken. For as soon as
Faust reveals uncertainty about what course of conduct to follow,
Mephistopheles adopts the technique of persuasion by taunt he has
so successfully exploited earlier and leaves with a Faust already
no longer protesting.

The first lines spoken by the returning Margarete are more a 2753-82
premonitory statement of the direction in which the dramatic action
is to develop than an expression of her sensitivity to the recent
presence in her mother's house of an evil spirit. Yet her feeling of
oppressiveness may also be interpreted psychologically; she has been
feverishly preoccupied with romantic dreams which make her desire
the stabilizing presence of her mother—hence her revealing reference
to herself as "woman" and the themes of the ballad which she sings
to quiet her "foolish" womanly fears. Although "There was a king

in Thule" is for Margarete a familiar and therefore reassuring folk-song, it is a folksong in *Faust* only by virtue of literary convention, for it is an original text which, coming after the fourteenth line so far spoken by Margarete, must fulfill a complex dramatic-symbolic function. An inconspicuous regularity of meter and rhyme hardly characteristic of genuine folksong,[2] and somewhat unusual in *Faust*, marks the ballad as a whole and helps a listener to give undiverted attention to its meaning, while the opening introduction of so literally indefinite a place as Thule and its use as a rhyme-word for *Buhle* ("beloved," "sweetheart"—a word for which German folksong had no rhyme) warn that the ballad is to have a definite literary significance. The emphasis on *Buhle* makes clear Margarete's identification of herself with the royal mistress faithfully loved in life and after death. Her "Liebestraum," like Faust's, reveals the same impulse to conceive of true happiness as something which must be eternalized, and there is powerful dramatic irony in the pathos of her unconscious announcement that her love and Faust's is to be a love unto death and beyond into the uncharted depths of the sea of eternity. But the supreme irony is that her ballad of love, except in the second of its six stanzas, ominously concentrates on the dying of two lovers whose love is only a sad memory symbolically embodied in the sacred fetish of a golden cup.

2783–2804   After the goblet of love from which living warmth is imbibed has filled with the water of the sea, has been itself lost in the primal element, Margarete's discovery of the jewels left by Mephistopheles marks a return to immediate realities. Her fatal curiosity, the naïve vanity which inspires her to deck herself out in what she has found, and her awareness of the material factors that make the fulfillment of sentimental dreams almost entirely improbable, are phenomena so prosaically familiar in life—and sentimental literature—as to be somehow reassuring.

2805–48   The touching picture at the end of Evening—the stage would show a pretty girl in finery inappropriate to her dress—is immediately followed by the less sympathetic realism of the comic picture of lower-middle-class manners that constitutes the larger half of Promenade. Mephistopheles' burlesque account of the fate of the

---

[2] The printed text, like folksong texts as transcribed in Goethe's day, resolves into their normal orthographies contracted phonetic forms, archaic or colloquial, demanded by the ballad's metrical pattern. The apparent substitutions of dactyls for iambs thus do not affect the basic *da capo* song form of each stanza: five involve syllables ending in a nasal, which can be read as semi-vocalic; one involves the ending -*e* (l.10), often suppressed (compare the following form *Städt'*); and one an unstressed *i* between stem and flectional ending, normally suppressed in German iambic verse.

jewel offering is filled with comically irrelevant digression well designed to keep Faust from pursuing further the meditations it has interrupted. Its emphasis on the magico-religious attitude of Margarete's mother—"By smelling any object she can tell / If it belongs to Heaven or to Hell"—and on the devouring materialism of the Church recalls Faust's repudiation of conventional religion and his fundamental unconventionality. And its verbatim report of incongruous quotations and garbled paraphrases from scripture and popular theological literature[3] again makes the language of religion, so recently echoed by Faust and Margarete in passages of sublime rhetorical and lyric intensity, the medium of comic relief and a symbol of the Mephistophelean amoralism that threatens Faust's spiritual integrity.

If Mephistopheles' malicious irony does not excite Faust, neither 2849-64 does it favor his turning his thoughts to larger ethical issues. His inquiry about Gretchen, whom Mephistopheles has with pseudo-sympathy just called Margretlein—the tardy revelation of her name further emphasizes that in the large design of *Faust* she is primarily a symbolic figure—lets Mephistopheles picture her restless and perplexed, and for a moment the sentimental story once again follows familiar lines. The fact that Faust has Mephistopheles undertake the petty details of the seduction intrigue is nicely obscured by the comic stage business of Mephistopheles' exaggerated servility at this otherwise melodramatic point, and by the unusually brief comedy-servant monologue with which the scene concludes. Theatrically, Faust does not appear as a low intriguer, so that his dignity as dramatic hero suffers only slightly at the outset of his cold-blooded involvement in a plot against Margarete. The selfishness of his love remains evident, but as a "tragic flaw" more easily reconciled with the grandioseness of his already demonstrated arrogant intellectuality than would be the calculating villainies of the standard sentimental Lothario.

At the end of Promenade Mephistopheles' role has been that of 2865-2913 Sganarelle, Crispin, and all comic servants since those of Plautus. The following scene, in neighbor Marthe's house, permits him to play the wandering rogue of late-medieval farce, and its Hans Sachs manner allows an admirably brief monologue exposition of Marthe's grass-widowhood and of traits of her character relevant to the immediate sentimental intrigue. Margarete's arrival with the second gift of jewels is a first overt act of duplicity, for the temptation to

---

[3] For example, *ungerechtes Gut*, "treasures of wickedness"; *Himmels-Manna*, "spiritual manna" (manna is *Himmelbrot*); "he that overcometh" (*wer überwindet*) may "inherit (receive of) the hidden manna," but he does not "gain" (*der gewinnet*).

keep the gift of her secret admirer compels her to confide in someone less scrupulous than her mother. She tacitly accepts Marthe's somewhat sophisticated proposal that the jewels be gradually brought into use, and the half-heartedness of her "What's happening is quite uncanny" is revealed when she automatically expresses fear lest the—nicely timed—knocking at the door which follows these words announce her mother's arrival. With Mephistopheles' entrance the dramatic style, which had momentarily become psychologically modern, is once again archaically naïve[4]—his suppression of the first person pronoun is as much archaism as it is the mark of flattering servility. In the stylized naïveté of the present context Margarete's naïve reaction to the very compliment that she had so sharply parried when accosted by Faust can seem as normal as Marthe's, although Mephistopheles pays it far more fulsomely than Faust did.

2914–3005   Mephistopheles' account of the death of Marthe's husband and of the events leading up to it reintroduces, now in capriccio form, the Rake's Progress theme of sexual license and its degrading consequences. The contrast between Marthe's first conventional expressions of unfelt grief and Margarete's sincere pity for her, like Margarete's evident failure to understand the medical and erotic implications of the story of Schwerdtlein's adventures, establishes the impression that Margarete's unaffected simplicity is that of innocence and inexperience. In naïvely asserting that she will never love, lest the loss of the beloved might be her death, Margarete gives extreme formulation to the tragic theme of "There was a king in Thule." And in her warmhearted sympathy for the "repentant" Schwerdtlein she takes no offence at Mephistopheles' suggestion that she find herself a lover, although the tale which he is telling in such a way as repeatedly to deceive Marthe's expections is one long account of deception and faithlessness. His conditional offer of marriage to Marthe, implying that Marthe's conduct has had as much for her husband to condone as his has had for her to overlook, sums up these two themes at the same time that it reveals how very dangerous is the company Margarete is keeping.

3006–24   Immediately after his jesting proposal, Mephistopheles turns from Marthe to Margarete and asks, "How is it with *your* heart?" Her failure to understand the question's relevance guarantees the helpless inexperience—hence Mephistopheles' malicious aside, "You

---

4 In Marthe's eight-line soliloquy, pronoun subjects are omitted four times; also archaic are her use of the auxiliary verb *tun* to express past time and the paratactic character of all her utterances. She blurts out in definitely archaic word-order Mephistopheles' complimentary aside to the effect that Margarete seems a lady ("Der Herr dich für ein Fräulein hält," normally "Der Herr hält dich für . . .").

good and innocent child!"—which will permit her to come all unsuspecting to the evening rendezvous in Marthe's garden. Marthe's comic-anachronistic desire for death certificate and newspaper obituary furnishes the occasion for a final variation on the theme of deception—the introduction of Faust as a false witness—and to the would-be seducer of Margarete Mephistopheles lends biblical dignity by alluding to him, in words applied in the Lutheran version of *Tobit* to the angel Raphael, as "a fine companion."

The news that he is soon to meet Margarete is received with almost brutal impatience by Faust (second scene Street), who ignores [3025-72] the aspersion on her character implicit in the description of Marthe as a woman perfectly fitted to act as procuress and go-between. In a work of the age when Kant could teach that no lie of any kind was ever justifiable, his reluctance to bear false witness implies a degree of intellectual sophistication consonant with his years of search for ultimate truths, while the repudiation of Mephistopheles' sophistic analogy between falsehood and hypothetical assertions he made as a professor indicates that he still retains some measure of moral dignity. To the question whether he will not soon swear true love, he answers without hesitation "Of course, from my heart," and when Mephistopheles reformulates it, introducing more hyperbolic language, he can still assert that his protestations will be heartfelt. Then, after a marked pause (dash after his "Desist! They will"), he is impelled to defend lovers' dubious promises of "faith and love eternal" and asks whether to call the burning turbulence of his feelings "Infinite, eternal, eternal" is to lie. Since his "infinite" and "eternal" are rhetorical substitutes for "of an intensity not satisfactorily definable," Faust can only rudely silence his alter ego, not refute him. And so Faust once again confronts, now in the world of ordinary human experiences, the insufficiency of words that was so important a factor in his original ill-fated resolution to seek ultimate truths by turning from traditional modes of knowledge to a magical one. For the moment driven by an almost biological necessity to feel that he "must" accept Mephistopheles' dishonest plan, he still has much to learn from life before he will formulate effectively and objectively his growing awareness of its many-sided complexity.

The meeting of Faust and Margarete takes place as planned, but the curtain does not rise on the two couples in Marthe's garden [3073-3148] until all preliminary formalities have been disposed of. The regular alternation of moments of dialogue between Margarete and Faust and between Marthe and Mephistopheles is a happy adaptation to sentimental drama of the Renaissance-classicistic comedy device of a plurality of love plots, allowing in the dialogue of the "low" characters a rapid development of themes which in that of the "high" ones could not with verisimilitude be so briefly treated. The final impression of the scene will be that Faust and Margarete have in their own way discussed the topics touched upon by the other couple as well as those actually mentioned in their own bits of conversation, that Faust, for instance, like Mephistopheles answering Marthe's first question, has given Margarete evasive explanations of who he is, where he comes from, what he does, and where he is going, and that he too has perhaps been urged to settle down as a solid citizen in good time. The low comic relief thus permits syncopation of the stage action at the same time that it cuts to the minimum Faust's appearance in the role of wily seducer, and although Margarete is allowed to talk far more than Faust, whose longest speech comprises but seven lines, what she says makes it possible to imagine the missing dialogue quite satisfactorily. Faust's opening assault with conventional flattery must be deduced from Margarete's first speech, and his two-line reply to it—depreciating to her advantage with sentimental-religious extravagance what St. Paul called "wisdom of this world"—contains his only obviously artificial compliment in the course of the scene.

From Margarete's remarks it soon becomes clear that the responsibilities which she has been forced to assume and the way of life imposed upon her by a somewhat parsimonious mother have limited her social life and left her dangerously inexperienced. Although she knows theoretically that compliments can be meaningless, that men are fickle and do not find permanent satisfaction in the company of women their social and intellectual inferiors, she is sufficiently impressed by Faust's no doubt genuine appreciation of her simple virtues to confide loquaciously the details of her life and present situation. Her interruption of the beginnings of a Rousseauist hymn to the virtues of simplicity, innocence, and humility with the almost prosaically realistic remark, "Though you but think of me for a brief moment, / I'll have quite time enough for thinking about you," reveals a pathetic need of companionship—hence, Faust's leading "You must be much alone?"—that will compel her to enjoy his company while she may. In Margarete's account of her life there is much that is idyllic in an eighteenth-century sentimentally primitivistic way—there is even a delicate allusion to diapers in her mention of having had to be at the washtrough early in the morning— although it is primarily the picture of a way of life which, unlike Faust's, is distinctive for the inner harmony it affords. At the same time her story reveals her strong maternal instincts and a willingness to immolate herself for others, and so it is again suggested that she is doomed to be the victim of Faust's passion.

After a brief exchange of thrusts and parries by the almost 3149-83 evenly matched adversaries Marthe and Mephistopheles, Faust and Margarete again take the center of the stage. That they are already on more genuinely familiar terms is evident from his endearments and from her tacit pardon of his first, bold advances. Her account of how she reacted when he accosted her is significant because it reveals both an extremely strong sense of the proprieties and an almost abnormally scrupulous sense of personal moral responsibility, although the implications of these traits are lost on Faust, whose sole comment, "My sweet love!," would indicate that he sees in them only evidence of simple goodness and sweetness of disposition. Yet the desperate straits to which seduced innocence—*vide* the heroines of eighteenth-century moral and sentimental literature—can be reduced should make the revelation of this side of her character seriously disturbing. For all her naïveté, for all the patriarchal simplicity of her rigorous life at home, Margarete is no stolid peasant girl, and it is with most unpeasantlike incaution that she at this point lets the petals of an aster determine whether she is to believe Faust's protestations of love.

The favorable oracle allows Faust to retain hold of Margarete's 3184-3204 hands for the first time and to press his suit in ecstatically enthusiastic words. At first more honest than in the previous scene with Mephistopheles, he calls what he wants to express "ineffable," only subsequently defining this as the feeling that the bliss of love must be eternal. Momentarily transported by emotion, he can in all sincerity declare that the end of such bliss could only be despair, can assert that such bliss must know no end. His moment of thoughtful silence as Margarete runs down the garden path shows that he is aware of the insufficiency of his protestations, but by following her he indicates that he has chosen to sacrifice Margarete to the compulsion to experience "eternity" in the "moment" of love. And so, with symbolic appropriateness, twilight gives way to night. At Mephistopheles' announcement that he and Faust must leave, Marthe significantly emphasizes the risks attached to any apparently improper conduct in an "evil-tongued town." And apropos of her evident approval of Faust's interest in Margarete, Mephistopheles may well observe that this interest and its reciprocation is "the course of the world," for St. Paul wrote to the Ephesians that it was "according to the course of this world" that they had walked in time past when they "were dead in trespasses and sins."

3205-16   The scene shifts briefly to a Summerhouse—the setting in which so many eighteenth-century Lotharios and Casanovas sought to press their suit. For a moment Faust appears as the playful sweetheart of the girlishly coy Margarete; kisses are exchanged, and Margarete for the first time addresses him with the intimate pronoun "du." The entrance of Mephistopheles cuts short the official beginning of Faust's and Margarete's courtship, the foredoomed clandestine nature of which is clearly marked by Margarete's refusal to let Faust escort her home. When he and Mephistopheles have left, Margarete expresses an admiration of Faust's intellectual powers hardly justified by what he has actually been heard to say to her. A sense of social and intellectual inferiority combines with her desire for love and companionship to deprive her of any effective defense against the dangers of love become infatuation and passion.

CHAPTER IX

The Affirmation of Passion

Into seven short scenes covering two days' time have been compressed all important motifs of psychology and intrigue typical of eighteenth-century and earlier treatments of the first stages of a sentimental attachment, yet these six-hundred-twelve lines with their twenty-three entrances and exits contain enough passages of leisurely exposition to leave a final impression that Faust and Margarete have endured the temporal delays which custom and convention regarded as proper and which Mephistopheles had at the outset declared would be inevitable. When, in sentimental literature, a love relationship has been established, its further development is usually traced slowly and carefully up to the moment when at long last its protagonists are swept away by passion and surmount the often difficult obstacles to its fulfillment. In *Faust*, however, a now well-established technique of impressionistic syncopation—and the fact that Margarete is more a symbolic foil to Faust than an independent character—permit direct transition to this moment of crisis.

Faust's monologue at the beginning of Forest and Cave reveals 3217-39 that a period of sentimental idealization—one fairly long, hence the settled regularity of blank verse after the highly flexible versification of his utterances in recent scenes—is being succeeded by one during which passion will voice its claims ever more insistently. Although love seems to have endowed Faust with the power to commune disinterestedly with Nature, here represented by the life of the forest; and although he momentarily achieves a sense of oneness with Nature—his feeling of brotherhood with all "living creatures"—to

which he could not attain through metaphysical or magical speculation; yet the detachment and objectivity to which his measured words
make as it were audible claim are belied by more than the ultimate
revelation of his restlessness and self-dissatisfaction. Despite his
opening evocation of the Earth Spirit—of God-Necessity—Faust's
new insights are not the answer to any prayer but the corollary of
heightened sensibility, and if his earlier wish to commune, disburdened of all learned obfuscation, with Nature has been granted,
this is at best an indirect consequence of a despairing sense of human
finiteness only intensified by the Earth Spirit's words of rejection. In
the light of his observations on prayer in the scenes Night and
Outside the City Gates, the prayer form of the soliloquy marks a
reversion to patterns of anthropocentric magical-religious experience,
even though Faust now makes no direct appeal for supernatural
help. The potentially dangerous egotism underlying his hardly
fraternal assertion that Nature has been given to him as "kingdom"
will be laid bare in all its monstrousness by the end of the scene,
although it is already made evident within his soliloquy by a frequency
of self-reference far greater than in any previous—or subsequent—
reflective monologue of his.[1]

When, on Easter Eve, he gloomily surveyed the scientific
apparatus in his study, Faust asserted,

Mysterious by Day's broad light,
Nature will let no man remove her veil,
Nor will you wrest from her with screws and lever's might
What to your spirit she refuses to reveal.

Now closer than ever before to an objective understanding of Nature
—hence the new purity of his diction—he feels that his is the power
to look deeply into her breast "as into the bosom of a friend." The
cave to which he has turned for refuge from violent storm thus
symbolizes Faust's newly gained sense of a secure and stable
relationship with Nature, above all of close and meaningful parallels
between macrocosmic phenomena and the microcosmic ones of
man's inner life, between Nature's profound mysteries and those of
his own breast. But he cannot long sustain "contemplation's austere
pleasures," for contemplation is an insufficiently dynamic mode of
experience now to satisfy the impulse that has taken him so far
from the cloistered study. With the digressive vision of "the past's

[1] In the thirty-five lines of this soliloquy there are twenty-four self-references; there
are but thirteen in the first thirty-five lines of Faust's last previous soliloquy (in
Margarete's room), and but nine—of which five are generalizing first-person plural
pronouns—in the first thirty-five lines of his next one (opening scene of *Faust II*).

silvery forms," his thoughts turn by way of historical memories to personal recollections, and he is again aware of his immediate situation, again prey to feelings of dissatisfaction and self-pity.

"That nothing perfect ever can be man's, / That now I feel!" 3240–50 With these words Faust reveals his sense of the discrepancy between his insight into Nature's order, the "bliss" that brings him "ever closer to the gods," and his burning desire for Margarete. His world-outlook is still strongly sentimental and subjective, for he is unable to derive from it ethical principles which will give him a corresponding sense of inner order. Indeed, he is not only beginning to persuade himself that the course of conduct to which he inclines is unavoidable, but even preparing to shift as much as possible his reponsibility for it from himself onto his "now indispensable companion" and the Spirit which he asserts has burdened him with that companion. In the violently subjective context of the conclusion of his soliloquy, Faust's reference to "that fair image" is ominously impersonal, for even if he is alluding to the "heavenly image" of the recumbent beauty he glimpsed in the mirror of Witch's Kitchen, it is embodied at this point in *Faust* by Margarete only.[2] The brother-hood of living creatures within the realm of God-Nature is about to be succeeded by an absolute despotism of self, and Margarete about to become the thing sacrificed to Faust's ego. As he has just declared, perfection is not granted to man—and we know from Prologue in Heaven that error is the corollary of even the noblest human striving —but if he can now dedicate his energies to a seduction incompatible with his new insights, he will ultimately recognize that his has been no noble error and will suffer terribly in consequence.

With the entrance of Mephistopheles the action of *Faust* returns 3251–92 to the plane of normal reality, marked in the verse by the reintro-duction of rhyme, of variation in line length, and of colloquial contraction. Acting as if Faust's communion with Nature were but the conventional solitary reveries of an eighteenth-century senti-mentalist, as if Faust's relationship with Margarete had reached a dead-end of permanent sentimental idealization, Mephistopheles maliciously suggests that it is time for him to go on "to something new." Coolly dispassionate while Mephistopheles plays the mis-judged friend, Faust is nevertheless constrained to repudiate the taunting charge that his new insights are speculations in no wise different from those which once reduced him to almost fatal despair.

[2] Faust's "Thus from desire to its reward I reel, / And in enjoyment languish for desire" must be read as a poetic hyperbole for "I am tormented by conflicting emotions," as anticipatory imagery rather than as dramatic exposition of event or events in the past.

Do you then see what new vitality
This being here alone procures for me?
Indeed, with but an inkling of all this,
You'd be enough a devil to want to spoil my bliss.

Understanding of Nature in both its cosmic and human orders has been and is a primary concern of Faust's. If it is achieved to his satisfaction, he must be forever alienated from Mephistopheles and the magical-unnatural modes of experience symbolized by Mephistopheles. And so the latter nicely brings to his attention the disturbing element of self-preoccupation in his recent reflections before taking up the more immediate theme of his incompletely sublimated erotic desire.

3293–3344   After briefly insisting that Faust will suffer a psychological breakdown if he continues to live the lie of sublimation, Mephistopheles—now the voice of Faust's worser self—paints at length a touching picture of Margarete tormented by longing for the man who has awakened love in her only to desert her. Perfectly aware why Mephistopheles is appealing to the sentimentalist in him, Faust cries to his tempter "Get thee hence" and forbids him to name "that fair woman." But paraphrase defeats itself when he utters the words "desire for her sweet person," for the word for person is also the word for body, and in a moment he is declaring that he cannot forget, cannot bear to lose "her," admits to envying "the body of the Lord / When her lips touch it even for a moment." When the symbol of God's physical presence on earth, of selfless sacrifice and—as in the text of the chorale heard by Faust on Easter Eve—of the triumph of the spirit of mortal man over the forces of stagnation and death, can be regarded solely as a physical thing, then spiritualizing love can no longer hold in check the destructive power of selfish desire. There may still be obstacles to the affirmation of passion, but they are now only external. For, as Mephistopheles blasphemously observes, God helps those who boldly help themselves.

3345–73   Certain that the seduction of Margarete will have disastrous consequences for her, Faust sees himself as a "monster" which, like a plunging Alpine stream, will have destroyed the quiet idyll that was once her self-contained way of life. But since he cannot persuade himself that he is a mere natural force, he finally seeks to evade personal responsibility by simply asserting that her destruction is fatal necessity. Faust's adduction of the "higher" principle of deterministic fatalism is perhaps less subtly dishonest or evasive than the usual sentimentalist's equation of his personal desires with principles for which seemingly impersonal authority is claimed, although it is still hardly consistent with his recent sense of a harmonious order in Nature or with the high value he clearly attaches to Margarete's life and happiness. In finally evoking for himself too the destruction which he foresees will be Margarete's, Faust expresses an awareness that he is becoming inextricably implicated in guilt, rather than a deep-seated conviction that he will cease to be a responsible moral agent. A Faust already "rather well imbued with devilry"—so Mephistopheles' concluding remarks imply—is not one of those souls so pure that a feeling of guilt can destroy them utterly.

The scene Forest and Cave marks the moment of crisis in the sentimental drama of Faust and Margarete, and illuminates every aspect of this crisis as it affects Faust. In *Faust* as a whole, however, this moment coincides with Faust's first great ethical crisis since he emerged from the cloistered study, with his full awakening to the complexity of nonintellectual human experience. By revealing that such experience can grant insights to which abstract speculation could not attain, the scene has made clear that the problems and concerns of Faust the would-be man of practical experience and action are still fundamentally identical with those of Faust the thinker. But only when his relationship with Margarete has run its fatal course will Faust be sufficiently dispassionate to perceive objectively and to act on the insights which he is now in the process of attaining.

To Faust's complex affirmation of passion is contrasted in the 3374-3413 following scene, Gretchen's Room, Margarete's directly but ominously formulated acknowledgment that without his love her life can have no value.

Life is only death
When he's not near,
And all the earth
Seems bitter, drear.

Whereas Faust analyzes his love and its implications, in her monologue at the spinning-wheel—as in Prelude on the Stage, spinning is a symbol of noncomplexity—Margarete reveals an instinctive readiness to live solely for the moment of love fulfilled. Obsessed with thoughts of the absent Faust, she is under a hypnotic spell the half-impersonal quality of which is reflected in the assimilation of the phrasing of her thoughts to the monotonous working of her spinning-wheel, and the rondo-like recurrence of the lines "I have lost all peace, / My heart is sore; / No rest shall I find now / Or evermore" suggests the narrow circle of ideas revolving with mechanical regularity within her mind. The Faust whose return Margarete so vividly envisions will find her defenseless, her once strong sense of conventional values temporarily neutralized by the natural magic of love.

3414–58   The scene Marthe's Garden shows the lovers reunited at their normal place of rendezvous, and the curtain rises as Margarete is introducing the serious issue of religious belief into their conversation. Her "Promise me, Heinrich," [3] the preamble to a request for an honest answer to the question she is about to put to Faust, is interrupted by his gallant "Whatever I can!" But at first he seeks to avoid any confession of faith, not because his views might cost him her already unconditional devotion, which here takes a form verging on maternal concern, but because he recognizes the great importance of orthodoxy for one basically so convention-bound as Margarete. Finally constrained to make some statement, he blends Old Testament imagery and New Testament phraseology with familiar motifs of deistic and pantheistic speculation—the regular motion of the stars, the mystery of the "invisible visible" presence of an all-encompassing and all-sustaining force—only to insist once more that

Feeling is everything;
Name is but sound and smoke,
Obscuring Heaven's warm light.

3459–3500   Although Faust has offered no credo, but only an affirmation of feeling in which Bliss, Heart, and Love are suggested as full equivalents of God, his passionate eloquence is concrete enough to persuade Margarete of his profound piety, and general enough to conceal from her the degree to which his faith is unorthodox. "All that is very fine and right," she says, returning the dialogue from psalm-like rhythms to rhyming verse, "We've heard almost the same when our priest spoke, / Although in slightly different words." But Faust, subscribing to no system of transcendental values, has gambled his life on the instinctive conviction that man's destiny can be properly realized in the realm of ordinary human feeling and activity, a realm now seen to be only seemingly lower than that of the

---

[3] Heinrich may be an alias, since it is used exclusively by Margarete, although it is possible that Johann, the traditional given name of Faust, is avoided simply to keep him from being addressed by a name reserved for servants in eighteenth-century life and literature.

spirit to which he had so long and so unhappily confined himself. Through love his sense of a cosmic order with meaning for man has been heightened, and in the naturalistic frame of reference established by the prologues to *Faust*, Margarete's cautious approval of his religious views is valid witness to their basic rightness. As she observes, Faust is no Christian, but because her Christianity is also an affirmation of the meaningfulness of human life it permits her to accept him as what he is—a good man, even if implicated in error. For the same reason it compels her, a creature "otherwise kindly disposed toward all," to abhor Mephistopheles, in whom she condemns solely, but at significant length, those traits revealing hostility toward life and love that make his presence a dehumanizing influence.

Like the more complex Faust, Margarete is fundamentally "a good human being." The rightness of her judgment of Mephistopheles places her on the side of God-Love and the angels, of God-Nature and the Faust who has had faith in man even in his moments of profoundest skepticism. Her love may blind her to the danger in identifying Faust with the fulfillment of her womanly instincts—how she envisages the development of her relationship with him is clear from her observation that a permanent association with his companion would be intolerable, that she "Would not want to live with one like him." But love has not caused her to err so far from man's proper course as to lose faith in human dignity, nor has it deprived her of awareness that love without human spirituality, the hypothetical bestiality of Auerbach's Cellar, is not love at all. Her comments on Mephistopheles thus reveal not only loving concern for Faust's welfare; they also insist that Mephistopheles is the antithesis of the best within Faust and herself. Simple feeling—her awareness that Mephistopheles' presence is the death of love—can be more right than reason confused by feeling, yet Faust is able to silence her simplicity because it has no weapon with which to counter the explanation, itself only obscuring verbalism, "You just have an antipathy."

From erotic religiosity to seduction is but a step in much 3501–20 sentimental literature, and in the sentimental drama of Margarete and Faust it is also but a step from serious religious discussion to the fatal plan which will mean Margarete's destruction. Defenseless against Faust's passion because she is a creature of right instincts, she agrees to use the sleeping potion which Faust has ready. If she is persuaded with unusually little effort to do so, it is less because the motif is traditional and all too common in sentimental novels, than because for her the great violation of her former ethical code has been the clandestine association with Faust—her "I've done so much for you already." Within the Tragedy of Faust the juxtaposition of religious discussion and practical seduction is dramatic restatement of the ironic principle, announced in Prologue in Heaven, that what is good cannot be realized by finite man without some degree of attendant evil. For all his recent awareness of the glory and divinity of Nature, Faust can now cavalierly refer to Margarete's mother as a mere "living organism"—also *die Natur*—to be agreeably put to sleep for his and Margarete's convenience. And so the unbolted door of the third bit of folksong sung by Frosch in Auerbach's Cellar becomes a motif of Faust's experience of the world of common humanity.

3521-43   The cynical humor of Mephistopheles' deliberate misinterpretation of why Margarete has "catechized" him wins from Faust an unqualified acknowledgment of her honest concern for his welfare, although he fails to recognize that her "faith" is not simply the church creed with which she herself identifies it. The epithet "suprasensual-sensual," which Mephistopheles so sneeringly applies to Faust, is applicable to Margarete as well, for in her too are commingled unreconciled scales of values. If her Christianity must be offensive to Mephistopheles the traditional devil, her naturalistic humanism—her instinctive repugnance against his inhuman qualities—must be even more so to Mephistopheles the exponent of bestialization and total negation. Accordingly, except for a brief Mephistophelean anticipation of the events of the coming night, the scene closes with a reminder of the instinctive rightness of her feelings about himself, a reminder the more emphatic by virtue of its somewhat anachronistic allusions to the fad of physiognomy and the cult of genius so influential in Germany toward the end of the eighteenth century.

CHAPTER X

The Sense of Guilt

Faust has completed the seduction of Margarete in full 3544–86
awareness of what must be its consequences for her, but she had long
before ceased to think in terms of consequences. Only subsequently
does she again come to appreciate that conduct apparently justifiable
by subjective standards of feeling and instinct may seem merely
reprehensible when judged by the standards of a particular social
community. In the scene At the Well—a setting with patriarchal
associations regularly evoked in eighteenth-century sentimental
treatments of lower-class life—she is reminded that in addition to her
private world there is a public one which regards the fallen woman as
a public menace, as a sinner to be shunned, even as a criminal to be
punished by the ecclesiastical authorities. Lieschen's account of
Barbara's seduction and desertion, and the envy, jealousy, and
malicious hostility which it reveals, constitute for Margarete a rude
awakening to social reality. Her assumption that an offer of marriage
will satisfactorily regularize Barbara's social position indicates she
has not as yet been deserted by Faust, but her recognition that her
tolerance toward Barbara would have been impossible before she
herself became "vulnerable through sin" shows she is at last conscious
of what may be the social consequences of her relationship with him.
With the pathetic cry "And yet, o God! that which brought me to
this / Was all so good, was oh such precious bliss!" she relegates
to time past the subjective factors that were the only justification of
her conduct. The idyll of love is ended, and in accepting society's
view that her love has been sinful, that there are absolute standards

of right and wrong, she becomes prey to all the destructive forces that a sense of guilt can release.

3587-3619   Margarete acknowledges that in her world ostracism is the lot of the fallen woman by seeking out a shrine of the Mater Dolorosa located in the desolate area by the town's outer bulwarks to offer flowers—it is presumably early the following spring—and prayers to the Virgin. Her "Oh turn, in thy gracious mercy, / O thou who art sorrowful! / Thy countenance down upon my suffering" can echo the Stabat Mater because hers is a supreme grief, an anguish no less terrible than that of a mother who sees her son suffer and die. After the broadly stylized realism of the preceding scene, the monodramatic lyricism of By the Ramparts insists the more effectively that Faust's desertion has meant brokenhearted loneliness as well as fear of public disgrace. The primary function of Margarete's prayer is thus expository, to show the latest development of her relationship with Faust and its consequences for her, but her final four lines incidentally hint at what is to be her fate, at what form the destructive havoc Faust is causing will take. The "shame and death" she begs to be spared is the public humiliation of the unwed mother still demanded by eighteenth-century society, a practice condemned by many humanitarians and humane jurists on the grounds that it created a motive for infanticide, for which the death penalty was obligatory. Apparently but a hendiadys for "mortal shame," taken literally the phrase "shame and death" is a prefiguration of what is to be Margarete's tragic fate; not only is hers an agony like that of the Mater Dolorosa, but like the latter's Son she is to know the agony of public execution also.

3620-97   That Margarete's disgrace has become common knowledge is a main theme of Night: Street before Gretchen's Door, which takes place two nights before St. Walpurgis' Eve. Many weeks or months seem to have elapsed since the preceding scene, and although Faust's first lines show that he regards his visit to Margarete with some misgivings, this can only be because he has long neglected her, not because he has any glimmering of what has developed in his absence. It may be somewhat shameful to return to her simply in order to rekindle the flame of passion—is not the periodic reawakening of animal desire the theme of Mephistopheles' answering remarks?— but Faust is so blissfully ignorant of the true state of things that he welcomes the suggestion that he make his sweetheart a gift of pearls, which are a popular symbol of tears and misfortune. Ominous only are his insensitivity to Mephistopheles' insinuation that Margarete has already been paid well for her favors and his brutal failure to interrupt the highly offensive song with which Mephistopheles serenades her.

By letting Faust kill her hotheaded brother—the duel motif is ₃₆₉₈₋₃₇₇₅ standard in treatments of the theme of seduced innocence—Mephistopheles makes it psychologically inexpedient for him to see Margarete for some time to come, and so Faust is led away before he can learn anything that might inspire him, who is never ruthlessly unkind, to attempt to alleviate her distress. What Margarete and the gathering crowd hear from the lips of her dying brother is condemnation unmitigated by the least touch of human charity. Valentin's belief in the doctrine that one error always leads to a worse one— the Rake's Progress theme, and the very doctrine inspiring Mephistopheles' attempts to corrupt Faust by implicating him in as many forms of guilt as possible—places him in another camp than that of the Lord of Prologue in Heaven. His words can only further undermine Margarete's already shaken self-confidence, and the sole voice to reprove him is that of the all-too-human Marthe. General hostility is what Margarete must now expect from society, hostility as irrational and brutal as that which causes Valentin to believe that the murder of Marthe would be an act of blood sacrifice sufficient to guarantee the forgiveness of all his sins. Valentin may be right in believing he dies a Christian soldier, for God's mercy surpasseth human understanding, but he is surely wrong in totally condemning his sister. If she, the embodiment of seduced innocence, can retain any measure of human dignity after this degrading scene and its consequences, there will be every reason to believe that Faust also need never completely lose his way in the labyrinth of human error in which he has involved himself; if the cult of willful evil is not to be the consequence of guilt for Margarete, neither need it be so for Faust.

All the voices raised in condemnation of Margarete, and the voice ₃₇₇₆₋₃₈₃₄ of her own conscience too, merge as the one cruel voice of the Evil Spirit standing behind her throughout the scene Cathedral. She has summoned up the courage to appear in public for what is probably her brother's Requiem Mass, but memories of earlier and happier moments in church give new intensity to her sense of guilt, so that she considers herself responsible not only for Valentin's murder but also for her mother's death, which we here learn has occurred at some point during her connection with Faust.[1] From the religion

---

[1] It is usually assumed that Gretchen's mother has died of an overdose of the sleeping potion given at Faust's suggestion, although nothing in the text of *Faust* except what Margarete says in her final madness would indicate that she was killed by anything except the shock of discovering her daughter's misconduct.

which is her faith she gains no consolation for herself or the child quickening within her, and her Evil Spirit pictures the Last Judgment, in images borrowed from the very text now being sung to organ accompaniment, as a day of punishment only, as the moment when a heart enjoying the peace of the grave must again experience the torment of living. Her neighbors turn their faces away when, identifying her sense of oppressiveness with physical confinement, she cries out for air and seeks to leave, despite the knowledge that her departure will be regarded as a futile attempt of "sin and shame" to seek a hiding place. As she imagines the Blessed and Pure similarly turning from her on the Day of Judgment, the choir is heard repeating the question—a repetition *not* in the text of the Mass—"Quid sum miser tunc dicturus?"[2] In a sense her fainting appeal for immediate physical assistance answers the question, for in the cosmos posited by Prologue in Heaven what may be said on a Day of Judgment is irrelevant, what must always come first are the physical and spiritual needs of finite human beings. And if these needs are not satisfied, to live is but to be brutalized and life only a meaningless existing. In reducing Margarete to her present straits Faust himself has shown brutality, but he is not a creature of circumstance and remains free to redeem himself under new conditions; for Margarete the only escape from the cruel world to which she is bound may well be the hypothetical peace of the grave.

3835–70   At various times in history satanism and witchcraft have been earnestly cultivated because men, despairing of the forces of light, were persuaded of the greater power of those of darkness. Although a visit to a witches' Sabbath is not a traditional motif of the Faust legend, the scene Walpurgisnight seems momentarily to return the action of *Faust* from an age of intellectual and sentimental sophistication to the one of fear and superstition in which the story of Faust was originally offered as a warning against godless intellectualism and sensuality. But Faust, still ignorant of Margarete's true situation, cannot regard an ascent of the Brocken as an act of moral self-annihilation, as a renunciation of life and aspiration that might correspond to the assumption of Margarete's tragic fate so grandiloquently invoked at the end of the scene Forest and Cave. The death of Valentin, in which his role was largely that of Mephistopheles' agent, may have left him temporarily dazed, but in retrospect he could not fail to see that he had acted, however unnecessarily or unfortunately, in instinctive self-defense. At the

2 "What shall I then say in my misery?"

opening of Walpurgisnight, therefore, he speaks not as one hesitating to take a decisive step or as one burdened with a *new* sense of guilt, but simply as one glad to enjoy the distractions of an invigorating spring-night excursion. Apparently a tangential interlude in the sentimental drama of Faust and Margarete, by virtue of its theme of deliberate sensualism Walpurgisnight actually precipitates the climax of that drama at the same time that it further clarifies that drama's symbolic function in *Faust* as a whole.

Hardly has Mephistopheles commandeered the light of a Will-o'- the-Wisp to supplement that of the gibbous moon when the realm of the natural is replaced by a "sphere of dream and magic." The stanzas of Faust, Mephistopheles, and their guide mark a rapid transition to a world of the grotesque in which configurations of landscape come to life and things and creatures of the night crowd about the trio. If for a moment Faust can fancy that in the echoed gushing of mountain streams he hears songs of love and hope, by the time a first vantage point for viewing supernatural phenomena has been reached he can no longer distinguish between rest and motion or between animate and inanimate things. Under Mephistophelean suggestion he has been transported to a realm of phantasmagoria which partakes of reality only because it is a projection of the human spirit, and so his visit to the Brocken is the dream companion piece to Margarete's waking nightmare at her brother's funeral. 3871–3915

In Auerbach's Cellar and Witch's Kitchen Faust remained a detached observer of the baser manifestations of folly there confronting him, but the Walpurgisnight is a dream sequence mirroring an inner state of moral and emotional confusion that has become ever more precarious in the course of his connection with Margarete. Nature, for Faust usually a symbol of order and harmony, now assumes a demonic appearance as he sees the landscape glow with magic light and hears and feels the great destructive wind that brings hordes of witches and warlocks to offer homage at Satan's throne. Spring rites in which Faust the humanist might discern survivals of ancient fertility worship are viewed, uncharacteristically for him, through older orthodox Christian eyes as a cult of obscenity and bestiality,[3] so that pregnancy and birth—the theme is traditional in the lore of witchcraft, but the emphasis given it would indicate that Faust has at least considered the possibility of Margarete's being with child—represent only ugliness and evil. 3916–85

[3] The only "witch" mentioned by name in the text is Baubo, not a figure from Northern folklore but the lewd nurse of Demeter mentioned in Orphic poetry and cited in the writings of the early Church Fathers as an example of pagan indecency.

3986–4143   Despite the perverted system of values that prevails in it, the world of the Walpurgisnight always remains an extension of the natural order that Faust has known. Voices from below, variously lamenting their inability to achieve perfect imperfection, are reminders of his repeatedly experienced feeling of human finiteness. When he is momentarily separated from Mephistopheles in the fitfully illuminated confusion of motion, noise, and smell, his indispensable companion quickly rejoins him and begins playing the role of knowing guide first assumed when Faust consented to quit his scholar's study. As then, Faust inclines to speculative concerns—his interest in the "riddles" of Satan-worship—but Mephistopheles insists that the "great world" of the witches' Sabbath must be disregarded so that Faust may be introduced to a "little world" of what would seem rather ordinary human pleasures and pastimes for so supernatural an occasion. A group of senescent "old gentlemen" sit apart from the center of activity, their aloofness like that of Faust in Auerbach's Cellar, lamenting the better days of their lost youth. A witch peddling secondhand goods displays a series of items all of which recall critical moments in the story of Faust's connection with Margarete. The figure of Lilith, like the recumbent form that Faust glimpsed in the magic mirror of Witch's Kitchen, is a symbol of seductive beauty, and like that image, it marks a moment of awakening sexual desire. On beginning their tour of this "little world," Mephistopheles had announced that he would be the matchmaker and Faust the suitor. Now Faust seizes a young witch and his companion an old one, and the suggestive and, in the case of Mephistopheles and his partner, obscene stanzas of the following dance song represent a climactic moment of erotic abandon.

4144–75   The entrance at this point of Sir Runic Rump (as Philip Wayne so nicely translates the name Proctophantasmist) introduces a note of satirical skepticism consonant with Faust's basically naturalistic world-outlook—and provides a passage of dialogue which in the theater can cover up the censurable text being sung by the second pair of dancers. Since Sir Runic Rump is an easily identified exponent of the German Enlightenment who in 1799 reported that he had been cured of hallucinations by the medical treatment which explains his name, his appearance temporarily destroys the atmosphere of frenetic supernaturalism that has gradually been created and effectively insists that the obscene, like the fantastic and grotesque, is primarily symbolic in this Walpurgisnight masque. What Faust has experienced in the course of a few minutes is thus the equivalent of a series of erotic adventures, comparable to Saint-Preux's Parisian experiences in *La Nouvelle Héloïse*, by which he tries to put thoughts of Margarete from his mind. The intrusion of the figure of Procto-phantasmist is an interruption of this development, and by the end of the Aristophanes-like digression Faust has withdrawn from the dance because he has remembered Margarete.

Faust's innate inability to conceive of love on the Mephis- 4176–4209 tophelean level of mere bestiality is represented dramatically as his recognition that the beautiful young witch is a creature of loath-someness symbolized by the red mouse he has seen jump from her mouth. His vision of Gretchen with her feet shackled and a red cord about her neck is less a premonition of her ultimate fate at the executioner's axe than evidence that he at last recognizes what the full consequences of his love for her may be. It is thus in character for Mephistopheles pervertedly to insist that Faust sees only Medusa and willfully deludes himself by insisting otherwise, but it is also in character for Faust to ignore attempts to explain away "facts" that, if true, must drastically heighten the sense of guilt already his. With the reaffirmation of his loving concern for Margarete, Faust falls silent, and the Walpurgisnight ceases to be a dream of menacing satanic elements.

Faust has escaped complete dehumanization, has discovered 4210–4398 that in the realm of the satanic he is but an imperfect amateur, a dilettante. The remainder of Walpurgisnight is a brief dream play of little intrinsic interest, a masquerade[4] whose predominantly satiric tones once more insist that in *Faust* the supernatural has only a symbolic function. Of large thematic importance are the amateurish imperfection of the performance and the motif of a loving couple reconciled; a secondary theme quite relevant to *Faust* is the implication, ironically expressed in the lines of Materializing Spirit, that poetry must mirror life if it is not to be merely grotesque and meaningless; and in the spirit of Faust himself is the skeptical treatment of exponents of organized piety and formal philosophy. As more and more groups of figures crowd on to the stage, the

[4] Accordingly, some stage directions identify a speaker or speakers, while others simply indicate what character or characters pass as the Herald describes them. Although some critics have found the masquerade "delightful," they are a small minority. All the specific satiric allusions, with possibly one or two exceptions, are to minor eighteenth-century contemporaries of Goethe's; all but the last two of the intermezzo's forty-four stanzas are sheer doggerel, their metrical monotony relieved only by a far greater incidence of strikingly clever rhymes than is normal in the text of *Faust*. The rhyme scheme *abab* is strictly maintained except for three stanzas—that of Materializing Spirit, where the incongruous non-rhyme *nicht* (not) replaces an expected *auch* (too), and those of The Massive and Puck at the end of the scene, in which effects of clumsiness and mock-clumsiness seem intended.

intermezzo seems to become purely digressive, but at the very end the song with which Ariel summons the nature spirits of the masque to (Oberon's) rose-covered hill reestablishes for the terms "Nature" and "Spirit" the high value that the waking Faust has ever attached to them. The Orchestra's pianissimo heralds the first signs of dawn, the creatures of the witches' Sabbath disappear, and, as the curtain falls, Faust and Mephistopheles stand once more in the realm of visible Nature, the realm of possible realities, the all-comprehending realm in which alone imperfect man's worth can be fully tested.

The action of *Faust* moved from the world of autonomous human behavior to one of dreams and phantasmagoria when Margarete swooned at the end of the scene Cathedral. Walpurgisnight has represented symbolically Faust's unsuccessful attempt to forget her, his inability not to feel a sense of guilty responsibility for what happens to her. How well and wisely he stands the tests which the resumption of personal moral autonomy must entail is the one important theme still to be developed within the sentimental drama of Faust and Margarete, and in various guises it remains the central theme of all his subsequent dramatic adventures as well.

CHAPTER XI

The Compulsion to Atone

The climax of Walpurgisnight showed Faust's instinctive Trüber Tag feeling of responsibility for whatever might become of Margarete. His reaction to the actual facts of her desperate flight and eventual arrest for infanticide is the central theme of Field: Overcast Sky, a scene whose dynamic prose rhythms audibly insist that Faust has returned from the realm of dream fantasy to a world of starkest realities. No less than his opening reference to Margarete's "long" wanderings, the disheveled turbulence of his language marks a considerable temporal distance from the end of Walpurgis Night's Dream and its light verses, and the effect of the shock produced by the belated revelation that Margarete has been condemned to death is reflected in the fragmented structure of his sentences, which are predominantly exclamatory and nondeclarative. Pity for Margarete and horror at her sufferings from man's inhumanity are experienced by Faust with tragic intensity, but cathartic release is impossible, so terrible is his anger with Mephistopheles' perfidy and indifference and at his own disastrous blindness and the helpless irrationality of his present impassionedness. In identifying himself emotionally with Margarete, he experiences one important aspect of mankind's common lot so magniloquently invoked when he concluded his compact with Mephistopheles, although he does so with none of the egotistical fatalism that made his evocation of her fate at the end of the scene Forest and Cave so ambiguously rhetorical. On the Brocken he toyed with evil; now fully implicated in it, he feels only compelled to mitigate its consequences for Margarete.

If Faust rightly laments the perpetual repetition of human

suffering and rightly wonders that an all-forgiving God can ever anew demand mortal atonement of guilt, there is nevertheless a certain measure of unwarranted self-righteousness in his condemnations of Mephistopheles, who at last momentarily silences him with a blunt reminder that he, not Mephistopheles, "has caused her ruin." In accepting the companionship of Mephistopheles, Faust voluntarily chose to know joy *and* sorrow, so that it is only fitting for him to experience fully man's tragic sense of helplessness in the face of disproportionate "misery," a word he uses four times to characterize Margarete's human situation. As an autonomous moral agent, however, he can and must ignore his alter ego's warnings of the risks attendant upon an attempt to help Margarete; he shows the courage and will to act, and with this the moral clarity to recognize, as he has apparently not recognized before, that the killing of Valentin is one crime for which he cannot properly be held responsible. Unable to frighten Faust, or silence the voice of his conscience, Mephistopheles puts a good face on what for him is a bad business and agrees to provide the conditions necessary for Margarete's rescue. And so the "Up and away!" with which Faust exits is a cry for release in action as well as theatrical anticipation of his and Mephistopheles' hurried departure on magically provided horses.

4399–4404   The last moments of the wild ride back to Margarete take Faust and Mephistopheles past the place of execution to which she is to be led at dawn. Since her imminent death under the executioner's axe has already been clearly foreshadowed by the red line Faust saw about her throat in his Walpurgisnight vision, it is only a secondary motif of the scene Night: Open Field, which with its rhymeless verse provides a stylistic transition from the prose of the preceding scene to the normal metrical patterns that are reintroduced in the following one. Although witches may be expected to congregate about a gallows, busily concocting some brew, Mephistopheles' explanation of what the aerial figures discerned by Faust are and of what they are doing does not quite fit the ritual solemnity of their activity as Faust describes it. Creatures of evil or not, their endowment with angel-like motions by Faust at least reflects his conviction that Margarete is a good and potentially redeemable human being. The sums total of finite man's achievements and failures cannot simply be balanced against each other like ledger entries but must remain incommensurable, else there could be no propriety in ever speaking of tragic failure, an all-too-human concept perhaps, but one which even poets who have consciously tried to believe that the good man is rewarded in this or some other life have in their practice never ceased to acknowledge as valid and viable. The final entry for Margarete is to be suffering surely disproportionate to her responsible acts, and Faust's first great experience outside the cloistered study is to end with his helpless discovery of tragic necessity.

The scene Prison opens with Piranesi-like effect as Faust stands 4405–22 before Margarete's cell in the darkness into which he has brought the feeble light of a lantern. A sense of the immensity of human pathos, "of all the misery of man," evokes in him a feeling of dread and awe which he has long not known and which he has not claimed to know since the moment when the Earth Spirit was about to appear to him in his prison-study. Of his own free will he has returned to the stifling narrowness, from which he had hoped forever to escape by joining Mephistopheles, that in *Faust* symbolizes man's oppressive awareness of his finite physical limitations. If Faust is right in asserting that the crime of her behind the damp wall was "a brave illusion"—a series of actions that seemed the best possible at the time they were resolved upon—then even in this prison man's powers of aspiration may be heroically affirmed. Not by Faust, however, who must summon up courage even to face Margarete, but by the fear-crazed girl who is heard singing within the words of the reincarnated victim in a German folk tale of Atreus-like infanticide. Opening the door to her cell, he may still think of himself as "the one she loves," but he is just beginning to experience at first hand some of the horror that has emptied her life of meaning and so altered the character of their relationship that her rescue could have no constructive value except to palliate temporarily his own sense of guilt.

Margarete's failure to recognize Faust immediately is a symptom 4423–69 of this fundamental change in their relationship, not one of blind fright only. If she protests that her "executioner" has come too soon, it is less because she fears death than because she is trying to understand herself and what is happening to her, less because she suffers physically than because she needs human sympathy to help her regain some measure of human dignity. "If you are human," she cries groveling before Faust, "feel my distress." Her insistence that he is a stranger is thus symbolic, although it also is evidence of an examination of her past experiences so engrossing that she cannot bring herself at once back to the present. Her words recall her desertion by Faust, Lieschen's malicious remarks at the town well, the child she is charged with killing, the popular condemnation to which she has been exposed and, in language echoing that of the scene Cathedral, her religious fear of eternal damnation. In his feeling of the terrible pathos (*Jammer*) of Margarete's condition, Faust at last becomes a man whose actions are simply the natural reflexes of common humanity. His heartfelt cry, "Gretchen! Gretchen!"—this is the first time he is heard to address her by name—succeeds in penetrating Margarete's consciousness; in "the beloved's voice" she recognizes a power more real and immediate than that of the hell of "weeping and gnashing of teeth" she has been envisioning.

4470–4550   Margarete recognizes her rescuer, but she can conceive of rescue only as a return to a past when she had not yet experienced the anguish of guilt or the fear of retribution, as a return to the time of her first meetings with Faust. That haste is urgent is thus beyond her comprehension, and Faust's unconcern with caresses seems to her to be the coldness of a dead love. Death is indeed in the air of her prison, but not until Faust's reassuring "Soon will I press you warmly to my heart" does she pointedly ask Faust, and herself, if he knows whom he wants to set free. When he does not reproach her for the death of their child—the motif of her madness leaves uncertain whether this was a crime or an accident—she seizes his hand and at last grasps the immediate situation clearly. The clamminess of Faust's touch may remind her of blood-covered hands, of Valentin's death, but she is no longer confusing past and present. Accordingly, she repudiates Faust's injunction to let bygones be bygones and makes it plain—in her touching instructions for the final interment of her mother, her brother, her child, and herself, and in her refusal to leave her cell except to die—that she is instinctively resolved to atone by death for the fatal consequences of her past conduct. Although Faust has returned to her, and although she discerns true kindness and goodness in his eyes, she knows that never again could happiness with him be possible. Hers is not the power of will that could sustain a guilt-racked existence in some strange new environment, even though it were not, as she naïvely imagines it in terms of the period of flight which ended in her arrest, a life of physical want and perpetual fear of recapture. To live with her memories and her conscience, even in the companionship of Faust, would be for Margarete but a joyless existing, completely unlike the good human life as she understands it, something so alien to reality as known to her that she again begins to relive the past even while she explains why she cannot go with him.

4551–96   Margarete's visionary state, her reëxperiencing of their child's drowning and of a moment of flight when she nightmarishly imagined seeing the seated figure of her dead mother on a mountainside, is now the means by which her own free-unfree will excludes further

discussion of what Faust is urging her to do. Only a strangely
incongruous "Those were happy times!" reveals that in her heart,
as opposed to her conscience, she still feels her love for Faust was
somehow good and fair. At Faust's attempt to rescue her forcibly
her resistance again becomes conscious, and in refusing to leave
with him she can remind him with terrible clarity that "Once I did
all for love of you." Faust's last attempt at verbal persuasion, his
warning that day is at hand, only turns her thoughts to the public
ceremony of her execution. The great occasion of her life should, as
she says, have been her wedding day—the day of fulfillment of the
eternal romantic dream that has so fatally involved her with Faust—
but this day's climax will be no gay wedding dance, only the silence
of spectators "mute with the muteness of the grave." Margarete has
accepted and anticipated her death, no longer belongs to the world
of the living, and Faust knows that her will has triumphed over his,
can only helplessly wish that he had never been born to experience
the anguish he has here seen and felt.

The appearance of Mephistopheles in the outer darkness of the 4597-4612
prison and his cynical "Futile faint-heartedness! Waiting and
prating!" underscore the moment of Faust's tragic defeat. Margarete's
horror at this intrusion into the place where she has made her peace
with her God and has achieved tragic dignity is entirely consonant
with her earlier recognition of the essence of evil in Mephistopheles'
inhumanity; and Faust's dazed inability to understand her compulsion to atone—his mechanically reassuring "You shall live!"—
constrains her to recoil from him as well. Sadistically reminding
him that Margarete is now irrevocably condemned to death,
Mephistopheles disappears into the darkness with Faust, whose will
has been paralyzed by the horror of his guilt. If a voice from above
somewhat superfluously insists that guilt and redemption need not
be mutually exclusive,[1] the voice of Margarete heard crying Faust's
name less and less audibly from within her cell as the curtain falls
emphasizes that her loving concern for him remains to the end the
highest value given her to know in the course of her ill-fated life.
Terrible though have been its consequences, Margarete's love has
potentially revealed to Faust all the sustaining and transforming

---

[1] The words of Voice from Above—"She is redeemed!"— were not superfluous
when *Faust I* appeared in 1808, since no one except Goethe could then guess that she
would appear as a heavenly figure at the end of the whole *Faust*. They served to make
clear that Mephistopheles' "She is condemned" meant only "She is not to be saved
from execution" and not "She is eternally damned," which the parallel to the ending of
old Faust plays, "Fauste, in aeternum damnatus es," might have unintentionally
conveyed.

force which the Lord of Prologue in Heaven attributed to divine love itself.

The second large section of *Faust* has seen its protagonist exhaust the whole gamut of emotions to which he surrendered himself with willful imprudence when he entered the realm of common humanity; if he now again leaves a prison in the company of Mephistopheles, it can only be to enter new spheres of life and new realms of experience in which the supreme values must still remain those revealed to him by his love for Margarete. Given the apparently inexhaustible recuperative powers which Faust demonstrated in the first scene of the Tragedy by recovering from seemingly bottomless despair, his recovery from the tragic shock of her final sufferings can be but a matter of time. He will then be able to see, although he will come to do so only gradually, that a girl remarkable only by virtue of her aptitude for selfless love has shown him the height of dignity to which mortal man can attain—what has been dramatically represented in Prison by her secular-sentimental apotheosis. Although Margarete's simple religious faith can never be his, she has demonstrated to Faust once and for all that man lives fully only when his way of life fully expresses the compelling ideas to which he gives supreme allegiance. During the denouement of Margarete's tragedy, as he has suffered by being the cause of human suffering and so has in some measure atoned for the *hubris* which occasioned his original decision to venture forth from the cloistered study, Faust's part has been a passive one, ultimately because at the critical moment represented by the scene Forest and Cave he deliberately renounced responsibility for the consequences of the seduction of Margarete. The hurt he has done to Margarete, and himself, cannot be undone or effectively atoned for in the realms of human experience still ahead of him; but Faust is surely free to choose a more active, responsible role in those new moments of critical decision which a life of many potential labyrinthine paths of human error still leaves open to him.

CHAPTER XII

A Prelude on Earth

The Second Part of the Tragedy opens with the scene 4613–33
Pleasant Landscape, the foreshortened dramatic representation of
Faust's recovery from the paralyzing shock of Margarete's terrible
last hours and what he then himself suffered.[1] A dream technique
like that employed at the end of his first interview with Mephistopheles and for the Walpurgisnight sequence permits a highly
economical variation in the treatment of the already familiar motif of
Faust's recuperative powers. It also makes possible the introduction
of echoes of the first prologues, echoes which strengthen the scene's
incidental function as the prologue to a new section of *Faust*. As at
the critical moment in the development of his relationship with
Margarete, a restless Faust has sought the solace of Nature, and
while dusk becomes darkness he falls into a healing sleep on a bank
of grass and flowers to the song of Ariel, the one harmonious voice
of his Walpurgis Night's Dream. The accompanying music of
Aeolian harps—Dedication's symbol of "natural" art—emphasizes
that Ariel and his elfin companions symbolize those natural forces
which enable "Every scion of the earth" and "Saintly man and
sinner too" to know a rebirth like that of plants in spring. As rest

---

[1] Unlike the First Part of the Tragedy, the Second Part is divided into "acts."
Act I consists of the present scene and a series of scenes at a German imperial court,
II of two scenes in Faust's university quarters and a "Classical Walpurgisnight"
localized in Thessaly, III of scenes taking place on the Peloponnesus, IV of scenes in a
mountainous region of the German Empire, and V of scenes taking place on the coast
of the Empire and a scene amid mountainous ravines. Since these divisions are not
dramatically functional, but only mark large changes in style of scenery, they are ignored
in this interpretation.

and time quiet "the heart's fierce strife" and remove "the incan-
descent-bitter darts of blame," the series of feverish moments that
began with Walpurgisnight ends with Faust in a state of protective
oblivion, remembering few specific details of "horror experienced"
but restored "to the sacred light" which is life.

4634–78   In four lyric stanzas the various voices of the spirit chorus
successively evoke the twilight in which Faust is lulled to sleep, the
nocturnal quiet in which he obtains the "blessing of complete
repose," the first tokens of the new day to which he will awaken
renewed, and the dawn which comes as his sleep, symbol of will-less
passivity, is about to end. "Sleep is husk to cast away! / Although
others drag and dally, / Do not hesitate to dare; / All is done by
spirits lofty/Of bold action's need aware." The complete disappearance
of narrative-descriptive elements from these final lines of the elfin
chorus marks the imminent restoration of Faust's active will, of the
attitude which one Easter night inspired him confidently to substitute
"Deed" for "Word" in his fatally interrupted translation of the
opening of the Gospel according to St. John. At the approach of
the sun, announced by a majestic reverberation that recalls its
"thunderous course" in the Archangels' hymn of Prologue in
Heaven, Ariel and his spirits withdraw to the silence of stone and
plant, and a waking Faust once more communes with God-Nature.
Still the paramount symbol of the source of light and life, in the now
well-established humanistic context of *Faust* the sun no longer needs
to be approximated to the God of Judaeo-Christian tradition; the
sound heralding its arrival—and the natural resurrection of Faust—
is now identified with that of the noisy gates of Homer's heaven
and that of the wheels of Apollo's chariot.

4679–4703   With Faust's soliloquy, a more usual, though no less direct, form
of dramatic exposition replaces that of allegorical projection.[2] No
longer Ariel's "man of misfortune," Faust notes approvingly the
signs of Nature's awakening, "Life's pulses beat with fresh vitality /
To hail in tenderness etherial dawn," and rightly attributes to God-
Nature, to Earth—the personification is his—the stimuli which
arouse in him "a strong resolve / Ever to strive for life's most perfect
forms." Then he surrenders himself to contemplation of the world
about him, offering a description which superficially resembles the
picture of spring he painted in tripping rhythms for Wagner on
Easter Sunday but which is free of its sentimental glossing over of

---

[2] Readers familiar with the enthusiasm of Goethe and his romantic contemporaries
for the dramas of Calderón will recognize Calderonian techniques both in the device of
lyric-allegorical exposition and in the use of *terza rima* for dramatic monologue.

the fundamental difference between Nature's unconsciousness and man's distinguishing attribute of rational awareness. In *terza rima* as majestic as the blank verse of his Forest and Cave soliloquy, though less statically regular, he describes only what he actually observes, accurately and vividly, with none of the insistent intrusion of his ego that there belied the apparent objectivity of his measured words. Nature is still God-Nature—hence the "paradise" in which he places himself as almost impersonal observer—but there is no equating of the dynamic interplay of its forces with the very different phenomena of sentient human life. Faust marks the signs of approaching day about and below him—the noises of the somber forest, the fog, the light penetrating the valleys, and the emergence of visible forms, first as the larger shapes of branch and bough, then as colors, and finally as flower, leaf, and even trembling pearl of dew. He then looks up to the mountain summits, already directly illuminated, and watches the green contours of their slopes become clearer and more brilliant as the rays "of the eternal light" strike ever lower points. At last "he" appears, and Faust, dazzled, turns, so that he is not forced to look into the symbol par excellence of the visible mystery of God-Nature.

Only now does Faust reflect upon what he has just seen, and he does so in a manner inconceivable at any earlier point in his development. He is not crushed because communion with Nature has again wrung from him an admission that her veil is impenetrable even in day's broad light, nor do his heightened powers of observation afford an occasion for immoderate self-exaltation. If he ventures an analogy, it is not between Nature and Man, but between man the observer of physical phenomena and man the observer of spiritual or moral ones. Thus, as when Faust evoked the flaming shape of the Earth Spirit, men may strive with apparent success for the realization of their highest hopes but find the momentary vision of perfection so overwhelmingly bright—"From those eternal depths breaks forth / Excess of flame, we stand confounded"—that the fiery intensity of their pain and pleasure prevents certain identification of what the Poet of Prelude on the Stage termed "The power of hate, the force of love," normally recognizable as polar opposites. And so Faust at last acknowledges that man is necessarily and rightly earth-bound, constrained to look "to the earth" and there find security "within the ever-youthful veil" of self-renewing Nature.[3]

[3] The epithet "youthful" is employed by Faust with the positive connotation "vitally fresh" attached to it in Dedication and by the Player of Prelude on the Stage, rather than in the meaning "young in years" that the Prelude's repudiated Poet gives it

4715-27   In resolutely leaving his back turned to the sun, Faust affirms
that the limits of finite man as he now understands them are essential
positive values. Although he does not say so, this implies the
corollary, confirmed by the action of the remainder of the Tragedy,
that he will be content with a normal lifetime and renounce the
madness of seeking literally that infinite totality of human experience
he invoked for himself when he made his compact with Mephistopheles. During his Easter walk with Wagner he had regarded as
intolerable frustration of man's highest aspirations the impossibility
of fulfilling his dream of perpetual flight into the setting sun. Now he
accepts human finiteness not merely gracefully—fluidly graceful as
is the verse in which he speaks—but with heroic confidence in man's
power to place himself in a harmonious relationship with the large
design of infinite God-Nature. If, in terms of the theology of
Prologue in Heaven, the dignity of man is indeed the dignity of God,
then now Faust is making no tragic sacrifice in any absolute sense
and may turn, without regret or frustration, a delighted gaze to the
observation of a plunging mountain stream. A waterfall like the one
to which (at the end of the scene Forest and Cave) he compared
himself, the monstrous destroyer of the Alpine idyll of Margarete's
life, this cascade is for him simply a fact of nature, not something
arbitrarily perverted to a symbol of one individual's momentary
emotions. Indeed, such is his present objectivity that the rainbow
appearing and disappearing in the shifting cloud of vapor above the
falls suggests to him not the usual symbolic associations of hope or
transcendental promise but, as its impermanence demands, a
mirroring of human endeavor. Although man's strivings may seem
to be ineffectual diffusions of energy, they must be part of a large
design no less regularly ordered than that which makes inevitable the
projection of a spectrum under the right conditions. In this sense
Faust can properly assert that we have the essence of life in its
varicolored facets. Like the insubstantial rainbow, the seemingly
insubstantial achievements of man are realities mirroring whatever
ultimate reality there may be.

Attaining the insight posited in Dedication—that mere appearances can be supreme realities (applied only to the realm of art,
though Prelude on the Stage added the corollary that life and art
are of one essence)—Faust possesses a fuller understanding of life's
significance and man's divine dignity than has yet been his. His new

and that is Mephistopheles' value for it when he is goading Faust to leave his prison
study. As in Prelude on the Stage, youthfulness is thus here synonymous with the
power to grow and develop.

clarity of vision may be regarded as a consequence of the cathartic experience from which he has just recovered; how well it sustains him in coming vicissitudes must be a central theme of the subsequent dramatic action. In "the little world" of Margarete he largely failed to act in consonance with the best insights to which he had then attained. It remains to be seen whether, in "the great world" which comes next on the program Mephistopheles originally mapped out for him, Faust's actions will be more consistent with the insights he has now achieved.

THE REALM OF THE
GREAT AND POWERFUL

CHAPTER XIII

Man and History

The scene Throne Room of an Imperial Palace represents the theoretical center of the society to which Faust historically belonged; it motivates his introduction into the sphere of temporal greatness and power. In the light of his resolution "ever to strive for life's most perfect forms," it must be deduced that this is the setting in which he hopes to find a worthy outlet for his energies, although in the event he will prove to have played here a role no more permanently constructive than that which was his in Margarete's little world. This does not mean that his experiences will be valueless, or that history—the imperial court is a historical world, not the one of timeless individual experiences in which Faust has so far moved— will remain for him the unreadable "book with seven seals" he once told Wagner it was. But he has grasped the seeming fact that the rainbow's "changing permanence" is the symbol of human endeavor. He has generalized his personal conviction, ultimately a consequence of the tragic ending of a love to which he willfully insisted upon applying the epithet "eternal," that life's meaning can only be grasped "in its varicolored forms" through the observation of phenomenal reality, that is, *sub specie temporis* and not *sub specie aeternitatis*. Rightly or wrongly, therefore, and unlike totalitarian thinkers whose premises have enabled them to justify visions of ideal static societies, Faust is committed by a potentially tragic sense of human finiteness to a non-utopian vision of history. While he may for a time incline to the view that society can somehow be wiser and more consistent than its individual members, in the end he will recognize that "changing permanence" describes man's collective endeavors no less well than his individual efforts.

Although the Second Part of the Tragedy, like the First, is basically the drama of one individual, it places him in large social contexts, the satisfactory representation of which demands dramatic techniques other than the lyrical and impressionistic ones chiefly employed up to this point. In various scenes collective entities have been represented—by types and groups in Outside the City Gates and Auerbach's Cellar, by single speakers in At the Well and Cathedral, and by even more patently symbolic figures in Witch's Kitchen and the Walpurgisnight sequence. But these have served only to place the individual concerns of Faust or Margarete in clearer focus. In Throne Room and subsequent scenes, historical and social phenomena which Faust is to observe or reflect upon are most frequently presented with the techniques of Renaissance theatrical pageantry that romantic and later writers copied from Shakespeare and Calderón, in Goethe's day the almost equally esteemed models for grand-historical drama. But drama of this kind usually treats only the private concerns of some individual who is historically important or to whom historic importance is fictitiously attributed, and Goethe's ironic use of its salient features indicates he is fully aware of this. And so the sudden change in stage technique announced by a fanfare of trumpets—the obviously "historico-dramatic" entrance of an Emperor accompanied by splendidly accoutered Courtiers into the presence of a Council of State—marks, not a lessening of interest in Faust as an individual hero, but simply one more of the variations in theatrical technique promised by Prelude on the Stage and already frequently illustrated.

4728–60   The Emperor's speech from the throne begins in the best ceremonial manner, only to be interrupted after two lines so that he may inquire into the whereabouts of his Fool, who it transpires has collapsed on the way to the throne room. His place has been immediately taken by a stranger, exquisitely though grotesquely costumed, who forces himself into the Emperor's presence and attests his professional qualifications with a riddle or, perhaps, a flood of riddles.[1] This figure, Mephistopheles in a new and obviously

---

[1] If Mephistopheles' eight questions constitute a single riddle, its answer might be The Fool. He "approaches the steps of the throne" in jester's garb, and his predecessor there "has banished himself" simply by not turning up; this answer reduces his earlier questions to mere distractors, since they really fit neither A Fool nor The Fool. The first two pairs of questions concern something completely ambivalent, like money (which can be both "accursed" and "ever welcome") or one's own weaknesses (which can sometimes be "defended," yet at others be "scolded and lamented" in self-reproach).

"Shakespearean" role, is accepted as court fool by the Emperor, who punningly but revealingly equates questions raised by his Councilors with a jester's conundrums.[2] The Emperor's indifference to the fate of his old fool and his carelessness in letting an unvouched-for stranger succeed him, no less than his inability to give undistracted attention to matters of importance, have shown him to be personally and politically irresponsible even before he is seen confronted with any specific problem of state. So this brief but dramatically important digression ends with the Court's murmuring that the advent of a new favorite will mean new sufferings.

The historical pomp and circumstance of the opening of Throne Room ironically emphasizes the Emperor's personal insignificance. It also serves to place the action of this section of *Faust* in a past far more sharply differentiated from the present than in Faust's first two realms of experience, where vaguely sixteenth-century settings afforded convenient backgrounds for economical poetic statement of the timeless theme of individual human finiteness. There the historical Renaissance was a source of motifs; here it is a theme, the symbol of historical change and social crisis, of the historical process as it came to be understood in the eighteenth century by thinkers like Vico, Montesquieu, Hume, and Herder. There largely the age which saw a successful reëstablishment of the arts and sciences despite survivals of medieval superstition, here it is a period of transition from feudalism, which long survived anachronistically in the Holy Roman Empire, to national states more viable in a world of expanding capitalism. Although the important factors for understanding German history on the eve of the Reformation had been clearly discerned by historians of the romantic period, for romantic poets the middle ages were a sacrosanct golden age the termination of which they could with propriety lament, and they tacitly ignored historical phenomena that might reveal the instability of a theoretic-ally harmonious and static feudal world and so explain the emergence

A plausible answer to the third pair of questions would be *One's Self*, which cannot be summoned to where one is no matter how much one may like to hear his name mentioned. And even the last pair could as well be answered with *Wisdom* as with *Folly*; banished from the Emperor's presence by his frivolity, it can be reintroduced inoffensively by a court fool. Given Mephistopheles' predilection for barbed remarks, his "riddles"—the plural is the Emperor's—seem to me to suggest a series of impudent allusions to the Emperor's financial distress, his personal irresponsibility, his vanity or self-centeredness, and his unreceptiveness to wise counsel.

[2] Pointing to the left side of his throne, the Emperor orders Mephistopheles to occupy his former jester's place, saying "Da löse du! das hört' ich gern" (both "I'd like you there as his replacement" and "I'd like you to do some unriddling in that matter," "that matter" being "the riddles which are the concern of these Lords Counsellors").

of new social patterns. To place Faust in a historical milieu illustrating the disintegration of medieval society is to repudiate romanticism in its most popular early nineteenth-century German form, that of nationalistic medievalism. The middle ages, and two other great golden ages of European romanticism—that of primitive and Arcadian man, and that of classical Greece—provide the historical settings for most of the rest of *Faust*, but at no point will romantic medievalism, romantic primitivism, or romantic hellenism represent more than the variable substance which mirrors the "changing permanence," the patterned constants, of individual and collective human endeavor. Similarly, the utopia which Faust will seek to establish at the end of his career will not be a romantic one, and at that point he will even repudiate romantic supernaturalism—perhaps the only perpetually recurring form of romanticism and the one which, with its universal myth of the magus, provides both the plot and the machinery of *Faust* as a whole.

4761–4851 With Mephistopheles now at his left hand, the Emperor again begins to welcome his "faithful vassals and beloved subjects." Hardly has he alluded to the favorable auspices of the occasion when he once more shifts suddenly from formal eloquence to a more colloquial style and expresses his petulance at having to devote himself at carnival time to serious matters. The Chancellor—it will later appear that he is an Archbishop—answers in kind what should have been a convocatory speech from the throne, first praising the Emperor as the living embodiment of justice and then offering a general description of the Empire paralyzed by monstrous disorders and legalized injustice. When his elegant generalizations, formulated with frequent recourse to parallelism and personification and nicely adorned with exclamation, rhetorical question, simile, and antithesis, fail to evoke an imperial rejoinder, he goes on to paint a black picture of universal corruption in which he fleetingly alludes to "rebellion's growing tumult." Having again paused and received no reply, he concludes his speech with a blunt warning that, unless decisive action is taken, the Emperor's personal interests will be adversely affected. The Grand-Master of the Imperial Forces completes the picture of lawlessness with his account of burgher and knight rebelling successfully against imperial hirelings who plunder and lay waste the lands they should protect, so that half the Emperor's world is already lost. The Intendant-General, taking his cue from the Grand-Master's concluding allusion to the indifference of other monarchs, opens his statement of imperial finances with a reminder that subsidies promised by allies have not been forthcoming. After noting that in an ever less feudal society the crown has no salable rights left to alienate, he pessimistically expatiates on how, in an apathetic body politic, self-interest has so barred "the gates of gold" that the imperial coffers remain empty.

It is noteworthy that the Intendant has illustrated the enervation 4852-76 of the Empire with the same polar opposites that Faust in the preceding scene declared were indistinguishable in moments of abnormally intense aspiration. For a society in which "love and hate are both become the same" is in an abnormal state, is suffering from a psychic disintegration that is the collective counterpart of the individual breakdown from which Faust has just recovered. If Faust's principle of "changing permanence" is valid for the group as well as for the individual, time and rest may restore the Empire to health, although it will necessarily be a different sort of Empire because the conditions which it meets will have changed. The Intendant's is thus, historically, the most important speech in this whole historico-dramatic scene; it implies what is to be demonstrated in the course of the historical action of the Second Part of the Tragedy, that political activity which simply seeks to bolster a moribund social order by preserving unhealthy conditions is doomed to failure. In contrast, the speech of the Lord-Steward, with its picture of the extravagances of the imperial household, of an intemperate nobility, and of deficit financing, reflects only concern with immediately pressing difficulties, yet it alone evokes comment from the Emperor, who with fatalistic passivity asks his new fool if he knows no other source of distress.

With Mephistopheles' reassuring denial, the function of the 4877-4916 Lord-Steward's homely observations becomes clear. They make obvious to all but the Emperor that Mephistopheles is deliberately dishonest in his panegyric argument from visible but mortgaged magnificence, that he is a sycophant who will gain favor only to foist upon the court some disastrous "scheme," a term evoking memories of John Law and Cagliostro as well as of countless royal alchemists. Declaring that money is all that is wanting, he proposes that the situation be remedied by locating gold buried as treasure or as yet unmined with the aid of a magus, a competent natural philosopher. His cautious circumlocution for Faust, "A man of talent's innate mental powers," occasions an angry tirade from the hostile Chancellor-Archbishop, who protests the favorable mention of human Nature and the human Spirit—for neither of these is a highest value in Christian theology. Heedless of the principles of Ciceronian oratory of which he is a demonstrated master,[3] the Chancellor pictures the fate of heretics, describing with typical late-medieval allegory Doubt as the misshapen bastard child of Nature-Sin and Spirit-Devil, and is out of breath and forced to speak elliptically by the time he warns Mephistopheles "[Talk] not so to us!" After a necessary pause, marked in the text by a dash, he goes on to castigate as heretical the liberal tendency to grant political influence to nonmembers of the two traditional estates of medieval society, the clergy and the nobility, and ends in such passionateness that the remote antecedents of his pronouns let him unintentionally suggest that "these high circles," rather than "heretics and warlocks," are somehow "closely akin to the Fool."

4917–46   With the Chancellor reduced to verbal helplessness, Mephistopheles can impudently attack him in his own theological territory and charge him with the heresy of somatological materialism. The Emperor, too frivolous to enjoy a "Lenten sermon" or theological disputation, but accepting as sound the thesis that money will solve all problems, demands action. For the rest of the scene Mephistopheles plays on the Emperor's cupidity like a cat with a mouse, alternately raising and dashing his hopes of sudden wealth. A true mystagogue, he ironically mixes truth and falsehood, sense and nonsense. The task the Emperor has set is "easy, yet easy things are hard." There is subterranean wealth and an art of winning it, but "Who knows how to undertake this art?" That treasure trove belongs to the crown is a principle whose validity is acknowledged by the still disinterested Intendant-General, but no one questions his insinuation that European history has been an almost perpetual reign of terror from "time immemorial . . . till yesterday—and till today." The Chancellor may recognize that Mephistopheles is making a diabolic appeal to human avarice, is perhaps laying the groundwork for recourse to impious magic, but the Lord-Steward, thinking only in terms of immediate advantage, is willing to risk "a little injustice," while the Grand-Master, a military realist who regards himself simply as an instrument of policy, is frankly indifferent to ethical considerations.

4947–76   By calling on the court astrologer to testify, not to the truth of what he has been saying, but to the auspiciousness of the hour,

---

[3] Although the Chancellor is too impassioned to organize his ideas coherently, his innate formalism is reflected in the verse structure of his speech, which follows the rule of the fifteenth-century Mastersingers that a stanza should consist of two *Stollen* with the same rhyme-scheme followed by a dissimilarly rhymed *Abgesang* longer than one *Stollen* but shorter than the two of them together. (The rhyme pattern of the German text is *aabccb, ddeffe, ghghiiih.*)

Mephistopheles uses him—the murmuring crowd rightly recognizes that "the seer" is prompted by "the fool"—to proclaim the coming of a master. The Astrologer's "man of greatest learning" is Faust, and his horoscope, so transparently filled with double and triple meanings that even the Emperor finds it unconvincing,[4] is dramatically important because it announces Faust's imminent reappearance in a role often played by the Faust of history and legend, that of magician-alchemist. Although Faust has renounced alchemical magic to seek more ordinary forms of human experience, he is to be introduced at court as a magus, esteemed by some but regarded by others—thus by one of the murmuring voices of the crowd—as "a charlatan." Any wisdom he can offer will be disregarded by an Emperor and advisers anxious only to exploit his highly praised magical powers. So Mephistopheles has already doomed his first efforts in "the great world" to failure.

Mephistopheles now takes open cognizance of the murmurings   4977–5032 of opposition, whether timidly superstitious or ironically skeptical, and assures his listeners that Nature will tell them by various bodily sensations where to begin to dig for treasure. Mass suggestion at once produces the expected symptoms, which seem to be those of the dancing madness of the later Middle Ages, and the voice of reason is silenced as the scene turns into a sort of Witch's Kitchen transposed from a romantic-supernatural setting to a romantic-historical one. The Emperor himself announces his readiness to put his hand to the spade and again demands immediate action, threatening Mephistopheles with death if he is lying. But the latter, a demagogue who has completely captured his audience, chooses further to excite its cupidity with a Land-of-Cockaigne-like picture of the delights of finding gold and plate, goblets carved from precious stones, even wines preserved in their precipitated tartar, now all shrouded "in awesome night." "Here undeterred," he declares, "the Sage pursues his quest; / To know a thing by daylight's but a jest— / The home of mysteries is darkness hight." Without these concluding lines his speech would be a purple passage only, a counterpart of the Queen Mab speech in *Romeo and Juliet*; with them, it is a challenging denial of Faust's view that life and light are one, of his awareness that Nature is mysterious even in day's broad light, and establishes obscurantism as an important symbol of error for that part of his dramatic career now about to begin.

[4] Mars is thus not only both planet and the element iron; he is also the threat of war and, given the erotic allusions of the speech (the symbolic marriage of elements, gold as means of buying sexual gratification), the danger embodied in outraged parent, guardian, or husband.

9—G.F.

5033–56   While he disavows all interest in Mephistopheles' "mysteries" and counters his praise of darkness with a series of proverbs of the class "All cats are gray at night," on mentioning pots of gold, also colorless in subterranean darkness, the Emperor reawakens his own cupidity and interrupts himself to order immediate action for a third time. Mephistopheles now boldly assures him that by taking mattock and spade in hand he can in a trice release a herd of golden calves, although the line "This peasants' work will make you great," an ironical repetition of the Witch's Kitchen motif of the benefits of physical exercise, hints that the only practical result of the scheme which has won the Emperor's support could be to teach the dignity of labor. But then, having raised the Emperor's expectations to fever pitch, Mephistopheles suddenly unbinds the spell which he has worked upon his victim and, through the Astrologer, proposes postponing action until carnival is over, insinuating with truly diabolic irony that Lenten devotions which strengthen the faith of the believer will also increase the credulity of him who hopes for (profane) miracles.

5057–64   In docilely proclaiming that joy shall reign unconfined until Ash Wednesday, the Emperor does exactly what he had vainly attempted to do at the opening of the Council of State. When the figures who represent the pomp and circumstance of historical drama have withdrawn to the sound of trumpets, Mephistopheles is alone on the stage. Now simply the wise fool of Shakespearean and pseudo-Shakespearean tragedy, he points out the obvious lesson that simpletons never realize that there may be a causal relationship between merit and fortune. His epigram is banal, but his illustrative assertion that the philosopher's stone demands the presence of a philosopher to use it is dramatically functional, for it is a final reminder that the scene Throne Room has prepared Faust's introduction to the imperial court in his old-new role of philosopher-magician.

The second and larger theme of the Herald's prefatory speech is its equation of pageantry and life, the first recapitulation within the dramatic action of *Faust* of an important aesthetic principle posited in Dedication and Prelude on the Stage. Since it will eventually transpire that the whole Masquerade has been prepared by Faust, the assertion that the folly of carnival is an extension of the folly of life must be regarded as an aesthetic corollary of his insight in Pleasant Landscape, that meaningful appearances have absolute symbolic value. It is another matter, however, whether the bastard art form of a court pageant, in which great concession must be made to rank, occasion, and the acting talent available, can effectively embody highest human insights. Thus, the intrinsic dramatic interest of Masquerade largely centers in how well Faust succeeds in creating this his first but not last self-contained work of art.

The first group of masks consists of Florentine flower girls, who 5088–5157 identify themselves and their artificial wares in a song paying appropriate tribute to the "Splendor of the German court" and appropriately insisting—this the Herald's art-life theme—that feminine nature is closely related to art. At his order they dispose of their flowers, demanding that each purchaser describe in epigram what he acquires. These impromptu verses, surely *impromptus faits à loisir* if there ever were such, present two symbols of peace and prosperity (Olive Branch, Wreath of Grain), two of artificiality (Artificial Wreath, Artificial Bouquet), and one of naturalness (Rosebuds) challenging art to rival nature. Thus, by the time the Flower Girls set up their displays under the green arcades that decorate the great hall, the motif of art as artifice which they primarily represent has been balanced by that of nature the touchstone of art; then a new group, consisting of Gardeners, immediately takes the center of the stage.

This is possible only because Faust's pageant is composed in 5158–77 accordance with the best principles of masquerade writing, one of the most important being that the text not only be suited to the talents available for its performance but that it also be performable without deadly silence between its separate parts. What on a program may look like an unwieldy number of *dramatis personae* must at performance break down into distinct groups and a few easily identified main figures. What in a libretto may seem to be an endless number of speeches written only to give as many persons as possible speaking parts, should, when heard, fall into two very different categories. The first consists of matter subordinate to the introduction and placement on the stage of the customarily numerous actors. This includes the songs and speeches of groups and their members, and frequently separate pieces given to minor figures so that there will be a break between the successive entrances of large groups otherwise not effectively distinguished from each other. The second consists of elements—lyric, allegorical-symbolic, narrative, or dramatic—entrusted to better qualified speakers and placed at points when stage movement and spectacle will not distract attention from them. At this point in Masquerade matter of the first type predominates, but when the stage has been properly filled with a lavish variety of figures, elements of the second kind will assume primary importance.[4] The episode of the Flower Girls has illustrated the principles just outlined, for they enter to five stanzas of song, the last and presumably most audible of which introduces the important art-nature theme; they disperse during the verse impromptus, the last and most serious of which comes at a moment when no stage business is required; and then the Gardeners in their turn enter, at the end of their song joining the Flower Girls in the background as both groups sing alternately.

5178–5262   Another principle frequently followed in court masquerades is to build steadily to a climactic final moment, introducing the most important figures—and highest court personages—at the very end.[5] In Faust's masque this principle—which may be good theater or spectacle but which is certainly bad drama, allowing as it does little occasion for suspense or reversal of situation—is applied with a novel variation. Each successive episode represents a "higher" subject in accordance with late Renaissance art theory, which established an order of subject-values ascending in gradual stages from still life to landscape and landscapes with figures, then to portraits and genre scenes, and so on by way of mythology to allegory and, highest of all, the equally esteemed genres of history and tragedy. The Gardeners with their useful—and "real"—fruits have already represented an advance beyond the "merely beautiful" flowers of the first carnival group. They are followed by figures from pastoral life, the mute fishermen and bird-catchers who enter and mix with the crowd in the chatter that follows the Mother's advice to her still unmarried Daughter to use this occasion to catch herself

---

[4] At no point are the limitations of a stage hall, as opposed to the greater floor space of an actual palace, forgotten. Solo interludes not only serve to keep large groups discrete; they also permit superfluous figures, or figures needed to enhance the size of later groups, to disperse inconspicuously through the adjacent apartments mentioned in the opening stage direction.

[5] This is not merely a matter of inverse precedence, since first-comers must stand patiently silent the longest.

a husband. Noisy Woodcutters, representing the coarseness of village peasantry, furnish a butt for the remarks of Idlers (Pulcinelle) and Parasites, low forms of urban life. The three groups constitute one episode and therefore all speak in the same short dipodic lines (which may correspond successively to the short breaths taken by those who perform heavy labor, by those who run aimlessly about killing time, and by those who must watch the effect of their every phrase if they are to continue to enjoy patronage).

Again a soloist, this time a Drunkard whose tipsy unselfconscious- 5263-98 ness is a wholesome antidote to the Parasites' "double-breathedness," allows an overcrowded stage to be made ready for new mass entrances. By the time he collapses in the middle of the last stanza of his song, a drinkers' chorus has been organized on benches and kegs somewhere to the side of the stage. So, at the end of this musical interlude there is room for a procession of poets, descriptively announced by the Herald as "Poets of Nature, Court Singers, Poets of Chivalry, Sweet Singers, and Enthusiasts." Their simultaneous desire to take the center of the stage produces such confusion that they are unable to display their talents, only Satiric Poet getting in four lines on the apt theme of poetry no one would want to hear. Straggling behind come Poets of Night Thoughts and Graveyard Poets, by their animated conversation with a Vampire, "visibly fresh from his grave," patently about to become poets of the grotesque in some late-romantic form. Granting their pantomimic request not to be inter-rupted and made to speak their piece,[6] the Herald now calls forth the female figures from Greek mythology inevitable in any Renaissance masque. These are led by Greek Mythology herself and, like her, are pleasingly dignified despite their being "in modern mask," in conventional classical costume.

The Graces—the briefness of the lines assigned them suggests 5299-5344 that they represent court beauties to whom the memorization of more than one couplet each could not be safely entrusted—succinctly urge graciousness in the giving and receiving of gifts, a theme nicely suited to an occasion when all present are the beneficiaries of lavish imperial hospitality. The Fates, who need not be beauties, have more lines to speak than the Graces, although what Atropos and Clotho say is not very important—the former warning against immoderation and the latter, who has been entrusted with the cutting of the life

---

[6] Although songs of groups of poets were common in Italian *trionfi*, the satiric stage business here permits maximum economy in the use of a motif that, if developed, would duplicate themes already exploited sufficiently in Walpurgisnight and Walpurgis Night's Dream.

thread because of general dissatisfaction with Atropos' practice, paying tribute to the auspiciousness of the occasion by placing her shears in their case. The words of Lachesis, however, are serious; reflecting Faust's awareness (vision of the Earth Spirit) that weaving is a valid symbol of life's meaningful complexity, they recall the existence of an immutable natural order which no masquerade make-believe can conceal or prettify for more than a fleeting moment.

Should I once forget my duty,
World might then no life sustain;
Hour and year must aye be counted
Till the Weaver takes the skein.

5345–92   The third and last mythological group, the Furies, has to be explained by the Herald, for it consists of three beauties—apparently with considerable dramatic ability—whose identities are to be deduced neither from their appearance nor from what they say. Here the ever-wrathful Alecto is a malicious belle of a comedy of manners who delights in alienating lovers, confident that her efforts will have lasting harmful effects regardless of apparent reconciliations. The envious Megaera could be the moving force of a comedy of humors, a personification of Mephistophelean-diabolic as opposed to divine discontent, although her association with Asmodeus makes her primarily Alecto's counterpart for married couples.[7] And so Tisiphone, the avenger of murder, is correspondingly the murderous avengeress of infidelity, the betrayed operatic heroine who in breathless lines, shorter than those of her companions, operatically proclaims that rocks echo "Revenge!" to her lament.[8] With the tragicomic figures of the Furies, Faust's masque has attained something near the level of simple dramatic action, above which come only allegory (anticipated to the extent that the Furies incidentally represent Calumny, Inconstancy, and Jealousy) and the coequals history and tragedy. Almost all the remainder of Masquerade takes place in the realm of allegory, of novel poetic invention, and when the allegorical action finally merges with the dramatic action of *Faust* the whole gamut of Renaissance art subjects will by a unique theatrical tour de force have been successfully represented in an art form which by its very nature cannot ordinarily transcend the limits of allegory.

[7] The simultaneous use of Greek mythological figures and one from the Apocrypha is a typical pagan-Renaissance motif.
[8] Her "He who changes must not live" is a villainess' denial of Faust's affirmative concept of "changing permanence" in Pleasant Landscape.

Up to this point Masquerade has been largely mere divertissement, of perhaps slightly more than average interest if the principles governing its structure have been recognized, and it has actually disappointed dramatic expectations raised by the scene preceding it. Since its empty splendor can hardly have dimmed the picture of a frivolous Emperor unstably enthroned, it may, like Walpurgis Night's Dream, be regarded as marking a significant passage of time—the interval between Mephistopheles' arrival at court and the formal climax and conclusion of pre-Lenten celebrations. During these days Faust, whose services the Emperor expects to use on Ash Wednesday, has had to be presented to him and be persuaded to assume the office of master of the revels that corresponds to the traditional Faust's role as court magician-entertainer. If the hand of Faust has been occasionally evident in earlier episodes, with that of the allegory of victory Masquerade becomes primarily the expression of the best insights to which he has so far attained.

From the Herald's descriptive commentary, and from the 5393–5456 speeches of Fear, Hope, and Understanding in the Old Testament sense of the means by which wisdom is achieved, it is clear that the moving tableau of Victory is more than mere local-historical color, is not simply a motif copied from a bas-relief depicting a Roman triumph or from a painting of a Renaissance triumphal procession in the style of Mantegna. To be sure, Italian *trionfi* were mounted on occasions when there was no triumph to celebrate, but it is surely ironical that a figure so inappropriate to the state of the Empire is here introduced. Victory is "Goddess of Activity" because she crowns all wisely directed human striving. She may safely stand in resplendent triumph so long as Force—in the more special political-historical context the Power of the Nation as in the great elephant fountain planned by Napoleon for the Place de la Bastille—is guided by Understanding, so long as unfounded Fear and self-deluding Hope are kept by Understanding from producing panic paralysis or optimistic passivity. Faust's allegory is therefore didactic rather than sycophantic, a warning both against pessimistic despair such as was expressed by the Emperor's advisers at the opening of Throne Room and against wishful thinking like that later encouraged by Mephistopheles. And through the veil of allegory may be glimpsed not only his new resoluteness, but also the past when he vacillated between happy imprudence and fatalistic passivity, finally to experience the horror of Margarete's last hours.

As then, the voice of evil intrudes, in the unheralded person of a 5457–93 double-dwarf who vituperatively abuses "Dame Victory." (The medieval title before Victory is a deliberately discordant note, a reminder that classical elegance is largely veneer in this Renaissance world.) Although the stage figure of Zoilo-Thersites—a name suggested by the carping Alexandrian critic of Homer, Zoilus, and the scurrilous enemy of Achilles and Odysseus in the *Iliad*—is hardly Mephistopheles', the voice surely is; for in *Faust* only he can be imagined so boldly asserting in the rhythms of Walpurgisnight witches' choruses, "Raise high what's low, what's high pooh-pooh! / Put crooked straight, what's straight askew! / Nothing else gives me such mirth, / That's how I want things here on earth." To what has been an Allegory of High Purpose is opposed a symbolic embodiment of cynical realism, over which Foresight, the Herald's "pious wand," can triumph. Smitten with a "compelling blow," the dwarf must withdraw, but its retreat becomes a semi-victory for Mephistopheles when, first changing into a loathsome mass, it departs in the double semblance of an adder and a bat.

The uncanny episode produces confusion among the spectators, most of whom fail to recognize it as an antimasque. It thus emphasizes the fact that what up to now has been treated with the freedom of an outdoor set is indeed a large and crowded hall, over whose dusty floor the adder crawled, toward whose ceiling flew the bat, and to whose windows and main door the Herald will allude in his next speech. Before the entrance of Victory daylight had begun to fail; the stage is now lit only by the flickering torches, lanterns, and candles to which Fear first drew attention and to which even blindly optimistic Hope alluded disparagingly. The dangers of fire and panic in a closed room filled with inflammable decorations are main conditions of the theatrical effectiveness of the climactic ending of Faust's pageant; accordingly, this bit of seemingly gratuitous stage magic is functionally important in terms of the larger dramatic action as well as thematically relevant as counterpoint to the Victory allegory.

5494–5639 The episode of Zoilo-Thersites has allowed the stage to be cleared for the entrance of a new allegorical group, which arrives on a dragon-drawn and star-surrounded quadriga that the Herald has claimed to see approach with magic insubstantiality through crowded off-stage anterooms. His protested inability to identify the new arrivals—a handsome Boy-Charioteer, Faust on a throne in the rich oriental costume so long standard for magicians and, crouching behind him, Mephistopheles, still in fool's garb but looking thin from starvation—emphasizes the importance of this allegory by permitting a more dramatic form of dialogue to replace that of set speeches. Although Charioteer disarmingly declares that he and his companions are allegories come to honor the Emperor's halls, from the Herald's description emerges a vivid picture of a warm-blooded and attractive youth, while the long familiar figures of Faust and the half-hidden Mephistopheles clearly represent a first introduction of familiar reality into the self-declared world of make-believe which is Masquerade. And since Charioteer serves Faust as Faust-minded Understanding served Victory, it is to be deduced that this allegorical episode is to complement the first by offering corollaries of insights there expressed. For to strive for high achievement, as an insatiable and unhappy Faust so long did, and to achieve victoriously, as may but need not necessarily happen when Understanding controls Force, are both to express some part of man's innate divinity. Yet neither separately nor together can aspiration and success constitute the only supreme values discerned by one who has resolved to seek all life's most perfect forms. Isolated from his fellow men, Faust gained only the bitterest satisfactions from his triumphs as scholar, physician, and philosopher-magician, and he learned at least one thing from his relationship with Margarete—that to receive more from others and from life than one gives of one's self is to know only an empty victory.

If Faust now appears in the mask of Wealth, as Plutus, it is not only because he hopes to gain power in the great world which is any seat of empire by assisting the Emperor with financial wizardry, but also because Wealth is the symbol of power enabling one to act for the benefit of others as opposed to power from which only personal advantages accrue, is potentially Prodigality in its best meaning. That his Charioteer should be "the Poet, for whom fulfillment is / The giving freely of what's uniquely his," is thus something more than the traditional motif of Wealth the patron of art and Art the servant-equal of wealth, so popular since the Renaissance raised the artist above the artisan. The giving of spiritual things is at least as important as the bestowing of material gifts, and Charioteer represents the complement of Faust-Wealth, to whom he refers as his equal when he says, "I can distribute what he lacks." Accordingly, the first and far the longer part of the Plutus episode is dominated by Charioteer; only after he and his quadriga have disappeared is the sub-theme of the limitations of material prodigality allegorically developed.

There is nothing ambiguous in the symbolism of the legerdemain of Charioteer's pulling favors of jewelry and bits of flame from the air and his distributing them among a crowd whose members have already forgotten the Graces' recent injunction to accept gifts graciously. The complete materialist cannot successfully grasp the creations of the spirit, whose "greatest gifts"—the flames that hover over some spectators' heads like secular equivalents of the cloven tongues of fire that sat upon the apostles when they were filled at Pentecost with the Holy Ghost—seldom find recipients even temporarily worthy of them. As Plutus, Faust wears a wreath of laurel that confirms the parallel between himself and Victory, that hints at his hope of achieving victories for himself and the Emperor. But in rewarding Charioteer's services with the green branch which he regards as his most precious crown he testifies that, whatever his immediate concern with sordid realities, his highest loyalty continues to be owed to things of the spirit. In bestowing this accolade upon his servant to the solemn words heard when the Holy Ghost descended upon Jesus—"My beloved Son, in thee I am well pleased"—Faust is not merely blending Christian and secular motifs in the manner of pagan-humanistic Renaissance art; he is also emphasizing for more sensitive modern ears the solemn significance of the moment.

5640–5708   After the quasi-tragic sub-episode of fire magic has visibly completed the parallel between a highest Christian mystery and a highest humanistic insight, there is a moment of comic relief as Chattering Women, calling Faust a charlatan, draw attention to Mephistopheles, whom they recognize to be the Emperor's new jester. Identifying himself as Sir Miserliness, a modern masculine counterpart of Dame Avarice who has come into being because of the ever growing extravagance of the other sex, Mephistopheles arouses the Mob of Women, encouraged by the boldness of their Leader, to a show of open hostility. But before they can lay hands on him, the Herald intervenes, and the dragons which their better judgment (and ours) knows must be machines of wood and cardboard warningly spread their wings and snort fire from scale-covered jaws. The crowd gives way, making room for Faust to descend regally from the quadriga and give a gesture at which the dragons place at his feet the chest where Mephistopheles-Miserliness still crouches. He dismisses his Charioteer, bidding him quit this motley and grotesque confusion—a place where art can only with great difficulty and much indirection rise above the level of artifice and so partially escape subservience to empty spectacle, banal allegory, and the adulation offered by venality and ambition—to create his own poetic world "Where naught but what is good and beautiful / Does please—in solitude!" Charioteer's farewell reply completes the allegorical parallels between Material and Spiritual Prodigality by noting that the followers of Wealth are always potentially creatures of idleness, while those who devote themselves to Poetry will always be effectively active. And so, after wryly confessing that the Poet—even the poet of solitary withdrawal—does not keep secret what he achieves, he leaves as he came, with a final promise to return should Faust[9] express the faintest desire for him and what he symbolizes.

When Faust-Plutus now touches its locks with the Herald's 5709-5800 wand, the chest he has brought opens to reveal golden vessels, coins, and jewelry heaped beside cauldrons of molten gold. The crowd's amazement turns to greed as coins spill out onto the floor; while some grab for these, others propose to seize the source of wealth itself. In order to quiet these "simpletons" the Herald reminds them that everything this evening is "pleasant illusion," "truth" of another kind than that of "coarse reality," and order is restored as Faust dips the wand in the seething chest and, having sprayed the more temerarious with singeing sparks, protects it with a magic circle. Thanked by the Herald for controlling the situation with his "wise power," Understanding's guiding control of Force, Faust warns him to expect more disorder—that of the next and final allegorical episode of the masque. In the lull before this storm Mephistopheles again plays the exhibitionist, now quite literally, by using the magician's plastic gold to make pantomimic sexual overtures to the Women upstage. Although the Herald wishes to intervene, Faust assures him that no action is necessary, since new arrivals are about to deprive Mephistopheles of space for the continuance of his "harlequinade." "Our law," he says to the Herald, "is strong, but stronger is necessity," lack of physical room. And hardly has he uttered these words when the stage begins to be filled with the noisily singing Host of Pan.

The members of this army of wild, primitive, and elemental 5801-97 creatures claim to know some great secret—"For they know that which no one knows"—but Faust of course knows it too, knows, as he says, their identities and that of their great Pan, and so he "dutifully" admits them to the magically reserved space around the chest of wealth. His ironic aside, however, warns that a surprise is in store for them and their leader.

I hope good luck will now attend them!
The strangest things can happen here;
They know not where their road will send them,
They have not looked ahead, I fear.

9 Faust is here having Charioteer address himself as Court Poet no less than as the allegorical mask Plutus.

The masks of earlier episodes, disparagingly termed "tinsel display" by the newcomers, constitute the audience for the antics of various folkloristic figures. Dancing Fauns boast in irregular verse of their animal attractiveness; a goat-footed Satyr proclaims his scorn of comfort and convention; and Gnomes, the choral description of whose straggling entrance suggests that these masks with miners' lamps are children, disclaim responsibility for the perverted uses to which the gold and iron they make accessible are put in violation of the commandments against murder, theft, and adultery.[10] Finally Great Pan himself enters with his Wild Men, club-bearing giants in loincloths of natural greenery who are "naturally naked" because they symbolize primitive strength. He is surrounded by dancing Nymphs whose presence helps preserve the incognito of the only masker who, as will soon be noted in the text, wears not the usual scanty visor but a full mask with scraggy beard. Although their praise of Pan as supreme symbol of Nature consists chiefly of familiar classical motifs, there is again an echo of Walpurgisnight, this time ominous, in their concluding "So honor to him to whom honor's owed, / All hail to him who led our road!," which half repeats the words that then greeted Baubo's arrival, "So honor to him to whom honor's owed, / Dame Baubo front! Then on our road!"

5898–5986   The moment of catastrophic climax and happy denouement has now arrived. A Deputation of Gnomes draws Pan's attention to the chest symbolizing the wealth that Faust the magician-sage can place at the Emperor's beneficent disposal, and Faust warns the Herald— the warning is surely *pro forma*—not to intervene in the terrifying spectacle about to be seen, but to describe and record it for skeptical posterity. As Pan bends over the alternately glowing and dark volcano-like mouth of the chest, his bearded mask falls in and then shoots up out of it in flames, causing his costume to burn. As members of his retinue seek to beat out the fire it spreads to them, and cries of "The *Emperor*'s the suffering victim" reveal his identity. The Herald now draws the episode's moral by asking whether youth will ever learn moderation, whether imperial highness will ever be as wise

---

[10] The usual punctuation of Gnomes' last eight lines conceals the fact that these constitute a single loosely constructed sentence; the first period (after *ersann*) could be replaced by a comma or semicolon, the second (after *macht*) by a colon, although this would destroy the perhaps intentional effect of children reciting their lines badly. The gist of the sentence is: "Even if the gold we bring to light is misused, and even if those who defy the three mentioned commandments also ignore the other seven, we are not to blame; therefore you must be patient (with us), as we are patient (in our work as miners)."

as it is powerful. Then, at the height of panic confusion, as the burning "forest" of greenery seems about to set fire to the ceiling timbers and produce a general conflagration, Faust smites the Herald's wand against the floor. Having emphatically represented the allegorical dangers of easy wealth, he now clears the hall of smoke and flames with the help of magic rain and fog, and the curtain falls to the traditional magician's formula, "If spirits threaten to do us hurt, / Magic then should be alert."

Faust's final lines have a triumphant ring, but in *Faust* a triumph in the realm of the supernatural is by definition specious, since it is a premise of the drama that the only sphere of valid activity is that of finite human life. His masquerade has been an artistic triumph in its kind, but it is a kind of art of dubious value, one in which theatrical and spectacular elements too easily obscure the allegorical statement. The artistic ambivalence of the masque form may heighten the immediate effectiveness of a didactic allegory of the ambivalence of prodigality, but it is to misunderstand the nature of poetry to expect that art serve as an instrument of direct moral instruction. Faust's partial recognition of this was symbolized by his dismissal of Charioteer before taking up the theme of material wealth. As Dedication and Prelude on the Stage insisted, the symbols of poetry can only state a vision of what life is or seems to be, and they cannot properly serve some ulterior purpose, whether it be that of teaching lessons directly or that, as in Mephistopheles' ironic proposal at his second interview with Faust, of courting favor by direct and indirect adulation. From the next scene, as well as from later ones, it will be clear that the improper means of Masquerade do not achieve the proper ends that Faust envisaged, and so the scene has prepared for his subsequent turning to new spheres of interest and new forms of activity. At the same time it has represented the introduction into *Faust* on a larger scale than in Walpurgisnight of a pageant technique that, with certain of its motifs, will later be developed in forms both fuller and more intimately connected with Faust's personal destiny, so that certain scenes to come will gain greatly in dramatic economy.

CHAPTER XV

The Price of Success

5987-6030   The scene Palace Garden takes place the following morning.
Faust and Mephistopheles are seen kneeling in ordinary attire before
the Emperor, who replies to the former's deprecating "Do you, my
lord, forgive the fire magic?" by giving them a sign to rise. The
ingenuous wish for "many more such jests" leaves Faust speechless—
the pause is marked by a dash after the Emperor's first line. And so
the Emperor goes on to expatiate on the pleasure Faust has afforded
him, giving no indication of having glimpsed the allegorical significance of a masque in whose molten display of symbolic wealth he
simply imagined a setting where, like the god of the underworld or
a prince of salamanders, he received the homage of his peoples and
his courtiers. This expression of irresponsible egotism is parodied by
Mephistopheles, who adapts the Emperor's fire fancies to the
demands of water, characteristically adding erotic motifs. Neither
the irony of being pictured as a submarine King Canute nor the
gross compliment of being called a second Peleus offends the
pleasure-loving prince, who only finds his flatterer long-winded and
cuts him off with a humorous reminder of man's brief time on earth
before he can be portrayed as Olympian monarch of the aerial
element.

6031-82   Turning again to Faust, from servant to master, the Emperor
promises him the highest favors if he will always be ready to help
him escape from the world of everyday reality to one of pleasant
fantasy. Again Faust is unable to reply, this time because they are
interrupted by the entrance of the Lord-Steward, joyously reporting
that the imperial household has been freed of debt. He is followed

by the Grand-Master, whose troops have been paid and are no longer disaffected, and then by the Intendant-General, who urges the Emperor to seek the explanation of this change of fortune from Faust and Mephistopheles, from "these who did the feat." Faust, however, wisely lets the Chancellor, the only imperial adviser openly hostile to Mephistopheles' original scheme, have the honor of explaining what has happened. When the Emperor learns that the new source of wealth is simply a piece of paper for an amount of money secured by still buried treasure and guaranteed by his signature, he is outraged and suspects impious forgery, but the Intendant-General reminds him that during the previous evening's masquerade—apparently while eagerly awaiting the moment of his triumphal entry as Pan—he had signed the note at the Chancellor's request; since then it has become the model for paper currency of all denominations and so revitalized the Empire's financial life. The unscrupulous boldness of the whole operation reveals the hand of Mephistopheles; if the Intendant-General's account of "magicians" making the original note multiply is simply an allusion to the magic of the printing press—the printer Fust and the charlatan Faust were long confused—the bold sycophancy of his asserting that the letters of the Emperor's name as inscribed on these notes is sufficient alphabet for every need, and the hint of sacrilege in his calling the imperial signature a sign in which all can find salvation, are both clearly Mephistophelean.

Since the new money has won acceptance as currency, the 6083–6118 Emperor forgets his scruples and does not repudiate it. The Lord-Steward's account of how it is accepted for gold and silver—"at a discount to be sure," that is, in accordance with the law formulated by the historical Faust's younger contemporary Gresham—and circulates rapidly everywhere is meant to reassure him further. Actually, it is a picture of incipient inflation nicely glossed over by Mephistopheles' mock enthusiasm for the convenience of bank-notes in connection with erotic matters and for breviary-laden priest or once purse-impeded soldier. In the end, however, Mephistopheles is careful to insist that he too really regards the issuance of paper currency as an "exalted accomplishment," and these words strike a responsive chord in Faust, who now speaks for the third and last time in the course of an audience during which he has so far uttered but two lines.

That superfluity of frozen treasure
. . .
Remains unused. The greatest mind, 'tis evident,

10—G.F.

Could never grasp such riches' full extent;
Imagination in its highest flight
Can only grope, unsatisfied, for light.
Yet spirits that deserve insights profound,
For what is vast, vast confidence have found.

He alone thinks of the great enterprise which is essential if the new notes are to have full monetary value, and it is evident that he conceives of himself as the person with the will and wisdom necessary for undertaking it.

6119–72   His impulse to devote his energies to something worthwhile is frustrated by Mephistopheles' arguments of the convenience of paper money and the futility of undertaking more mining activity than necessary to keep it circulating. The Emperor appoints Faust and Mephistopheles custodians of the Empire's subterranean wealth— "If there be any digging, be it as you direct"—and enjoins them to unite with the Intendant-General in a triumvirate of treasurers symbolizing the harmonious union of this world with that below. After Faust's departure with the Intendant-General, who welcomes as colleague the magician whom he naturally regards as master of the apostolic mountebank Mephistopheles, the scene develops briefly the theme that few appreciate the potential value of unearned good fortune. Even the Emperor, who though frivolous has demonstrated that he has imagination, is disappointed that his largesse evokes no "courageous zest for new activity," and only the Court Fool, "resurrected" from the drunken stupor which had let Mephistopheles replace him earlier, has wit enough to seize the opportunity to better himself economically and socially. More important than their theme, however, is the stichomythic form of these final lines, whose classicistic simplicity—especially after the earlier classical device of having the news of the Empire's financial recovery reported by actors entering in messenger-like succession—firmly reëestablishes the dramatic style as one of normal unpretentiousness rather than of grand-historic proportions. Palace Garden can thus appropriately end with a one-line soliloquy creating again the direct rapport between actor and audience that has been regularly characteristic of *Faust* since its prologues and first monodramatic scene.

6173–6202   If Faust has had poor success as poetic pedagogue and has failed to achieve by honest merit a position of influence at the seat of empire, it is because he has used means, including the assistance of Mephistopheles, which in the bright light of day have been nakedly revealed to be unworthy of his high aspirations. The scene Ill-Lighted

Gallery—its semi-darkness is symbolic—shows how error breeds error, how his success as a magician forces him into a position in which he must again seek his indispensable companion's help. Mephistopheles' feigned ignorance of why he has drawn him aside, the taunting insinuation that he is bored in crowded palace rooms that afford plentiful opportunities for amusing chicanery, are recognized by Faust as worn-out tricks, and he bluntly orders him to cease being evasive and help him fulfill his promise to produce for the Emperor the figures of Helen and Paris "as distinct forms," not as images magically projected by mirrors or other devices but in three dimensions. Put off his guard by the reprimand that he was foolish to make frivolous promises, Faust momentarily takes an easier tone—"You didn't think, my friend, / To what your tricks would bring us"—and so Mephistopheles, now insinuating that Faust had wanted the production of "spectral paper coins," can continue his delaying tactics and protest inability to provide any creature that could pass as a classical heroine.

The situation is comparable to that when Mephistopheles claimed   6203-12
it would take a full two weeks to find an occasion to bring him and Margarete together, and although Faust rightly recognizes "the old familiar tune," his self-control is insufficient to prevent a note of rhetorical pathos from creeping into his reply.

You always land one in uncertainty
And are the Father of Contrariety,
Wanting a new reward for each expedient.

His words here and later suggest the line of withdrawal Mephistopheles will follow—from a position of stubborn intransigence to one of diffident but helpful cooperation which will, as always, hasten a never-too-patient Faust's implication in new labyrinths of error and truth. Still insisting that he has no connections with the world of classical paganism, the very world which furnished Baubo for Walpurgisnight and with whose mythology he demonstrated thorough familiarity at the opening of the scene just concluded, he now concedes that there is an expedient available. What it is to be he has apparently not yet decided, however, for there is a moment of hesitation during which Faust utters an impatient "Then tell it instantly!" and still another moment of thought-taking after Mephistopheles has portentously announced, "Revealing higher mysteries comes hard to me.—"

Poetically effective and novel as is the myth which Mephistopheles   6213-16
now develops, dramatically it is first and foremost a brilliant

improvisation. If it is adapted to exploit Faust's mood of irritated frustration at being unable to realize at court the aspirations he had expressed in Pleasant Landscape, in the Victory allegory of Masquerade, and, more briefly, in Palace Garden, it is equally well suited to work upon one subconsciously vulnerable to a sense of guilt not only because of the dubious value of his actual achievements at court but also because, underlying his new impulse of Pleasant Landscape, is an unconscious will to atone by worthier efforts for the fatal consequences of his love for Margarete. Taking literally Faust's charge "You always land one in uncertainty," Mephistopheles proposes to send him to seek out goddesses enthroned in a "solitude" without the attributes of time and place usually regarded as the necessary preconditions of factual certainty. Solitude is the sterile isolation from which Faust sought to escape when he entered, so tragically for Margarete and himself, the realm of common humanity. It is the perilous sterility of solitude he seeks to avoid by undertaking activities like the creating of masquerade *poésie de société* as opposed to the supposedly purer poetry of solitude represented by Boy-Charioteer. And these goddesses are "the *Mothers*," whose name alone may properly startle one who, on first visiting Margarete's room, sensed with awe her "maternal" spirit, perhaps because of some latent feeling of guilt in the attraction which she, surely a mother-image in the best sense of the term, exercised over him; one who was deeply touched by her account of maternal devotion to her dead sister during her mother's long illness after the child's birth; and one who has perhaps been ultimately responsible for that mother's death and on whose conscience certainly weighs the death of the infanticide mother who in *Faust* is the supreme symbol of motherhood.

6217-21   But Faust's awe at the thought of a lonely realm of the Mothers need not derive only from the vicissitudes in which he has been involved in the course of the dramatic action of the Tragedy of Faust. Their name suggests both the mystery of birth, with which a feeling of awesome and at times guilt-laden reverence is often associated, and the mysterious mother-gods of primitive religions, such as those mentioned in Plutarch's life of Marcellus. Their abode evokes associations of afterworlds of disembodied spirits, like the realm also described by Plutarch, in his treatise on the decadence of oracles, in which elect souls may at ten-thousand-year intervals contemplate the basic forms of all existing things. Yet, if the Mothers are his invention, Mephistopheles can properly claim that they are "unknown to you mortals." If they are goddesses of birth, he and his kind, as spirits of denial and destruction, can properly be loath to name them. And, if their abode is really nowhere, he can properly assert, "To find their dwelling place you'd plumb the deepest depths [in vain]."

Still awed by their very name, Faust disregards what might seem 6222-38 to be the "nowhereness" of the Mothers and, instinctively eager to act, asks "What way goes there?" For all its effective mysteriousness, Mephistopheles' answer to this query is characteristically negative. If there is no way to where none have trod and none can tread, no way to the inexorable that none has ever solicited, Faust may well not answer the question "Are you ready?" There are of course "no locks or bolts" in the solitudes that surround the solitude of the Mothers, but Mephistopheles' apparently otiose mention of these absent physical barriers is an allusion to Faust's desperate situation immediately before he availed himself of his services, to a time when Faust in anguished solitude repudiated his scientific instruments as keys unable to open the bolts of the gate behind which Nature, "mysterious by Day's broad light," remains forever veiled. In Forest and Cave Faust asserted that Mephistopheles could only begrudge him the renewed vitality he had then gained from being alone. Now he is sufficiently angered by the question whether he has any real idea of "desolateness and solitude" to accuse him of uttering nonsense reminiscent of Witch's Kitchen—"empty nothings" like those he had to endure in ordinary social intercourse, and inanities like those he had to learn as a student and teach as a professor until attempts to speak "reasonably" made him the butt of attacks and constrained him to seek the figurative "wilderness of solitude" from which he escaped by placing himself in a devil's hands.

Faust's angry outburst, his use of *das Leere* for "emptiness" and 6239-64 "inanity," has provided Mephistopheles with a new motif, emptiness or the Void, which he develops with the image of an ocean vastness[1]— the commonest metaphor for boundless space in eighteenth-century poetry inspired by the newly popularized concepts of astronomical immensity and mathematical infinity—in which nothing is to be seen or heard or felt. Although he recognizes that Mephistopheles' is the voice of the supreme mystagogue, unusual only in that it does not promise the neophyte admission to some only too tangible inner sanctum, and although he thinks that he is to be used to pull chestnuts out of the fire, he urges him to continue. With skepticism justified by

[1] The motif is derived from Faust's wish, in Outside the City Gates, that he might fly forever over the ocean's waves into the setting sun—the wish explicitly repudiated by him when he resolutely turned his back to the sun in Pleasant Landscape.

Mephistopheles' propensity to represent the opposite of what really is, he adds "We'll fathom this,—no longer stall!— / For in your Nothingness I hope to find the All." The "vast confidence for what is vast" momentarily revealed by Faust in the preceding scene, is seeking an outlet worthy of itself, but it is being directed into a new path of error—symbolized as so often in *Faust* by theatrical magic, which here takes the form of an unprepossessing key that Mephistopheles, having ironically praised his understanding of the Devil's true nature, offers his dupe. This key, which apparently is produced from nowhere or nothingness, grows in size, shines, and gives forth flashes of light as soon as Faust has had it forced upon him by his magician-companion, who assures him that it will "smell out the right spot" and lead him "down" to the Mothers.

6265–80   Hearing the name of the Mothers "with a tremor of awe," Faust again becomes reflective and seeks to identify its disturbing associations. The taunting questions—"Are you a dullard by new words disturbed? / Will you but hear what you've already heard?"—are well designed to reawaken the frustrated impulse of self-expansion which originally brought him into his relationship with Mephistopheles and which has still found no worthy outlet. Faust, however, is so seriously disturbed that he repudiates in complete seriousness Mephistopheles' encouraging "Let nothing you dismay."

By feeling's death I do not seek salvation,
For awe's the best thing given to humanity;
Although it cost a great consideration,
Within, it lets one sense infinity.

These words constitute an unqualified repudiation of impassiveness, but are hardly an affirmation of the value of adventure simply for the sake of a thrill. Yet Mephistopheles chooses to interpret them as an expression of Faust's readiness to depart for the abode of the Mothers and bids him descend or—he makes it clear that the direction Faust may take is unimportant—ascend "from things with being / Unto the independent realms of shapes," there to "enjoy what long since ceased to be."

6281–6306   As he automatically follows Mephistopheles' directions for the use of the magic key, Faust expresses a feeling of heroic inspiration typical of the neophyte who has been properly worked upon. Then Mephistopheles gives—the technique is that of suggestion—final instructions which complete the picture of the realm of the Mothers he is extemporizing. Amid shapes drifting in cloudlike fashion he is to find a glowing tripod and see by its light the Mothers, some sitting, some standing and walking. About these symbols of "Formation, transformation, / Eternal Mind's eternal conservation" who see only what has no substance, what has ceased to be or, like Paris and Helen, exists only as idea, "Pictures of all things created hover." In this realm of the dead past Faust is to touch the tripod with the key—here Faust, completely under the spell of Mephistopheles' hypnotizing words, uncharacteristically strikes "a vigorously imperious pose"—whereupon it will follow him back up to earth and provide a cloud of incense that can be metamorphosed into godlike shapes. He stamps his foot and sinks out of sight, leaving Mephistopheles to express the pious hope that the key will prove useful, and cynical curiosity about whether he will ever return from what must—in view of the fact that the injunction to "strive downward" occurs in a text that has attached positive value only to onward or upward striving—be an ordeal leading Faust still further astray. If, unlike several earlier scenes, this does not close with Mephistopheles gleefully anticipating a new triumph, it is because, in adapting his myth to Faust's temperament and mood, he has had to make the Mothers symbolically meaningful and fill his Void with something more than merely awesome guardians of a magician's tripod.

The brief scene Brightly-Lit Rooms, which shows Mephistopheles 6307–76 back in the Emperor's entourage, coincides with Faust's absence. Now the one importuned, Mephistopheles assures the Lord-Steward that Faust is busily preparing "to raise the treasure which is beauty." Soon finding himself overwhelmed by demands for assistance medical and magical, he advances the time for the appearance of Paris and Helen by immediately releasing Faust from the spell of the realm of the Mothers. Candles burn more dimly, and the court moves off in almost magical silence to what he identifies as the old knights' hall of the palace. And since such great halls, with their ancient tapestries and their quoins and niches decoratively filled with ancient armor, were the interior set par excellence of the literature and painting of romantic medievalism in both its earlier Gothic and its later popular-national forms, he can well assert, "No magic words, methinks, are needed here, / Where spirits on their own appear."

The curtain rises on Knights' Hall as the Emperor and his court 6377–6420 take their places facing a tapestry-covered wall—an arrangement which the Herald, who has been deprived of his usual office of descriptive commentator, finds strange. At a fanfare of trumpets the Astrologer whom Mephistopheles had so effectively prompted in Throne Room assumes the Herald's function, describing how the tapestries disappear and the wall behind them moves apart and back to reveal a mysteriously lighted stage, on the proscenium of which he takes his stand conveniently close to a prompter's box that is seen to hold Mephistopheles. The interior of a massive Doric temple next becomes visible, whose great columns inspire an Architect to disparage classical architecture at the expense of the spirituality of aspiring gothic. This in turn affords the Astrologer occasion to declare with Mephistophelean irony that now is a time not for reason but for fantasy, that what will now be seen is "impossible, / And for that very reason credible." The theological argument is one familiar ever since St. Paul, but in a drama in which reason is an established symbol of man's highest powers it only insists that to believe literally what follows, or even to believe that what follows represents worthwhile human effort, is to confuse error with truth.

6421–38   At this moment Faust rises up with a tripod at the opposite side of the proscenium. Appropriately attired as a priest of ancient Greece he makes preparations for what the Astrologer interprets to be an invocation of divine approval for the "exalted accomplishment"[2] he is about to undertake successfully. If Faust was the neophyte in Ill-Lighted Gallery, here he is the mystagogue. Speaking with uncharacteristic grandiosity, he invokes the Mothers, but now he adapts the myth freely to the situation in which he has placed himself. In their vast solitude all are seated on thrones; they constitute a company rather than a number of isolated individuals; the shapes hovering about them actually stir, though still lifeless; their realm is specifically that of things which have once existed and which know the all-too-human impulse to eternalize themselves; and the Mothers, like the Fates of his masquerade, actually determine which phantoms shall again see the light of day and which be lost in perpetual darkness unless "a bold magician" rescue them. Faust's magic is not merely that of the vulgar theatrical illusionist. His current role of magician-priest is an extension of that of showman-poet which he first consciously essayed in Masquerade. Only to the extent that he is effectively prodigal with the inner riches of poetry can the dumb show which now follows justify his bold claim of being able to recreate imaginatively a past itself but imaginative. But, in any event, his transmutation of the realm of the Mothers from one of esoteric solitude to one of potential realities, from one like that he envisioned as the Poet's in his farewell to Boy-Charioteer to one closer to that of Poetry as posited in Dedication and Prelude

---

[2] This is the same phrase that Mephistopheles used in Palace Garden to characterize the creation of unsecured paper money!

on the Stage, reveals a growing insight into the function of art which augurs well for his future efforts as a creative artist.

Faust's key, now simply a substitute for a magician's wand, 6439–78 touches the basin of incense, and the inner stage is obscured by vapors billowing to aerial music which suggests to the Astrologer that the whole temple sings; one remembers that a romantic-minded Architect is present and recalls the romantic conceit that architecture is frozen music. From the sinking veil of mist emerges Paris, who, to comments ranging from enthusiastic feminine approbation to severest faultfinding on the part of the men present, sits down, reclines, goes to sleep, and, snoring, emanates an aura of youth. What now happens is essentially the story of the Rape of Helen— so the Astrologer will entitle the piece—in the pseudo-contemporary account of Dares the Phrygian. This tells how Helen, having come to Cythera because she was curious to see the handsome Paris, was seized by him as she offered up a sacrifice to Diana; only the motif of Faust's disastrous intervention, which derives from popular superstition, will be new.

Whereas the appearance of Paris evokes little more than superficial 6479–6500 observations from the stage audience, that of Helen produces a profound effect. In earlier versions of the Faust legend a succubus who awakens in Faust strong erotic desires, here she is primarily his ideal of feminine beauty magically projected with the secret help of Mephistopheles, and may therefore be most appropriately imagined as Margarete in the classical dress so often worn by women in *tableaux vivants*.[3] That she is not the traditional diabolic temptress is immediately made clear by Mephistopheles' "So that is she! I don't find her exciting; / No doubt she's pretty, but to me she's not inviting." Unprompted by Mephistopheles—hence "as man of honor"—the Astrologer recognizes that she is one whose beauty is of the kind sung by poets since time immemorial, one too beautiful rightly ever to have belonged to any ordinary mortal. And Faust— no ordinary mortal but a tragic hero of extraordinary resilience and vitality—sees in her "the fount of beauty" that is his reward for undertaking his recent "ordeal" and that has given meaning to the world for him "now that I am become a priest." If he asserts that she must remain dearer to him than life itself so long as he lives, it is not because she is physically desirable only. Well aware that she

---

[3] As an ideal of Beauty, Helen is a counterpart of the allegorical figure of Freedom envisioned by the sleeping hero of Goethe's *Egmont*; the pantomimic role is played by Egmont's sweetheart, Klärchen, and Egmont declares on awakening, "They were one, the two sweetest joys of my heart—divine Freedom borrowed her form from my beloved."

represents something far better than the alluring figure he once contemplated in the magic mirror of Witch's Kitchen, he dedicates to her as tribute due "All forces' quickening, and passion's essence, / Affection, love, and reverence and madness."

6501–45   When Faust has been momentarily silenced by Mephistopheles, the dumb show proceeds. Again the audience's comments describe the action on the inner stage as Helen softly approaches Paris, like a Diana contemplates the Endymion-like sleeper, and kisses him. Faust's anger at this point threatens an interruption and forces Mephistopheles to warn him not to fall out of his role and intervene in what he makes clear is a performance of spirits not controlled by Faust—"Just let the ghost do what it wants to do." The remarks of members of the audience also make clear that Helen's beauty is womanly rather than girlish, that she represents experience and queenly maturity, not merely the attractiveness of youth which Margarete at first symbolized. Only the comment of the Man of Learning, whose age and profession permit him to be garrulous, raises the question of her literal reality. For to doubt "whether she's the right one" is to recall that even classical legend knew at least two Helens, one a shade which accompanied Paris to Troy, and one a "real" Helen who found refuge elsewhere. Faust, however, proves no better able to distinguish between poetic illusion and material reality than those who were duped by his symbolic display of wealth in Masquerade, and, as Paris seizes Helen to carry her off, orders him to halt.

6546–65   When reminded by Mephistopheles that the Rape of Helen[4] is a phantom play for which he himself is responsible, Faust challengingly asks if he who holds the key that has brought him back from seas of terrible solitude to firm land is to have no say at all in what happens. Calling the magic stage on whose proscenium he stands a place of "realities," a place from which "the spirit may with spirits strive" and so create "the great double realm" which will unite the Ideal and the Real, he announces that he will rescue Helen from Paris and make her his own—"doubly mine," because he will not only have projected her image but also actually possessed it. So he invokes the aid of the Mothers as he prepares to wrest Helen from the spirit-figure which is Paris. But, when he touches him with the key, both figures vanish in the smoke of a grand theatrical explosion. The past cannot be brought back to literal life, myth cannot become literal

---

[4] Goethe's own actually dramatic presentation of the Rape of Helen is apparently a unique tour de force, for this is one of the few very popular subjects from classical mythology that seems never to have lent itself to dramatization.

reality, and the Mothers, however vividly imagined, remain in a realm of the spirit apart from Faust and man. For a moment Faust lies unconscious, the epitome of helplessness and impotence, on an empty stage; then Mephistopheles slings the would-be hero over his shoulder and prepares to carry him off as the curtain falls on darkness and confusion.

The ignominious conclusion of Faust's pantomime seems another triumph for Mephistopheles, for its production has been an undertaking even less worthy of his high resolutions than was the great court masquerade, has symbolized in the realm of art a dragging of Faust through that "meaningless inanity" by which Mephistopheles originally resolved to destroy him. But, however obviously Faust has acted in error, the impulse which motivated his final disastrous intervention was basically noble, one chivalric, even heroic. Although he is as impotent to impose his will on the world about him as he was during Margarete's last hours, his guilt is venial; whatever hurt he has caused himself by his folly should be undone by time and rest less prolonged than that symbolized by the scene Pleasant Landscape. The poetic resolution of the apparent dilemma created by Faust's impulse to possess Helen will be the dramatic action of the next great section of the Tragedy of Faust, but it would be wrong to regard the scenes Ill-Lighted Gallery and Knights' Hall as having only the function of providing the premises of this action. For in each of them Faust makes allusions to his past—in the first to the experiences which caused him to enter into his compact with Mephistopheles, and in the second to an adventure that marked his symbolic initiation into the emotional life of common humanity. Thus, the scenes mark the beginning of that reintegration of Faust's personality without which the Second Part of the Tragedy would be at best only a Second Tragedy of an Alternate Faust. As Mephistopheles noted, Faust's first declaration of unconditional devotion to what Helen represents is a falling out of his role of magician-priest; but it is a return to a role that was characteristically his in the First Part of the Tragedy—that of a man equally capable of the most intense passion and the most idealistic and impractical speculation. Faust may be completely unmindful of Margarete when he declares that he intends to make Helen his inalienable possession, but the parallel between this new passion and his earlier one must eventually strike his attention. When it does, he will have reached that point in his development when all that he has been and all that he is are again integral parts of one dramatic character. But, before that moment of clarity is reached, Faust has a long and labyrinthine course to follow.

CHAPTER XVI

Under the Spell of Beauty

6566–69   The reintegration of Faust's personality will be completed in two great dream sequences that constitute the next large section of *Faust*. Before this begins, however, Goethe reëstablishes more firmly the identity of the dramatic character who has played the part of imperial magician and adviser with that of the unworldly scholar who left his study to learn about life in Mephistopheles' company. No measurable period of time elapses between Faust's collapse at the end of Knights' Hall and his discovery on the bed on which he is momentarily glimpsed as Mephistopheles emerges from behind a curtain into his unchanged study, the setting of High-Vaulted Narrow Gothic Room.[1] Again Faust has sought the impossible, and again he is helpless to achieve it, for he lies in a trance-like state which Mephistopheles informs him is the natural consequence of a paralyzing passion for Helen. This explanation must be regarded as highly suspect, since the essence of the myth of Helen is that beauty inspires the impulse to act heroically, even in "the gray-bearded elders of Troy" mentioned by Man of Learning at the end of the preceding scene. But whatever the actual motives of Mephistopheles' fiction, it is clear that Faust's sleep, like that into which Mephistopheles lulled him at the end of their first interview, is one in which he can understand what is said in his hearing and may remember it when he later awakens.

6570–91   Accordingly, Mephistopheles' leisurely and audible examination

---

[1] Referring to Helen, Faust will soon say to Chiron, "You saw her once; I saw her e'en today." Mephistopheles, referring to the Fates of Masquerade, will likewise soon assure the Graeae or Phorcides that he saw their sisters "yesterday—or the day before."

of Faust's old study not only emphasizes the passage of time since he and Faust first met, so suggesting that Faust is now a man of greater maturity, though freed by worldly experience of a scholar's oldish mannerisms; it also seeks to insinuate to one unable to protest and recall the actual terms of their compact that he really "indentured himself to the Devil," although at the time of their agreement Faust specifically repudiated as empty nonsense the traditional exchange of soul for services. Mephistopheles may speak with apparent disinterest of the value which Faust's pen might have for the collector of curios, but he is actually seeking to undermine in a spirit again precariously disturbed its sense of truth and falsehood, of right and wrong, of reality itself. Returning Faust to his study is thus no Mephistophelean whim, but a deliberate attempt to confuse him further by placing him in the hateful setting of that sterile isolation which originally persuaded him, as he has recently recalled in Ill-Lighted Gallery, to put himself in a Devil's hands. If, however, Mephistopheles is to exploit his present helplessness successfully, indirection is essential, indirection disguised as whimsical fancy, leisurely digression, or—and this will be most important— curious coincidence. Thus Faust's gown "reminds" Mephistopheles of his interlude with the Student and evokes a "disposition" to play once more the "university teacher." Although he has never been one to eschew positive assertions in his dealings with Faust, his monologues, or even his opening interview with the Lord, he now insinuates that such assertions, always so irksome to Faust, are a scholar's prerogative which the Devil—again this deliberately inexact form of self-reference suggested by Faust's loose usage in Ill-Lighted Gallery —has long since sensibly renounced.

When a chorus of speaking insects emerges from the fur of Faust's gown, all the main features of Mephistopheles' two original interviews with Faust, at both of which were heard the voices of his spirit dependents, have been effectively recalled. In dismissing them he is able to mention the manuscripts, scientific apparatus, and anatomical specimens by which Faust felt oppressed and mocked as he sat in what he called on Easter Eve the "moth world" of his study; while in insisting that there should always be *Grillen*—both crickets and whimseys—where there is such musty confusion, he punningly gives a glimpse of the method of his newest offensive against Faust. In order to have an audience or, more accurately, unwitting accomplices for his role of "Principal"—significantly, the title was that of the chief actor of a traveling troupe as well as of head professor—Mephistopheles makes his presence known by

6592–6635

pulling at the bell used to summon attendants. The result of this innocuous natural gesture is a shrill and penetrating sound that causes the building to shake and doors to spring open, a display of theatrical magic which reproduces literally the nightmarish imaginings which the sudden ringing of a bell can evoke in one who, like Faust behind the curtain, is not sound asleep. As in the scenes at the imperial court, where Mephistopheles used it first to counteract Faust's efforts as magician-sage and then to undermine his hold on reality, magic is one of Mephistopheles' weapons in a deliberate campaign against Faust's resolution "Ever to strive for life's most perfect forms." And so when Nicodemus—the name of the assistant to Faust's sometime assistant is that of the literal-minded Pharisee in St. John's gospel—appears in the doorway, his comic timorousness helpfully emphasizing the awesomeness of the effects which Mephistopheles has produced, and Mephistopheles lets himself appear to him as a figure of superhuman size before whose gaze and nod, reminiscent of those of Don Juan's great stone guest, he is ready to sink Leporello-like to his knees.

6636–84   Mephistopheles' interview with Nicodemus begins with a series of taunting ironic reminders that academic success such as Faust once knew may represent only the willy-nilly building by mediocrity of "a modest house of cards." Wagner, whose plodding unimaginativeness Faust so sharply condemned after his intrusion on Easter Eve, is praised as "augmentor of wisdom"[2] (emperor of the learned world, since one imperial title was "augmentor of the Empire"), pope of the basilica of knowledge, sun whose brightness obscures even Faust's fame, and "only begetter of all discovery." Nicodemus' polite but firm contradiction—his assurance that Wagner humbly awaits the return of the master to whose unexplained disappearance he has never resigned himself and for whom he has kept the study intact—is a further indication that Mephistopheles is being anything but truthful at this point in the dramatic action, while his refusal to summon Wagner from a great experiment to which he is giving constant breathless attention permits Mephistopheles to announce that he will then seek out Wagner, the happy event of whose experiment he is the very man to hasten.

6685–6720   After Nicodemus' departure, Mephistopheles prepares to receive "a familiar guest," the Student of his second interview with Faust. Now "completely up to date" and "vastly brash," this newly graduated Bachelor reveals by his opening remarks that Faust's absence

[2] During their Easter walk, Wagner had said to Faust, "If you, as man, augment our knowledge, / Your son can then attain a higher goal."

has been kept secret, for he interprets the opening of this part of the building to mean that its occupant is about to turn to some more vital pursuit than stultifying, solitary study. Despite his fears lest quake-weakened walls collapse, recognition of the study and of the man who there interviewed him on his arrival at the university resolve him to beard an academic lion in his den and so demonstrate the superiority of modern youth to what seemed cleverness when he could still think himself edified by the "prattle" of bearded professors and by learning which they themselves did not believe valid. The Student's hostility toward dead book-learning is a grotesque parody of Faust's original, better-founded disillusionment with academic life, and permits Mephistopheles to draw from him expressions of sentiment well designed to torment the paralyzed Faust who is his unseen captive audience. This second interlude of Devil and Student, which would be disproportionately long if it served only to establish a few more parallels between Faust's academic environment as he once knew it and as it is now, thus extends a nightmare of things and persons into the sphere of thoughts and ideas, so that it becomes in some respects a counterpart of earlier nightmarish passages in Witch's Kitchen and Walpurgisnight, with which it will even share the characteristic feature of anachronistic satiric elements.

With impudent allusion to professorial mummification—the ₆₇₂₁₋₄₃ mention of "Lethe's dark floods" also recalls Faust's earlier, more healthful immersion in "Lethe's flood" as he lay sleeping in Pleasant Landscape—the Student presents himself to Mephistopheles, who amiably agrees with him that he has changed, observing that caterpillar and chrysalis may well give promise of becoming a colorful butterfly, only to add the stinging insinuation that the bold young man before him, whose boyish curls have given way to a new-fashioned haircut, would do well not to return home completely bald. The play on *resolut* and *absolut*, bold and bald, but perhaps also bold and penniless or even resolute and absolute in the idealistic-philosophical sense, is caught by the Student, who warns his interviewer that in these times of cultural renewal he and his fellows are too alert to be the naïve butts of *double-entendre*. The renewal alluded to is of course Romanticism, whose early nineteenth-century German exponents often over-exploited the rhetorical devices of irony and ambiguity with disastrous unrestraint. But the Student gives no evidence of sensing that Mephistopheles' "absolute" or "bold" is a barbed allusion to his presumptuousness, which verges dangerously on solipsism of the kind that in the German romantic period proclaimed the sovereign freedom of the creative spirit and confused the freedom of Fichte's Absolute Ego (God) with the finite freedom of personal ego.

6744–69   The theme of man's limited freedom is a central one in *Faust*, but it is only tangential at this point, for Mephistopheles is simply reminding Faust that teaching, even when effective, is rarely recognized as such by the pupil, who will later think of his master as a "dullard." The Student suggests that "rogue" would be a better word, for he recognizes what Faust lamented in his opening monologue—that a teacher may distort truth for various reasons—and comes dangerously close to an unwitting description of Mephistopheles' present tactics with Faust. Hastily acknowledging that the Student himself is ready to teach, Mephistopheles changes the topic by tentatively complimenting him on the fullness of experience he has "no doubt" gained during the past years. To speak respectfully of empirical knowledge in the presence of a German idealist is to wave a red flag before a bull, and the Student automatically depreciates it to the advantage of what Kant and his romantic successors called Pure Reason and Spirit, challenging Mephistopheles to confess that nothing known before was worth knowing. For penitently admitting that he has been a "shallow simpleton," Mephistopheles receives the dubious compliment of being called the first sensible old man the Student has found; and when he heaps coals of fire upon his head by avowing that his search for hidden gold—the "treasure" is that superficial knowledge which Wagner sought, and, for being satisfied with it, Faust condemned him as one who sought "treasures" and found "earthworms"—has brought him only ugly coal, he is asked to confess that his bald pate covers a skull as empty as that of Faust's anatomical specimens.

6770–6806   Reprimanded for rudeness, the Student rudely counters with the proverb that says to be polite in German is to lie. The theme that courtesy is a condition *sine qua non* of human intercourse, having already been developed in both Witch's Kitchen and (by Faust himself) in Masquerade, needs no elaboration at this point; in any case, Mephistopheles' shifting of his chair closer to the audience with the words "Up here there is no light or air left me" is a patent indication that the Student self-sufficiently symbolizes Mephistophelean values. Heedless of his listener's complete alienation, he announces that it is presumptuous of useless age to want to exist, that the old and weak were best destroyed—a motif that will be developed dramatically on the final day of Faust's life. Although his case is weakened by the naïve assumption that thirty is the deadline of life, his blood-mysticism and cold-blooded formulation of the doctrine of the survival of the fittest constitute the *reductio*, not *ad absurdum* but, in the light of more recent historical developments, *ad horrendum* of subjective romantic speculation ruthlessly carried to its logical conclusions. As Mephistopheles concedes, there is nothing for the Devil to add to what has been said, but the Student, missing the point of his remark, takes the mention of the Devil—"Unless I will, no devil may exist"—as excuse to glorify the powers of the creative ego. And so his parting speech is a hymn to self verging on Chanticleer-like ridiculousness no less evident in the motif of evoking the sunrise than in the illogicality of having "brightness ahead and darkness behind" when one is following one's "inner light." This Beckmesser-like perversion of the dream of perpetual flight which Faust renounced as he turned his back to the sun in Pleasant Landscape is thus a last reminder of the concealed presence of one who could be kind and courteous even in moments of great stress and who is learning to accept human finiteness graciously and wisely despite the unconditional freedom he enjoys by virtue of his magical relationship with Mephistopheles.

Not to claim the departing Student for his own may seem 6807–18 undiabolic of Mephistopheles, the embodiment of the darkness to which the former's back is quite literally turned; but, as he says, the Devil is old and knows that improvement is always possible. His last asides are not for Faust, but only for those who know that what is possible for the Student is certainly more than possible for Faust. Except for these remarks, however, every bit of the action of High-Vaulted Narrow Gothic Room has served Mephistopheles' purpose of placing Faust in a dream world potentially dangerous because in it man is bound by no absolute finite restrictions. Asleep, Faust can hear; soon he will see and, like powerful magicians of legend (Nostradamus is the most famous of these), move effortlessly through both space and time. The suspension of time has been adumbrated by the unchanged study, which is both Faust's past and his immediate present, both a bit of the late medieval and early modern world of Faust and an early nineteenth-century contemporaneity also. Mephistopheles mentions the curio value of Faust's pen, but the avid private collector of curiosities and relics is a post-Renaissance phenomenon; in calling himself docent he uses a title unknown until the end of the eighteenth century and not employed officially until even later; the late-medieval Student has a nineteenth-century haircut and is suspected by Mephistopheles of never having worn a queue, old-fashioned long before the end of the eighteenth century; and both Mephistopheles and the Student are informed about philosophic developments since the *Critique of Pure Reason*. After the absence of anachronism throughout the scenes at the imperial court—paper money was known since antiquity, the principle of curing *similia similibus* long antedated Hahnemann— this heaping up of glaring anachronistic details announces clearly and effectively that historical time is to be suspended for the duration of Faust's trance-like state.

6819–35   With its clumsy alchemical apparatus grotesquely inappropriate to Wagner's obviously modern scientific pretensions and to his occasionally modern scientific terminology—interspersed among older terms are eighteenth-century ones like "organize" and "crystallize"—the scene Laboratory continues to insist that normal concepts of time are temporarily meaningless both to Faust and for the understanding of the dramatic action of *Faust*. In the world of dreams, even more than in Dedication's "spirit realm" of poetic creation, time, like place, is ultimately but convention. At the critical point in an often attempted experiment, as a white light of growing intensity appears in the innermost of a group of glass vessels, Mephistopheles intrudes upon the tense experimenter, Wagner. His entrance loosely parallels Wagner's forcing of his presence upon Faust after the vanishing of the Earth Spirit; but, whereas that un- welcome intrusion was genuinely fortunate, as Faust subsequently acknowledged, Mephistopheles' well-timed entrance is only delusorily so. For although Wagner will soon be persuaded that his attempt to produce human life has succeeded, he who enters, announcing "My intentions are good," is, as Faust pointed out early during their second interview, an egoist who helps no one disinterestedly.

6836–78   Mephistopheles' feigned ignorance of the nature of the experi- ment, like his maliciously ingenuous suggestion that there must be an amorous couple in the recesses of the chimney, evokes from Wagner justification of an enterprise which will enable man, that highly gifted creature, to dispense with old-fashioned procreation and achieve being in a less bestial manner. As the experiment seems to be going well, Wagner is persuaded that science has at last penetrated the mystery of organic Nature[3]—Nature whose visible manifestations Faust has come to recognize as a veil always ultimately impenetrable. Wagner's living human substance is to be created by "crystal- lization," a process which might seem more likely to produce a petrefact than protoplasm, but the irony of Mephistopheles' prompt and sententiously flavored remark that even in his earlier years he

---

[3] During Goethe's last years Wöhler achieved the first synthesis of an organic substance, rightly heralded by Liebig as the dawn of a new era—in chemical science.

has seen "petrified people" is wasted on one engrossed in demonstrating that a human intelligence can from now on be created in a test-tube. Even as Wagner watches, the glass vessel begins to give a ringing tone, a diminutive man is said to be visible in it, and its hollow resonance—the effect is one of ventriloquism—becomes that of a speaking voice.

The Homunculus who now impishly addresses Wagner as 6879-90 "Daddikins" is the artificial man that late Greek, medieval, and Renaissance alchemists believed could be created with supernatural aid. Like others of his kind, who were dreamt of until the microscope disproved the theory of biological preformation, this "artificial" creature is born—"it was no jest," no easy delivery, he asserts—a miniature adult in possession of all his faculties. He is not, however, Wagner's creation, but the creature of the rogue and cousin whose timely presence he so gratefully acknowledges, a bottle-imp introduced with the familiar magical effects of mysterious sounds and gradually dissipating obscurity that have regularly characterized Mephistophelean hocus-pocus from the comic seance in Witch's Kitchen down to the recent evocation of the figures of Paris and Helen. Accordingly, he keeps Wagner at a safe distance and, after his opening words, addresses himself almost exclusively to the master who may be presumed not only to suggest his presence but also to project his voice. For it is to Mephistopheles that he, a Lilliputian Faust unconditionally welcoming the chance to avail himself of a devil's useful services, at once turns for tutelage with the Faustian sentiment, "Since I exist, I must be active too. / At once I'd like to gird myself for work."

The traditional homunculus was supposed to be omniscient, 6891-6920 which explains why Wagner hastens to seek an answer to the age-old question how soul and body can be in harmony, and also why Mephistopheles, urging the prior importance of Homunculus' will to do something, hastens to silence him with an equally old jest and so momentarily conceals the fact that his homunculus is anything but omniscient and autonomous. Dummy-like, Homunculus promptly asks what it is that he wants to do and is directed to demonstrate his talents in connection with the sleeping Faust, whose recumbent figure is revealed by the magical opening of the door to the adjacent room. Playing the mind reader, Wagner's "loveliest of boys" pretends to be much impressed by what he claims to see in Faust's dreams, slips from Wagner's hands, and floats over to Faust. The vision of Leda and the swan which he attributes to Faust is a bit of Mephistophelean suggestion appropriately inspired by Helen's miraculous conception and replete with Mephistophelean suggestiveness. Instead of Wagner's fatherly pride, there is now voyeuristic delight in "loveliest of women" undressing; no fragile vial but pliant water is the crystal enveloping Leda; Jove chooses to procreate in a manner considerably more bestial than the one Wagner hopes to make unnecessary; and, with pleasurable anticipation like that expressed by Mephistopheles on the evening of Margarete's seduction, Homunculus declares that the suddenly veiled climax of what he has so enthusiastically described is "The scene that's loveliest of all."

6921–44   Ironically charging that Homunculus' vision has been pure invention, Mephistopheles interrupts himself to let Homunculus make the countercharge that he is a creature of Northern Europe's dark ages, one only "at home in gloom."[4] In the Faustian role of Renaissance Graecophile, which is that of Romantic Hellenist also, Homunculus sees Faust's environment with completely different eyes from those of the Architect who condemned as heavy and confining the Greek temple of Faust's Rape of Helen. Claiming it would be fatal to let one who dreams of "Forest springs, of swans and naked beauties" awaken in a depressing gothic building, he proposes that Faust be removed elsewhere. He whom Faust but recently called "the Father of Contrariety" immediately approves this suggestion, then conveniently remembers that "Right this moment . . . / Is classical Walpurgis Night," an opportune occasion for placing Faust in his proper element.[5] By definition, a Walpurgisnight should be a moment of evil and ugliness when erotic desires, perhaps awakened by the suggestive scene of Leda and the swan, will find an outlet unworthy of Faust's best impulses, will pervert to "meaningless inanity" his would-be heroic devotion to the classical ideal of beauty which Helen symbolizes. Of all Mephistophelean extemporizations, none is so brilliant or bold as this timely invention of a classical counterpart to the "sphere of dream and magic" which was the northern Walpurgisnight of Faust's experiences in the realm of common humanity. Yet the insistent establishment in this scene and its immediate predecessor of parallels with earlier periods of Faust's life has made possible the fiction of a classical witches' Sabbath

---

[4] Homunculus' line "The home for you must be a place of gloom," the only non-rhyming one in Laboratory, echoes the concluding line of Mephistopheles' Land-of-Cockaigne-like description in Throne Room of the delights of finding buried treasure, "The home of mysteries is darkness hight."

[5] Here and later "classical Walpurgis Night" means "classical witches' Sabbath." That section of Faust which bears the sub-title Klassische Walpurgisnacht (the scenes Pharsalian Fields and Rocky Inlets of the Aegean Sea) is always referred to as Classical Walpurgisnight.

which Mephistopheles can with impudent honesty confess never having heard of.

As a rabid Graecophile, Homunculus insists that Mephistopheles' 6945–69 ignorance—a motif developed from his claim in Ill-Lighted Gallery that he lacked connections with classical antiquity—is a consequence of knowing only romantic ghosts, although classical ones alone are genuine. This feigned ignorance, which Mephistopheles seeks to make more plausible by asserting that the mere thought of "colleagues in antiquity" offends him, permits Homunculus-Mephistopheles to fill in the details of this new myth and localize its setting. Faust is to be transported from the realm of Satan—again there is a deliberate misidentification of Mephistopheles—to the valley of the Peneios, a river winding freely, with pseudo-classical effortlessness, through the glades and forests of the Thessalian plain that stretches out below the old and new cities of Pharsalus. Mephistopheles recognizes that this is the plain on which Caesar defeated Pompey,[6] thereby reminding Faust of the less savory sides of ancient life represented by rival tyrants and revolting slaves, by the endless struggles—hence his mention of the Old Testament demon of strife that accompanied Megaera in Faust's masquerade—that made life in classical antiquity anything but the quiet idyll so often imagined by Renaissance and later Hellenophiles. His cynical observations are tacitly accepted as well founded by Homunculus, who justifies war with the equally cynical observation that through the practice of self-defense the boy becomes a man,[7] and then challenges him either to suggest his own "expedient" or else to leave the curing of Faust to him.

Much as when Faust declared that he "wanted a new reward for 6970–94 each expedient," Mephistopheles declines, though less categorically, to try the tricks of northern witchcraft. He contents himself with ironically derogating the Greeks as pagans who, he asserts with Student-like presumption, were never worth very much although— here his tone becomes one of Wagner-like moral indignation—they have dazzled mankind with a free sensuality that makes sin pleasurable rather than gloomy. But when Homunculus alludes knowingly to Thessalian witches, who were famous in classical times for their lewdness and viciousness and who accordingly represent still another dark side of ancient life and thought, he lets himself show more

[6] The opening of Classical Walpurgisnight will indicate that it represents the anniversary of the Battle of Pharsalus—which took place in August, or several months after Lent. The incongruity is deliberately comic.

[7] This seems to be a Shavian gibe, before the fact, at certain later German romanticists whose high-sounding pleas for a physically strong and healthy youth prove on closer inspection to be inspired by militantly nationalistic aims.

interest in Homunculus' proposal and, despite express doubts about the pleasurability of cohabiting with these witches night after night, announces his modern-scientific readiness to pay them "an *experimental* visit." Homunculus orders him to wrap Sir Faust in the cloak that will transport the two of them once more into a new realm of experience and proposes to light them on their way—for his luminous vial enables him to play the role of guide that was Will-o'-the-Wisp's at the opening of the genuine Walpurgisnight. Wagner, on the other hand, is left behind to repeat his experiment, for as Homunculus-Mephistopheles now makes quite clear, to produce life it is not enough to combine in proper proportions the elements that constitute a human body. Besides the problem of "the *what*" that is in a living organism, there is also that of "the *how*" of making it animate, and to discover the How would be to put the dot on the "i," which is what Homunculus now hopes to do for himself in the course of his travels.

6995–7004   If Homunculus should find the dot for the "i," and if he should impart this information to Wagner, Wagner is assured that his rewards will be "Gold, honor, fame, a long and healthy life"—the benefits promised the discoverer of the philosopher's stone of alchemical lore—"And, it may be, knowledge and virtue too," although these last seem deliberately Mephistophelean afterthoughts. Wagner may well take Homunculus' cavalier farewell sadly, for he is surely right in fearing that he will never see him again, but Mephistopheles is suspiciously cheerful about his own readiness to set out for the Peneios with his "not-to-be-despised cousin." His concluding aside, again one not meant for Faust's ears, explains both Wagner's sense of paternal loss and the irony of the uncharacteristic docility he himself has shown in seconding Homunculus' proposal. "The upshot is that we depend / Upon the creatures that we've made." The supreme irony of the whole scene, however, is the amusing yet easily overlooked fact that Wagner, still as engrossed in his own ideas as ever, should fail to realize that his mannikin is leaving him in the company of the very man for whose return he has so faithfully waited many a long year.

For the third time the curtain has fallen on a Faust about to leave one great human realm for another, and the drama of his first, abortive attempt to find a useful place for himself in the great world of state and society is ended. Although there is a superficial resemblance between the stupor into which he was plunged by Margarete's death and the coma which is the result of his attempt to change the fate of Helen, the present situation is as different from that when Mephistopheles snatched Faust from Margarete's prison as it is from that when he first transported him out of his prison study. On the earlier occasion he was so little worldly wise that he let himself be taken where Mephistopheles chose. On the other, he automatically sought out a milieu diametrically opposed to the little world that Margarete had represented. Now, however, he is entering a "sphere of dream and magic" that can only be an extension of worlds he already knows and that, if his resolutions of Pleasant Landscape have not been seriously weakened by his recent and surely venial errors and failures, he may shape successfully in accordance with his best insights. The quasi-tragedy of the scholar was followed by the middle-class tragedy of Margarete, and that drama has been followed by the tragi-comedy of Faust's experiences in a world of historical and social forces that included not only political, military, and economic factors but also didactic and artistic ones of central concern to him. From each of these spheres of experience and interest, but above all from that of classical myth and poetry symbolized by the figure of Helen, Faust will derive the elements of his classical Walpurgis Night and then order them as best he can. *How* he dreams, even more than *what* he dreams, will be the essence of the dramatic action of the fourth great section of the Tragedy of Faust.[8]

[8] All but the denouement of the dramatization of the Faust legend planned by Goethe's elder contemporary, Lessing—the first eighteenth-century German writer to attempt a serious literary treatment of the figure of Faust—was to be dream-play.

REALMS OF THE
CREATING IMAGINATION

CHAPTER XVII

The Affirmation of Myth

Faust's northern Walpurgisnight was a dream episode in the drama of his relationship with Margarete and depicted, chiefly with folkloristic and literary-satiric symbols, both his inability to find lasting satisfaction in the "meaningless inanity" of purely sensual pleasures and his fortunate, though in the event almost tragic, failure to persuade himself that her fate could be a matter of indifference to him. Its counterpart in the Second Part of the Tragedy is a Walpurgisnight almost four times its length, which is likewise followed by a dream intermezzo, though one of far, far greater scope, artistry, and dramatic significance than Oberon's and Titania's Golden Wedding. This Classical Walpurgisnight and the dream play which concludes it—the title of the latter when published in 1827 as a fragment of *Faust II* was "Helen: Classic-Romantic Phantasmagoria, a Faust Interlude"—together constitute the fourth large unit of the Tragedy of Faust. They differ from Walpurgisnight and Walpurgis Night's Dream not only in the importance they accord symbols from Graeco-Roman mythology and literature but also in their dramatic function, which is not to represent one episode in Faust's search for meaningful experience but to mirror as theatrical action the whole of his most important attempt in the development of his dramatic character to organize successfully his hard-won insights into the nature of man and the universe.

Classical Walpurgisnight, then, is the first half of a double dream play representing a victory of Faust over Mephistopheles. In form a series of carnival-like episodes (the scene Pharsalian Fields) that culminate in a grand *trionfo* (the scene Rocky Inlets of the Aegean

Sea), the pattern is that of Masquerade, but its execution is unfettered by any physical or occasional limitations other than those inherent in the fiction of a witches' Sabbath. It thus shows how Faust successfully counters both Mephistopheles' ridicule of his sympathetic enthusiasm for the grandeur of classical antiquity and Mephistopheles' attempt to insinuate ignoble elements into his would-be heroic devotion to that aesthetic perfection which is symbolized by Helen of Troy. During his northern Walpurgisnight Faust was largely under Mephistophelean influences; now he has achieved a considerable measure of spiritual, if not physical, autonomy. So this new phantasmagoria can, from the very start, be predominantly Faustian in character, can be a commingling of past knowledge and experience and of past and present aspiration so patterned by his latent poetic powers as to be both dream and work of art. The value and relative importance of themes and motifs, even those originally suggested by Mephistopheles, will be determined by Faust, who is free to endow them, as well as motifs ultimately deriving from the very bitterest experiences of his own past, with new and nobler significance. If he fails to exercise this freedom wisely, even his original splendid projection of Helen's ideal beauty must lose its pristine brightness and acquire a sullied Mephistophelean cast. If he does use it well, the extent of the triumph of a spirit of healthy affirmation over one of Mephistophelean negation will be the visible measure of his growing self-reliance and his increasing independence of all that Mephistopheles and his magic symbolize.

1. *Prologue*

7005-33   Like every great section of *Faust*, Classical Walpurgisnight opens with a prologue—this time one in unrhymed iambic trimeter, a verse form which, by virtue of its strict regularity, is the most emphatic equivalent in German of the flexible six-foot line used for the spoken word in Attic drama. With Euripidean directness, "Erichtho, I, the gloomy," announces that she comes once more with measured step— demanded by the wearing of the tragic buskin—to this night's awesome celebration. If she insists that she is less loathsome than slandering poets have claimed—the ghoulishness of this most notorious of Thessalian witches is a motif fully developed in Lucanus' epic of the Civil War, according to which she was consulted by Pompey's unworthy son—it is not only because Faust is arbitrarily idealizing even ugly classical motifs, but also because the expository repudiation of defamatory charges by god or goddess, hero or heroine (Euripides'

Helen, for instance), is itself a motif of Greek tragedy. The second reason is thus stylistic, and constitutes one of many Grecizing stylistic features whose cumulative effect is to endow her monologue with a sublimity normally associated only with Greek literature of the Periclean age.[1]

Erichtho's vision of a vale, gray with the phantom tents of dreaming Pompey's and waking Caesar's legions, is developed from Mephistopheles' cynical allusion to the Battle of Pharsalus as one battle in the endless, futile conflict between power-seeking factions, but the eternal futile repetition of a single battle by ghostly warriors is Faust's own mythologization of the motif, which now suggests the perpetually refought combats of dead heroes in Germanic mythology. What Mephistopheles claimed was a foolish struggle for illusory freedom, Faust regards as "a great example" of how power is misused when self-restraint is lacking—the theme is that of his Victory allegory—and of how "Freedom's lovely wreath," the olive branch which in Masquerade was a symbol of peaceful prosperity only, is destroyed so that "the rigid laurel" may be bent to crown a victor's head. If the laurel-wreath motif is a reminiscence of Faust's overconfident wearing of that symbol of victory at his great masquerade, the sentry fires about which Erichtho sees gather the fabulous creatures of Hellenic myth are "the hundred fires burning in a line" of the "little worlds" that on the Brocken symbolized foolish, criminal, and dissolute pleasures. Also from Walpurgisnight derives the motif of a rising gibbous moon, but whereas then the faint glow from its "imperfect disk" was not enough for a walker to see by, now its light is sufficient to make vanish the spectral tents and to fade the red of campfire to sickly blue.

When Homunculus comes into view, his luminous vial an 7034–61 "unexpected meteor" casting its light on the "corporeal sphere" of Mephistopheles' cloak, Erichtho scents life and, with prudent regard for her novel role of not-so-loathsome witch, withdraws. Classicizing verse gives way to normal rhyme, and for the duration of a song that opens with a succinct recapitulation of motifs from the one sung by Faust, Mephistopheles and Will-o'-the-Wisp as they magically ascended the Brocken, the new trio of aeronauts hovers over the battlefield. Its stanzas, in which Faust cannot share because his dream-awakening to consciousness is now contingent upon "physical" contact with classical soil, permit Mephistopheles to express

[1] Other strikingly classicizing elements are the generous use of inversion, harsh ellipses, postpositive noun-modifiers, sententious generalizations, separation of sentence parts normally or logically placed together, pathetic exclamations, and the use of chiasmic antithesis.

characteristic satisfaction at finding classical ghosts as horrible as Northern ones, and Homunculus to make clear that the life Faust seeks is to be one "in the realm of fable"—in a realm both of the fabulous and of poetic invention. No sooner is Faust set down on the ground than he asks, "Where is she?" Homunculus, who in Laboratory seemed endowed with clairvoyant omniscience, now protests his *and* Mephistopheles' ignorance of Helen's whereabouts, although he encourages Faust to "Go seeking her from flame to flame" with the assurance, at once Mephistopheleanly ironic and Faustianly self-confident, that one who has dared visit the Mothers can overcome any obstacle. Since Faust wishes to pay suit to Helen, the suggestion that he go from one campfire to another is a nice variation on the "let's go from fire to fire" with which Mephistopheles the matchmaker led aside Faust the suitor to view more intimate aspects of the Northern witches' Sabbath, while Homunculus' easy mention of the Mothers—of whom Mephistopheles has said, "To mention them makes one feel ill at ease,"—demonstrates both Faust's awareness that the bottle-imp is not what Mephistopheles pretended and his successful conquest of the feeling of superstitious awe that their name once evoked in him.

7062–79   On the Brocken Faust was continually in the symbolic company of Mephistopheles; now he marks his independence of him by having the proposal that each of the three shall go his own way accepted without discussion. (The undeveloped motif of a coming together at a signal from Homunculus furnishes the occasion for his vial to give off not the tinkling it made in Laboratory but the harsh resonance of the nightmarish bell heard in High-Vaulted Narrow Gothic Room, and so it further demonstrates that Faust has seen through Mephistopheles' recent tactics.) Left to himself, Faust repeats his "Where is she?" and then pauses significantly to add, "Pursue no further now the question . . ." For finding the person of Helen is already subordinate to enjoying the dream-miracle of breathing "the air that once her language spoke," and he is for the nonce content to investigate the curiosities of a Walpurgisnight in Thessaly—a region completely lacking associations with Helen of Sparta, of Troy, or of Egypt. Somewhat like the pliable poet of *Don Juan*, he is willing to identify geographical Greece with the ancient glory of its Isles. In his Hellenic enthusiasm he momentarily out-Byrons Byron when he claims that physical contact with Greece has inspired in him the spiritual equivalent of the strength Antaeus drew from (Libyan!) soil, although his tone is on the whole noticeably less bombastico-heroic than it had been in Knights' Hall.

2. *By the Sphinxes*

With Faust's announced departure into the "labyrinth of flames" 7080–7103
that is the counterpart of the "labyrinth of valleys" through which
he proposed to saunter at the opening of Walpurgisnight, there
begins a series of episodic entrances and exits by the trio of wanderers
very like those that succeed each other with such rapidity in Oberon's
"haunted grove" of *A Midsummer Night's Dream*. In Walpurgisnight
a single dimly-lit stage set could represent various parts of the Harz
Mountains; here a similar set represents the whole Pharsalian Plain,
a landscape-with-figures appropriate parts of which become visible,
as they should in a dream, without change of vantage point.[2] Taking
Faust's place, the investigating Mephistopheles espies two Sphinxes
and two Griffons, whom he politely greets after a soliloquy in which
are developed the motifs of his feigned unfamiliarity with things
Greek and his charge in Laboratory that the worthless Greeks were
shameless sensualists. The words "I find antiquity too vital" with
which he prefaces his uncharacteristic proposal that nudes should be
provided with fig-leaf or girdle also characterize him as a degenerate
modern by Faust's robust Graecophile standards. One of the
Griffons, who snarls his "r"s, acknowledges his greeting by reproving
him for calling them "old gentlemen"—this is Faust's delayed
rejoinder to Mephistopheles' taunting references at their second
interview to his advancing years—and gruffly insists that no one
should be addressed by a term (*Greisen*) whose "gr" suggests many
unpleasant words beginning with this sound combination. When
Mephistopheles counters his whim for romantic etymologizing,
which is simply dream word-association, by politely insisting that
the "Grei" in *Greifen* is pleasing, the Griffon expresses his agreement
with the Faustian sentiment, "Let one reach out"—to seize is also
greifen—"for maidens, crowns, and gold, / Dame Fortune often
favors him who's bold."

At this echo of the Victory motif of Faust's masque of wealth,[3] 7104–11
Giant Ants—Herodotus told of dog-sized ants that raise mounds of
gold while excavating their nests—complain that the Arimasps, a
race of one-eyed men, said by the same Herodotus to steal the gold
produced in northern lands, have seized their buried treasure. The

---

[2] The stage direction "On the Upper Peneios," found after 1.7079 in some editions
of *Faust*, is an interpolation of editors who consider scene changes in the interest of
geographical verisimilitude more important than the uninterrupted flow of dramatic
action for which Goethe's simultaneous stage set provides.

[3] The Griffons themselves, as guardians of treasure, are wealth symbols familiar
as such on many ancient coins.

Giant Ants are dream equivalents of the Gnomes of Masquerade whose miner's lamps made them look like "luminous ants," while the Arimasps, confident that they will have succeeded in spending their stolen wealth before the night of celebration is over, correspond grotesquely to the carnival masks who at the beginning of that scene were forbidden to economize when buying from the flower girls. The themes of subterranean treasure and misused wealth are not further developed at this point, however, and Mephistopheles is momentarily ignored by the Griffon, whose role of mythological examining magistrate is an Aristophanic comic invention highly appropriate to a "classical" dream-comedy inspired by Mephistophelean depreciation of all that Helen represents for Faust— especially in view of the ridicule Aristophanes heaped on Euripides in *The Thesmophoriazusae* for his treatment of the figure of Helen.

7112–37   Sitting down between the pair of Sphinxes, Mephistopheles expresses satisfaction at his quick acclimatization to a world all of whose creatures he can understand. Although his use of "man for man" for "all" is tactless in view of the Sphinxes' sex, the Sphinx who answers his remark is content to observe cryptically, "The spirit tones we aspirate, / Are made by you incorporate"—that is, mythological symbols are glorious or, as in this context, ugly, according to what one is able to make of them.[4] As when he emerged in the guise of a wandering scholar from behind the stove in Faust's study, Mephistopheles is asked to identify himself—as Faust then explained, the name of a devil should usually reveal its character—and, mindful of his role of leisured sightseer, he chooses to be a Britisher, Old Iniquity. The Sphinx's request for a demonstration of his power to cast a horoscope is Faust's taunting reminder of the astrological nonsense of Throne Room and Knights' Hall; and so Mephistopheles is here allowed to venture only simplest astronomical observations, although he does challenge the Sphinx to stump him with riddles "or, at least, charades." At his first interview with Faust he had defined himself in the riddle beginning "I am the spirit that ever denies"; now he is defined as the pious ascetic's plastron, the evil man's helpful companion in folly and, as both his first and his second, Zeus's amusement. By thus formulating Mephistopheles' function in terms close to the Lord's original definition of him as an unwitting stimulus to ultimately self-fulfilling activity, Faust reveals a new insight, one clearer and more objective than he has ever

[4] Goethe's was one of the first generations to recognize that many classical myths which had been rationalistically interpreted as distorted history or didactic allegories were poetic elaborations of earlier, more primitive religious beliefs.

expressed before, into what Mephistopheles and Mephistophelean negation represent.

If Mephistopheles is for him now only Zeus's roguish jester, the 7138-51
Lord's rogue-stimulus, Faust has reached that point on man's proper course when absolute evil and willful error can no longer symbolize threats to his moral integrity. He has potentially bested Mephistopheles, and so he may allow himself a pleasure previously reserved for his long indispensable companion, that of maliciously insisting upon his triumph. The Griffons snarl their open disapproval of one who has improperly intruded into their world, Mephistopheles for the first time demeans himself so far as to threaten a hostile opposition with violence, and a Sphinx gently announces that this intruder will soon withdraw from the uncongenial environment in which he finds himself. Although Mephistopheles quickly recovers his poise and alludes with ironic dread to the Sphinx's nonhuman body, the Sphinx gets the last word, invidiously comparing her own healthy claws to the twisted hoof of the "false one"—the motif derives from Witch's Kitchen—and again insisting that the present company inspires uncomfortable feelings in him.

The theme suddenly changes as introductory measures on the 7152-80
lyre draw attention to hitherto unnoticed Sirens swaying in the branches of poplar trees which Mephistopheles locates on the bank of a stream also hitherto unnoticed. They counter the Sphinx's warning that their songs have vanquished "the best of men"—the phrase patently excludes Mephistopheles—by brazenly reproaching him for consorting with "ugly monstrosities," and when the Sphinxes mockingly employ their own melody to describe them as they really are, they pharisaically profess to be above hate and envy and welcome him with a hymn to universal brotherhood and obscene joy. For their "most joyous gesture" is Faust's retaliation for the offensive "coat-of-arms" gesture of Witch's Kitchen which Mephistopheles repeated in Forest and Cave to describe the event of what Faust regarded as his exalted love of Margarete. And when Mephistopheles characterizes their singing as virtuosity that conveys no feeling, they are correspondingly quick to remind him, with clearly Aristophanic *double-entendre*, that a shrunken leather pouch would be the only 7181-94
heart in keeping with his (ugly) face.[5]

Faust's return confirms the truth of the Sphinx's oracular assertion that we see in the world about us a reflection of values we ourselves cherish. The half-human monsters to whose animal

---

[5] The physiognomy motif ultimately derives from Margarete's antipathy to the inhumanity evident in Mephistopheles' "repulsive face" (Marthe's Garden).

12—G.F.

attributes Mephistopheles has been repeatedly made to draw attention—very appropriately, in view of his bold development of the theme of human bestiality before Faust's eyes in Auerbach's Cellar, of his delight in the subhuman denizens of Witch's Kitchen and in the inhuman ones of Walpurgisnight, and of his recent metamorphosis in Masquerade from Zoilo-Thersites into adder and bat—afford Faust aesthetic satisfaction. In the ugliness of these monsters he can discover "traits of worth and grandeur." Regarding his pleasurable surprise as a good omen, he is content to recall briefly the noblest associations suggested by Sphinxes, Sirens, Ants, and Griffons, and to draw spiritual refreshment from "the memories great" that these "great shapes evoke." His power of disinterested contemplation again demonstrates a less complete obsession with thoughts of Helen than Mephistopheles has attributed to him, for since Longinus' treatise on the Sublime a feeling for grandeur has been frequently regarded by "classical" aestheticians as the true test of a selfless feeling for beauty. But it is also a tenet of neoclassical criticism that the highest beauty is that of the human form, so that he naturally thinks of Helen too, letting Mephistopheles suggest with characteristic cynicism that "Monstrosities are even welcome" when one seeks one's beloved.

7195–7213   If the Sphinxes protest their inability to give information about Helen by inventing a legend that "the last of the last of us" was slain by Hercules—before the Greek heroic age—the motif is both one of dream-frustration and a parody of Mephistopheles' earlier insistence that classical mythology antedates himself. There is also healthy humor in the grotesque motif of Chiron's restlessness, and in the Sphinxes' punning *Wenn er dir steht, so hast du's weit gebracht*, which means "You've made great progress if he stay still for you—and if he will to you an answer give." "Noble" by virtue of his high purpose, Faust can depart in search of Chiron so conscious of his new moral strength that, unlike the other hero Ulysses, he needs no bonds but those of the Sphinx's good advice to resist the Sirens' invitation to go with them to their green-sea retreats. (This last motif is the germ from which Faust will develop the idea of the water pageant that is to mark the triumphal conclusion of his Classical Walpurgisnight masquerade.)

7214–48   Mephistopheles now irritably remarks the croaking passage of creatures flying so fast as to be invisible—conveniently so for the stage director. The Sphinx's explanation that these Stymphalides (man-eating birds with iron beaks, claws, and wings, whose slaying was one of the labors of the just-mentioned Hercules) are well-

Chiron's reply to this exhortation is also surprizing. For if Helen   7399-7406
symbolizes ideal—though incidentally feminine—Beauty, is indeed
"the fount of beauty" of his original apostrophe to her, then Faust
may properly refer to her with an absolute superlative. But if she is
to be in any sense a reality, something more than what Chiron with
characteristically Faustian dynamism scornfully terms "a static
image," then her excellence must, like that of the "worthiest" Greek
heroes, be one of a peculiar and individual kind, and he accordingly
endows her with cheerful vitality and irresistible grace.[8] "Beauty's
blessing's its existing, / Grace's power there's no resisting." The theme
of Helen's twofold significance as a symbol of perfect beauty that
Faust has fatefully identified with a human personality is not,
however, further developed at this point, for the invention of a
connection between her and Chiron—there is no classical or later
authority for his account of having helped on the occasion of her
earliest rescue from unauthorized hands—conveniently permits Faust
now to recall her mythological background.

Chiron's claim of having carried Helen "on this back" makes   7406-12
Faust exclaim, "Am I not now confused enough? / To think I'm
blessed by sitting here!" If Chiron has ceased to be a man on horse-
back and become a hero-bearing centaur during the dream confusion
of mythological night—during an imaginary ride on a temporarily
darkened stage—his confounding metamorphosis is fittingly revealed
at the moment of Faust's first recognition of the confusing duality
of the object of his dream quest. However noble a centaur may be,
moreover, it is a beast symbol whose visible presence represents
Faust's renewed readiness to challenge the Mephistophelean premise
that in any human relationship between man and woman there
always intrudes a degrading element of bestiality. Unlike his attitude
on the occasions of his honest protestations of sincere and high-
minded love for Margarete, Faust's attitude now is not one of deadly
earnestness but is marked by healthy self-irony. His delight in sitting
where Helen once sat and his transports at grasping Chiron's mane
as she once did are comic variations on the modern-sentimental
motif of erotic fetishism that motivated his first, unexpectedly solemn
visit to the sanctuary of Margarete's room.

Asked where he carried Faust's "only desire," Chiron gives what,   7412-45
with a turn of phrase appropriate both to the ease with which new
details are added to an old myth and to Faust's imminent expression
of his desire to make her his very own, he calls "the easily provided

[8] Schiller had memorably defined grace as "beauty in motion" in a still classic
essay "On Grace and Dignity" (1793).

commodity" of the story of Helen's first rescue. Chiron's enthusiastic recollection of her charm and self-assurance evokes incongruous amazement from Faust that at the time of this adventure she was but seven years old—an age half the age of consent so cynically mentioned by Faust after he first accosted Margarete. Faust's comment on Helen's age, an echo of a Lady's remark in Knights' Hall that "Since she was ten she's been a good-for-nothing," permits him to remind himself directly for the last time in Classical Walpurgisnight that Helen is a poetic fiction. (This is the point of Chiron's insistence that "a woman mythological" exists outside time, and of his observation that philologists—too often concerned, like Man of Learning in Knights' Hall, with literal reality—have deceived Faust as well as themselves.) Then Faust announces his poetic intention of being bound by time no more than any (other) poet, of bringing to life "by the power of intensest longing" that "figure most unique" which is Helen, "coëqual of the gods." As precedent for what he intends to do he cites, quite appositely in view of the fact that he is only the shadowy hero of his own dream, the legend of the marriage of the shades of Helen and Achilles "at Pherae"—one expects "on Leuce," but Faust names the Thessalian city to which Alcestis was returned after Hercules, Faust's "fairest man," rescued her from the underworld, since his dream quest is to be patterned after Orpheus' descent to Hades. But although his precedents are classical, his sentiments are modern-romantic, like the language of hyperbole in which they are couched. And if his bombastic tone recalls the rhetoric of alternating exaltation and depression to which he was so prone in the first scenes of the Tragedy, his avowed compulsion to attempt the impossible at any price is the quintessence of romanticism.

7446–61   Yet Faust's resolution to obtain in person the Helen that he saw earlier "this very day" is no quixotic delusion. He is at last aware that the paradox of nontemporal existence which so disturbed him in connection with Mephistopheles' original invention of a realm of the Mothers may be resolved on the plane of poetry, and so he can let Chiron ironically observe that to spirit creatures he seems to be "really crazy." By a fortunate coincidence like Homunculus' original recollection that a certain day in Lent was the anniversary of the Battle of Pharsalus, Chiron is able to announce—"For your good fortune it so happens"—that he is about to pay his annual visit to a seeress medically qualified to cure Faust's madness; for that is what Manto of Delphi might have been were she not here conveniently made the daughter of Aesculapius and not of her proper father

Tiresias. That she should be praying to her deified father to enlighten physicians is a comic reminiscence of Faust's harsh condemnation of medical ignorance during his Easter walk, but that Faust should let himself be brought to her willy-nilly is outright farce, especially since he can assert, after just having declared himself quite sane, that it would be base of himself to let himself be cured. (The motif of curing strange maladies in a temple dedicated to Aesculapius is an Aristophanic motif recalling both the comic cure of Plutus in the comedy which bears his name and the account of Philocleon's incurable passion for jury duty in *The Wasps*, even as the motif of Faust's remarkable means of transportation has in *Peace* an Aristophanic analogue in Trygaeus' ride to heaven on a horse-beetle.)

Abruptly Chiron halts before a temple which suddenly becomes 7462-94 visible by moonlight; its situation midway between the Peneios and Olympus permits Faust again to repudiate Mephistopheles' too-inclusive condemnation of all war by letting it, with considerable poetic license, symbolize a battlefield on which republican Rome decisively defeated Macedonian tyranny in 168 B.C. As on the stage of Euripides and Aristophanes, a door opens to show a figure dozing within. Manto, who revealingly shares Faust's power to hear in her sleep, recognizes that "Demigods draw nigh," an appropriate self-tribute to one whose newest dream-role is that of mythological hero. Awakened by Chiron, she exchanges with him a few remarks—as so often in dreams, these are half commonplace, half cryptic—and is then told his diagnosis of Faust's disorder. As Chiron disappears, she unexpectedly announces, "I love the man who wants what cannot be," and without more ado starts to smuggle Faust down to what she implies will be a more profitable interview with Persephone than was Orpheus'. With dreamlike magic all obstacles to the fulfillment of Faust's poetic intention have disappeared, and the ordeal motif of Ill-Lighted Gallery repeats itself on the comic level of an almost effortless descent to Hades. An episode whose tone of sophisticated humor recalls Lucian's late-Greek *Dialogues of the Dead* has terminated, and as Temple, Manto, and Faust simultaneously vanish, the scene is once again the monster-populated river bank from which he and Chiron set forth on their strange ride through Walpurgisnight darkness.

4. *Again by the Upper Peneios*

Although Faust does not again appear in his own person during the remaining two-thirds of his Classical Walpurgisnight, what is still to be represented in his dream play is much more important for the revelation of his dramatic character than the part just concluded. To be sure, he has already expressed effectively his intuitive certainty that Mephistopheles' negativistic evaluation of the historical and mythopoetic achievements of classical antiquity is false; he has formulated certain of his highest insights—some old and others, their corollaries, new—with far greater poetic economy than in Masquerade and with none of the heavy didactic directness which marred that production's artistic success; and he has wittily demonstrated his growing power to see through Mephistopheles and what Mephistopheles represents, as well as his increased ability to resist successfully his indispensable companion's once all-too-effective tactics of direct suggestion and taunting countersuggestion. But because of its light charm, Faust's representation of his romantic-hellenistic enthusiasm has necessarily failed to present himself as a figure noticeably less ridiculous than Mephistopheles, for if the latter was sorrily treated by various classical monstrosities, Faust has had to play the role of a seemingly naïve visionary. Accordingly, he eliminates himself from the action of Classical Walpurgisnight and uses the figures of Greek mythology and history not only to ridicule Mephistopheles but as symbols with which to give a positive poetic formulation to his best insights, not least of which is his sense of civilization's deep indebtedness to classical antiquity.

7495–7518   Although the large line of progression in Classical Walpurgisnight is, as it was in Masquerade, from lower to higher forms—in the dream play from inhuman and half-human monsters to ever more perfectly human figures—for a moment we are returned to the world of Sirens, Sphinxes, and Griffons. Again the Sirens are heard inviting "unfortunate" creatures of the land to plunge into waters which their presence makes perilous, but before they can lure any victim into their stream an earthquake causes a blockage of its flow and sends them fleeing to the moonlit waters of the more congenial Aegean Sea. Singers of Water's saving supremacy, they are unabashed by what is a self-evident triumph of Earth and even in retreat enjoin the "merry noble guests" of this dream masquerade to hasten to the marine *trionfo* which they themselves are about to attend. And if they characterize this *trionfo* as a "cheerful festival" to which "every sensible person" should hurry, it is partly because they echo the opening assurance of Masquerade's Herald that "a cheerful festival" awaited its guests and that even a sensible man-of-the-world could with propriety wear Folly's mask on so auspicious an occasion, partly because the place where they are is "uncanny," and partly because monster-infested Pharsalian Fields are ultimately a Mephistophelean invention tainted with Brocken-like elements to which Faust will counterpose in the final third of Classical Walpurgisnight a nobler and completely different spirit-world of his own poetic invention.

Where but recently there was a rudely awakened river god now 7519-73 appears with much audible effort the torso of an Atlas-like strong man who supports a great mass of stone with his head and arms. This earthquake-god's exertions are halted at the point when they threaten the traditional immobility of the Sphinxes who have described his gradual emergence and have mistaken him, a mythopoetic invention of Faust's, for the sea-god whom legend credited with creating the island of Delos. His expression of self-satisfaction with what he has just done "all by myself" and his braggart account of earlier feats of strength make him a neo-mythological exemplar of youthful presumptuousness like that displayed by the newly graduated Student of High-Vaulted Narrow Gothic Room, but by virtue of his sense of beauty—both in landscape and in the arts symbolized by Apollo and "the blessed Muses' choir"—and hence of order he is something more than a rebellious, Mephistophelean descendant of "Night and Chaos." He may, like the Poet of Prelude on the Stage, exaggerate the importance of his contribution to mankind and the gods, but his exuberance is a generalized counterpart of that youthfulness of spirit which the Player there insisted was infinitely more important than mere physical youth. Seismos thus represents a new positive insight, a corollary of Faust's faith that it is man's proper destiny ever to strive toward life's most perfect forms, and one whose rightness may be confirmed by reference to that part of *Faust* which establishes the objective standards necessary for evaluating the rightness or wrongness of views expressed within the Tragedy of Faust. If, then, he incongruously blends elegantly poetic phrases with vividly colloquial expressions throughout his speech, which for the greater part is one long Homeric simile, it is for the healthy and pardonable reason that his fundamental sympathies are with that life whose representatives he now "loudly" summons to populate the territory he has newly created.

Although Seismos' earlier efforts may indeed have raised up the 7574-7621 throne of Zeus, his latest geological disturbance at once proves to have been a catastrophe of the class which the Sphinxes declared it was their destiny inscrutably to contemplate. No sooner is what the Sphinxes punningly call his "mounted fortress"magically covered by forest and underbrush and surrounded by rocks that metamorphose him into a miniature mountain, than the Griffons enjoin the Giant

Ants to pick from it the gold they espy in its crevices. When the "all-busy" Ants—their *allemsig* is also etymologically "all ant-like" —have taken the ore and left the "deads" (*Berg* is both the "mountain" and its oreless rock), and when "the supreme treasure" has been placed under the Griffons' guardianship, Pygmies appear and announce their intention of colonizing this new land—a motif which anticipates Faust's last great mortal enterprise. These dwarfs are dream counterparts of the miner-Gnomes who in Masquerade made their entrance in straggling pairs, and unlike the Pygmies of Greek myth, who were simply the warrior enemies of the Cranes, are neo-mythological miners and mining entrepreneurs. Their entrance as "model couples" suggests the dream word-association "Paradise" and so permits a characteristically Faustian repudiation of any regretted Garden of Eden, of any Judaeo-Christian golden age.

Yet we find things here are best,
To our stars our thanks we tender;
Be it East or be it West,
Mother Earth with joy engenders.

This assertion that man's life must be "best" here and now makes clear that Faust, however greatly he admires classical antiquity, is no longer likely to succumb to the fatal temptation of saying to the coming symbolic moment of his union with Helen, "Linger a while, thou art so fair!"

7622–75   The Pygmies are followed by still smaller creatures, the metalworking Dactyls of Greek mythology; here quite literally "Fingerkins," diminutive dream counterparts of the Pygmies or "Fistikins," they express almost childlike confidence in the power of their common Mother Earth to find them mates also. For the nonce, however, they and the Giant Ants are perforce "pliant" slaves of the Pygmies, whose Elders order them to implement a great armaments program, while the Pygmy Generalissimo orders the extermination of all the herons at a fortuitously nearby pond so that he and his men may have plumed helmets. This despoliation of nature is effected with dreamlike instantaneousness, and the Cranes of Ibycus—the cranes of a late Greek folktale of murderers who brought retribution upon themselves by carelessly mentioning the name of their victim—immediately appear to call for vengeance on the "fatbelly-bowlegged-rogues" who have wantonly slain their fellows. Faust's motivation of the never before explained hostility of Pygmies and Cranes is not only another neo-mythological tour de force but also the neo-mythological equivalent of his Masquerade warnings against the misuse of wealth and power, now formulated not as a didactic allegory but as a purely dramatic fable whose humanistic thesis is the natural inevitability of retribution. At the same time, his myth bears eloquent witness to its creator's hatred of the exploiter, to his understanding sympathy with the helpless victim of oppression, and to his wholehearted approval of the passionate indignation which inspires the champion of justice and makes condonable a hostility toward other living creatures entirely different from Mephistopheles' impotent hatred of all life. For all its high seriousness, however, his fable can appropriately be part of an Aristophanic dream-comedy by virtue of its grotesque motivation and the grotesque figures who are its actors—a grotesqueness nicely emphasized by the intrusion of comic Aristophanic compounds like "fatbelly-bowlegged-rogues" into the Cranes' otherwise passionately earnest declaration of a righteous war on "this spawn" of evil.

5. *Mephistopheles and the Lamiae—Homunculus and the Philosophers*

As the Cranes disperse to gather reinforcements, by natural 7676–7709 dream-association the primary symbol of Evil reappears, and the theme of Mephistopheles' discomfiture is further developed. He who produced the effect of an earthquake when he rang the bell in Faust's old study now is irritated because an earthquake has unexpectedly separated him from "his" Sphinxes by "A mountain hardly worthy of the name." Calling the spirits of the classical witches' Sabbath "alien"—as well he may, in view of the novel attributes with which Faust has endowed many of them—he confesses a characteristic preference for the static geographico-mythological figures of the Harz Mountains. Despite his evident homesickness, which is reflected in his homely use of *Abenteuer*, in Goethe's day an already old-fashioned word for "novelty," to describe Seismos' diminutive Brocken (which, like its Northern counterpart, is surrounded by darting lights), he is still resolved to catch himself one of the "gallant chorus" of ever-evasive, ever-luring Lamiae whom he has been unsuccessfully pursuing since his last exit. But they forestall "the old sinner" by suddenly whirling him about in a dance as wild as the Brocken one in which he so effortlessly participated with Faust and the naked witches, although now he can only stumble along clumsily because of the twisted foot to which the Sphinxes last drew his attention.

When the Lamiae release and again elude him, the ageless 7710–51 Mephistopheles who once tauntingly assured Faust that "there also comes a time / When one enjoys a bit of quiet feasting," now curses his own fate of being old and yet still foolish enough to want tangibly damaged goods, "rotten in every member," and to dance the tune of these "carrion" (*Luder*—also "loose women"). While these observations are appropriately couched in Aristophanic *double-entendre*, they also represent a penetrating insight of Faust's into the utter folly of evil becoming habitual. Accordingly, Mephistopheles returns to the pursuit with a resolution "not to be / Foolishly caught in scruple's web"—"For if there were no witches ever, / Who the devil would be a devil!" But as the Lamiae parade about him in best *maison-de-tolérance* manner, profiting from the discreet semi-darkness, an outsider pushes herself into their ranks. This new symbol of ugly folly is the Empusa, in Aristophanes' *Frogs* a protean vampire which in one of its rapid metamorphoses has one leg of brass and one of cow dung, but here a Bottom-like woman with ass's head and one ass's hoof who greets Mephistopheles as "Sir Cousin," the very title by which he let Homunculus first address him in Wagner's laboratory. The sovereign irony of her assertion that she has chosen her present form in his honor reflects Faust's increasing sense of intellectual and moral independence of his once indispensable companion, although the urbanity with which Mephistopheles repudiates the honor indicates that Faust by no means underestimates his wit.

7752–7800   Even as Margarete once sought to separate Faust from a companion whose presence emanated a spirit of inhumanity deadening to her power of selfless love, so now the Lamiae urge Mephistopheles to have nothing to do with a "nasty creature" at whose mere approach things seemingly "fair and lovely" cease to be so. Although he suspects "these cousins" of being capable of "metamorphoses too," he is now hoist with the petard of tactics he has so often used successfully with Faust, and lets himself be baited by their taunts. As he grabs hold of one after another of them, each immediately becomes something unlovely, and by a final metamorphosis all turn into bats—the motif derives from Masquerade's transformation of the Mephistophelean Zoilo-Thersites into an adder and a bat—who briefly circle about him before leaving him to a moment of peace and quiet. In Witch's Kitchen, to the nonsense of which Faust applied the epithet "insipid," and in connection with the evocation of the shades of Paris and Helen, Faust was the dupe of Mephistopheles; now himself deluded, Mephistopheles calls classical mythology as "absurd" as its northern counterpart and condemns as "insipid" the people and poets whose invention it was. The most important element in his brief soliloquy, however, is his observation that "As everywhere, so here today, / A masquerade's unreal ballet," for it is not only a reference to what he regards as the regrettable insubstantiality of Classical Walpurgis-night's masks, but also an expression of Faust's own regained ability to distinguish clearly between poetic symbols and literal realities and hence the objective dramatic demonstration that he well knows his successful quest of Helen can only be symbolic and poetic.

As Mephistopheles, still looking for his Sphinxes, stumbles over 7801-48 the "horrid stones"—*Graus* is both "horror" and "gravel"—of what he wittily calls a portable Brocken, an Oread invites him to climb the suddenly visible natural rock which she, an extreme outcrop of the Pindus Mountains, symbolizes. But before he has time to leave the "illusory formation" which the Oread warns will disappear at dawn—the contrast between artifice and nature was the theme of the flower auction at the opening of Masquerade, where Art and Nature were also simultaneously symbolized by things equally artificial—he espies Homunculus and asks him where he has been. No longer claiming omniscience, Homunculus explains that he has been floating impatiently about in search of something into which he might not hesitate to incorporate himself and so "come into being properly." If his caution reflects very real limitations in Faust's theoretical enthusiasm for the sublimity of primitive monsters, his hope that two philosophers will be able to help him because they have been talking perpetually about Nature indicates that he is now a genuinely Faustian Faustulus at a stage in his intellectual development approximating Faust's at the opening of the Tragedy. It is as much Faustian as Mephistophelean that Mephistopheles labels philo-sophical constructs "specters" entirely appropriate to a witches' Sabbath, but that he advises Homunculus to "come into being on your own" because "If you don't err, you never learn a thing," is purely Faustian and reveals that Faust at last understands the great truth posited in Prologue in Heaven, that error and effective human striving are inseparable.

As Homunculus utters the Wagner-like sentiment that "good 7849-58 advice should ne'er be scorned," Mephistopheles dissociates himself from him and departs, leaving Homunculus to become the pro-tagonist of Faust's Classical Walpurgisnight, a role which remains his until the very end of its concluding *trionfo*. His two philosophers now appear, disputing so passionately whether water or fire is the First Principle that they pay no attention either to his joining them or to his wish to achieve corporeal being. The motif of a comic dispute is in best tradition of Old Comedy, and it is a nice Aristophanic touch that the views of Anaxagoras, teacher of the Euripides whom Aristophanes so often attacked, are the ones dramatically demonstrated to be erroneous. For, as a fanatical exponent of the creative power of fire, Anaxagoras must inevitably be in the wrong, since Wagner's failure to crystallize life in the retorts of his laboratory is the original motivation of Homunculus' presence at the classical witches' Sabbath. But although the arguments of Thales and Anaxagoras superficially resemble those of early nineteenth-century geologists about the relative merits of Neptunism and Vulcanism as sufficient explanations of the formation of the earth, their function is not to afford an occasion for Aristophanic satire on the ideas of Goethe's contemporaries but to permit economical dramatic statement of Faust's highest insights into the nature of man and the universe at this point in his development.

7859–83   Anaxagoras' ridiculous self-identification with fire is perfectly evident in his question, "Did you, o Thales, in one night, / Bring such a mountain forth from slime to light?" Yet Thales ignores the opportunity this offers for a gibe at his opponent and contents himself with insisting that "Nature's living flow" is gradual, orderly and nonviolent, that an isolated volcanic mountain does not represent part of any large design—hence the indifferent "But what does such a mountain lead to?" with which he announces that further discussion is obviously fruitless. Less gracious than Thales, Anaxagoras pointedly brings to his attention the "Myrmidons" or ant-like creatures with which it teems before turning to Homunculus and proposing—this is a comically delayed response to Homunculus' originally ignored expression of his desire to begin to live—that he get used to being a ruler by becoming king of these creatures. Although Anaxagoras' presumptuousness in thinking himself the king-maker of any world created by fire is a comic motif, his observation that Homunculus has "lived in hermit-like confinement" is not only an allusion to the latter's glass container but also a reëxpression of Faust's awareness that isolation is sterile (the theme of Chiron's account of the Argonauts). Obviously of the opinion that Thales is the wiser philosopher, Homunculus hesitates to accept Anaxagoras' offer of kingship without the approval of "his" Thales, who advises him not to do so for the characteristically Faustian reason—Faust's resolution ever to strive for life's most perfect forms led him to the very seat of empire—that in a Lilliputian environment only petty activities are possible, whereas among great men "the little man" grows in stature.

The sudden defeat of the Pygmies by the Cranes demonstrates 7884–7929 the fortuitousness of Thales's advice, if not its wisdom. For a moment speechless, Anaxagoras announces that, although he has been praising "subterranean powers," he will address himself to "ones above" in the present "contingency" (*Fall*—also the Pygmies' literal and figurative "fall" just described by Thales). In the name of "my people's sufferings" he invokes the triple goddess who as contemplative Luna, the moon in the heavens, soothes the troubled breast; who as calm Diana, the moon goddess in human form, is yet capable of violent ardor; and whom as Hecate—underworld goddess of witchcraft—he actually enjoins to open her "shadows' horrid abyss" and demonstrate, although no "charm" has been pronounced, her "ancient power" on the Pygmies' behalf. The moon, for Faust a symbol of Nature's quiet harmony ever since he first expressed his longing to escape from his prison study to moonlit meadows, is simply a symbol of transcendental forces for the ever erring Anaxagoras, who can therefore presumptuously believe that a rapidly approaching meteor is "the throne disk of the goddess" come as the too hasty answer to his prayer, which has "the order of Nature now disturbed." If his surprise and fear at what seems to him the actual intervention of a divinity are a motif of both Old Comedy and New, they also constitute a burlesque variation on the theme of Faust's original inability to accept gracefully man's necessary finiteness. And so, even before the meteor lands, Anaxagoras is persuaded of the truth of the superstition, mentioned so matter-of-factly by Strepsiades in Aristophanes' *Clouds*, that Thessalian witches could change the moon's course, and when the great crash finally comes he calls upon his companions to humble themselves at the foot of the goddess' throne and, throwing himself prostrate, begs their forgiveness of what he has done.

Amazed at Anaxagoras' powers of self-deception, Thales points 7930–50 out that the moon is still where it was originally. Although Thales confesses that he cannot explain what has happened—he is a Neptunist—Homunculus asserts, perhaps under Anaxagorian suggestion, that the rock which has changed the round-topped "seat" of Pygmy empires into a craggy peak fell from the moon. It is at all events certain that Nature, for Faust now always the impersonal force that effected his recovery in Pleasant Landscape, has "crushed friend and foe alike." As for Homunculus' frank admiration of the "powers"—theatrical *Künste* symbolizing natural processes—which have created "in a single night . . . this mountain structure," it is nicely countered by the Faustianly modest "'Twas naught but

13—G.F.

thought" of Thales' terminal comments on the whole episode. Then the two set off for the great sea-festival (which is at long last really about to begin) without Anaxagoras, who presumably disappeared from view when he prostrated himself amid the debris of rock at the base of Seismos' mountain.

6. *Mephistopheles and the Phorcides*

7951–81   The final scene of Faust's Aristophanic comedy eliminates Mephistopheles from the action of his Classical Walpurgisnight and prepares for his appearance in a new disguise in Faust's second great dream-play, the Helen phantasmagoria. As he clambers into sight on the Oread's "natural" mountain, which is located at the side of the stage opposite to that where Anaxagoras and Thales stood, Mephistopheles is still grumbling about the Greek terrain, this time because he must stumble over the roots of ancient oaks that lack the compensating pitch-like smell of resin—"and pitch I like next best to sulphur"—which is characteristic of the mountains of the *Harz* (also "pitch"). The mention of these two substances suggests the natural association of hell-fires, and so hardly has a Dryad scornfully told him that he is "not clever enough" to adapt himself to a strange country and hardly has he once again lamented his lost Northern "paradise," when he espies in a faintly lighted cave three figures from the uttermost depths of the Greek underworld. The Dryad identifies them as the Phorcides—they are the Graeae of the legend of Perseus and the Gorgons—and tauntingly urges him to go and pay his addresses to them. Although he accepts the challenge, he is constrained to confess that he has never seen anything like this "trinity," whose members are "truly worse than mandrakes," are far uglier than "the oldest reprehensible sin," and would not be tolerated even on the thresholds "Of the most horrible of all our Hells." At his sneering observation that things like this are part and parcel of "the land of beauty" glorified by the epithet "classical," the Phorcides indicate that they are aware of an intruder's presence by stirring and by squeaking like vampire bats.

7982–8011   If Mephistopheles introduces himself to these monsters by paying them the compliment of knowing their family and its genealogy, it is partly because this survival of primitive etiquette had been taken over from heroic epic into Greek tragedy and then parodied in Old Comedy, partly because the destructive impulse to which he confessed at his meeting with Faust caused Faust then to call him "strange son of Chaos" and so justifies the fiction that he is a "distant relative" of sisters of Chaos and of the Fates whom he saw "yesterday—or the day before" (at Faust's masquerade). His claim of having offered homage to Ops and Rhea, however, is a barefaced lie constituting a new comic variation on the motif of his professed ignorance of things classical, since these are the Latin and Greek names of *one* goddess symbolizing the anti-Mephistophelean principle of fertility. As for his fulsome praise of the Phorcides' potential merit as artistic subjects, it permits them to be grotesque parodies of the solitary Mothers who he said Faust would see by the light of their tripod in the deepest depths of nowhere. For the Phorcides, "Sunk in solitude and deepest night," are not simply "unknown to you mortals," as Mephistopheles declared the Mothers to be, but are, as they say, "Ones born in night, related too to all that's night, / Unknown to us ourselves almost, to others quite."

In view of the lack of positive identity with which Faust has 8012–33 endowed his Phorcides, and in view of his growing awareness that Mephistopheles is but a symbol of negation, it is symbolically appropriate that the latter should now borrow the person or mask of one of them "for a short time" which will correspond to the remainder of Faust's double dream. As for Mephistopheles' argument that it would surely be mythologically as practicable for so unreal a trinity to embody itself in two persons as in three, this is simply an echo of the Witch's Kitchen theme of what Faust the non-transcendentalist there regarded as the feverish nonsense of numerology. But when Mephistopheles has closed one eye and turned his profile so that but one incisor is visible, he is at last as visibly ugly in human shape as he is in essence. The motif of transvestitism and the mock embarrassment with which he notes that his new role exposes him to the possible accusation of being hermaphroditic are final Aristophanic touches—in *The Thesmophoriazusae* Euripides' father disguises himself as a woman, in *The Ecclesiazusae* an old prostitute as an Empusa—before the falling of the curtain marks his departure to his own Hell and from a Classical Walpurgisnight where the presence of a diabolic bogey-man could only introduce a disharmonious note into what will be Faust's supreme poetic affirmation of life's positive significance.

CHAPTER XVIII

The Triumph of Life

8034–57   With the shift of scene from Pharsalian Fields to Rocky
Inlets of the Aegean Sea, light symbolically triumphs over macabre
darkness as Luna, graciously heeding the prayer of her willing
servants the Sirens, comes to rest at "her nocturnal arch's zenith."
In this new environment, no part of the world of "Thessalian
witches," the Sirens cease to be vicious monsters and become
elemental spirits—"daimons"—whose "lovely song" symbolizes
only the perilous call of the sea that ultimately permits the Nereids
and Tritons to adorn themselves with "shipwrecked treasures."
Whereas the *trionfo* motifs of Masquerade were ironically inappropriate both to the state of the Empire and to the consequences
for Faust of its success, the *trionfo* form of the present scene is
perfectly suited to his feeling of triumph at having apparently bested
Mephistopheles in a dream agon about whether broad human
significance could properly be attached to grotesque elements in
Greek mythology. Didactic solemnity was an incongruous element
to intrude into a supposedly carefree carnival entertainment whose
practical function of advancing Faust in the Emperor's favor was
itself inconsistent with the ideal of disinterested art proclaimed in
the allegory of Boy-Charioteer, and Masquerade's cheerful atmosphere was blemished by manifestations of Mephistopheles' malice
and by the more generally Mephistophelean phenomena of gross
materialism and ugly greed. The present *trionfo*, on the other hand,
can potentially be a flawless example of pure poetry mirroring, without the intrusion of constraining elements, Faust's vision and
interpretation of a large segment of the totality of human experience.

Serious but not solemn, pregnant with meaning but unmarred by didacticism, the great water-pageant which concludes Classical Walpurgisnight is, by virtue of its tolerant irony and healthy gaiety, the most convincing expression of Faust's sympathetic understanding of the universal harmony of Nature, and of his sense of man's proper place within that harmonious order, to be offered by him at any point in his development.

Urged by the Sirens to demonstrate that they are "more than fishes"—are demigods with human attributes—the Nereids and Tritons assure them that this was already their intention and swim off in the direction of Samothrace, leaving the Sirens to wonder what they plan to do "In august Cabiri's realm." Before resuming their hymn to Luna, however, the Sirens make a comment about the Cabiri—"They are Gods! Uniquely strange: / To breed themselves they ever do arrange, / And never know they what they are"—which is significant not only thematically but also for what it indicates about the style in which the musical passages of this water festival are to be rendered. As always in *Faust*, music is subordinate to the dramatic action, so that although the generous use of marine figures may suggest Baroque opera and a libretto like Dryden's *Albion and Albanius*, the vocal style must be that of cantata-recitative rather than that of opera-aria if the thematic significance of lines like those just cited is not to be lost. For the Sirens' words are not simply an anticipatory identification of relatively unfamiliar mythological creatures who are to be introduced later in the scene, but the first of a final group of variations on the theme of unknown divinities originally introduced with Mephistopheles' Mothers, "Goddesses unknown to you mortals," and then varied by Faust's invention of Phorcides "Unknown to ourselves almost, to others quite." Variously held to be of Egyptian, Semitic, and Phrygian origin; variously said to have been represented as embryo-like shapes, goblins, and human youths; and variously explained as divinities of navigation, as cult-objects of Samothracian mysteries of generation, and, at least by one German Romantic philosopher, as symbols of the Transcendental become Substance—the Cabiri are for Faust simply the third and final term in the series "Mothers-Phorcides-Cabiri" and represent the ultimate absurdity of beings ignorant of their own identity and yet capable of that eternal self-perpetuation which the realm of the Mothers symbolized in Mephistopheles' first account of it. And if it is to be remembered that one myth traced the descent of these dubious divinities from Leda and Zeus, then their introduction marks not only a repetition of the theme of Faust's

8058–81

growing independence of Mephistophelean suggestion but also a new demonstration that he no longer regards his dream-quest of Helen as a seriously literal attempt to make an ideal into substantial reality.

8082-8127   Thales now appears with Homunculus, whom he hesitates to bring to the seer Nereus, a grouchy misanthrope, nevertheless worthy of respect because of his many acts of benevolence. Like Mephistopheles on the eve of his departure for the Pharsalian Fields, Homunculus is willing to "try" a visit and knocks with his vial against the door of Nereus' conveniently handy cave. Like Faust when disturbed by Wagner after the vanishing of the Earth Spirit, the sea-god grumbles at the human intrusion and expresses Earth Spirit-like scorn of creatures "damned always to be like themselves" despite their divine aspirations. If he has vainly given men good advice although his has long been the right "to rest in godly wise," it is because he shares Faust's inability to enjoy idleness and Faust's awareness that "deeds accomplished" are perforce incommensurable with men's best intentions. Accordingly, Thales can well diffidently commend to his attention the submissively counsel-seeking flame, "manlike to be sure," that is Homunculus. Nereus' countering tirade on the futility of giving advice to mortals reveals why he, rather than Poseidon, is the sea-god of this *trionfo*; as the questing Faust found a Chiron who had known Helen, so Homunculus-Faustulus is to be helped on his way by one who has known Paris. And although Nereus' opening profession of misanthropic irritation is comically exaggerated, his "How earnestly I Paris warned with father's care / Before his lust an alien woman did ensnare" expresses a sense of moral responsibility of which Faust had been incapable when he resolved to seduce Margarete, while his brief prophetic description of the fall of Troy and its companion piece, the equally brief evocation of the adventures of Ulysses, magnificently demonstrate Faust's growing poetic powers. Most important of all, however, is the line "Troy's day of doom, in rhythms fixed for ever," for it marks Faust's achievement of full insight into the principle of Prelude on the Stage— there over-presumptuously announced by the Poet—that poetry is the rhythmic patterning of the stuff of life itself.

8128-53   Despite its Wagner-like sententiousness, Thales' assuring reply— that a good man, however pained by folly, will not be discouraged by failure or by ingratitude a hundred-weight of which is completely outweighed by a short-drachm of thanks—is a still more important echo of the prologues to *Faust*. For it marks the first time that the Lord's concept of "the good man" is mentioned within the Tragedy proper,[1] and, following immediately upon Nereus' sublime evocations of the *Iliad*—and *Aeneid*—and the *Odyssey*, it insists that Faust's moral growth and Faust's aesthetic development are but two different aspects of that one basic physical phenomenon which is man's innate power to strive toward the realization of his highest aspirations in whatever imperfect measure is granted him by the circumstances of his existence. The urgency of Homunculus' wish "to be wisely born" prevents the theme from being more than touched on in passing, although Nereus' gruff refusal to be helpful is nicely motivated by the all-absorbing natural affection and paternal pride—both clearly good human qualities—with which he awaits his (fifty!) daughters by the nymph Doris, whose oneness with Nature is patently symbolized by their sporting in the water "In perfect union with that element." And so, for all the eagerness with which he looks forward to the triumphal arrival of his fairest daughter, he does direct Homunculus and Thales to Proteus, the god whose miraculous powers of metamorphosis make it virtually certain that he can tell them "How one can get to be and change one's form."

While Thales, although doubtful whether Proteus will be of any help, leads his companion off so that they may at least "try the experiment" of asking his advice, the Sirens descend from their cliffs to welcome the returning Nereids and Tritons, who bring with them the Cabiri in the great tortoise shell of Chelone—a nymph whose mocking of the marriage of Zeus and Hera was punished by metamorphosis—and enjoin the Sirens to sing "Songs of Songs" in praise of these gods. It quickly transpires that the Cabiri are portable maritime divinities who will assure favorable auspices for the present celebration. Able to rescue shipwrecked sailors from the Sirens, only three are present—a Phorcides-like trinity—because the Cabirus who claims to be the "proper" god and to do the thinking for all his fellows has declined to come along. The Sirens may naïvely declare that even gods who mock one another should nevertheless be given every honor, but when the Nereids and Tritons now announce that there are "really seven," the three not at Samothrace presumably being on Olympus, and then suddenly remember an eighth of whom nobody ever thought before—this is nonexistence raised to the fourth power!—there can be no doubt that the worship of the Cabiri is here nonsense. Yet it is very Faustian nonsense too, not simply a final

[1] Wagner's use of the phrase "a good man" in Outside the City Gates comes in too unpositive a context to make it an exception ("A good man does enough, I've always thought, / If he employs the skills that he's been taught / With diligent, painstaking care").

turning of the tables on Mephistopheles, that the loveliest creatures of his Classical Walpurgisnight should worship deities "not yet completed."

8202-18   In having his Nereids, Tritons, and Sirens pay homage to imperfect divinities Faust is expressing not only his graceful acceptance of human finiteness, but also his clearest poetic formulation of the principle that life and growth are irreconcilable with the static and sterile condition which would be utopian perfection. And so for a moment he attains to that degree of insight possessed by the Player of Prelude on the Stage when the latter asserted, "Who thinks himself complete is never to be pleased; / One who is still becoming will always thankful be." Grotesque as may be "incomparable beings" whose perpetual aspiration makes them "nostalgic hungerers / For what's unattainable," they are extensions of man's essence as Faust understands it—hence the Sirens' almost parenthetical comment that it is rewarding to worship the Unattainable (wherever it may really be enthroned) "In Sun and Moon," as always in *Faust* and for Faust the supreme symbols of God-Nature. The episode appropriately ends with the comic motif of all-too-human pride as the Nereids and Tritons join the Sirens in singing that the winners of the Golden Fleece "come short of the glory"—the phrase is St. Paul's—of those who have found the Cabiri, while the parodistic "I and God" pattern of their hymn of praise now become one of self-praise demonstrates how far Faust has advanced beyond the egocentric forms of religious experience that he expressly repudiated in Outside the City Gates but still succumbed to in the opening soliloquy of Forest and Cave.

8219-54   As Homunculus, whose aerial vantage point permits him to look down into the great tortoise shell, reappears with Thales, he observes that the Cabiri are ordinary earthenware pots, are harder nuts than the heads with which scholars are trying to crack them. Thales's comment that learned interest is simply proportionate to the age and rarity of an artifact echoes the curio-theme of Mephistopheles' recent survey of the objects in Faust's old study, while his oblique allusion to the metamorphosing power of time affords a convenient cue for the humanly curious god of metamorphoses to make known his presence. If Proteus' first ventriloquistic tricks recall Mephistopheles' original projection of the voice of Homunculus, his entrance as a great turtle—the shell that bore the Cabiri is now reintroduced right side up—is a typical dream-metamorphosis. When what he calls Thales's "philosopher's trick" of concealing Homunculus from him has forced him to assume a "noble human shape," Proteus exclaims that "A dwarf who shines was never seen before!" Since Proteus is clearly the symbol of Nature's infinite variety, his failure to recognize Homunculus is Faust's final dramatic-ironic insistence that Homunculus is simply an insubstantial projection—hence also Thales's "Till now his glass alone gives him some weight." The Mephistophelean paradox of Thales's characterization of him as one "only half born," like Proteus' "Your's truly was a virgin birth, / For you exist before you live on earth," is a corollary of Faust's anti-transcendental, naturalistic view that spirit and substance must always be inseparably one, that pure idea is unreal abstraction only.

Homunculus' wish to be "substantialized" is thus very different 8255–74 from the announced quest for animation that Mephistopheles originally attributed to the stillborn mannikin of Laboratory, is the symbolic equivalent of Faust's own impulse to achieve a harmonious, natural wholeness of being. As a being still without reality, however, Homunculus may properly share with mythical monsters—Lamiae, Sphinxes, Mephistopheles-Phorkyas, or even Plato's eight-legged creatures—the trait of hermaphroditism to which Thales calls Proteus' attention and which Proteus observes with gently Aristophanic reassurance will make his finding of a suitable body no problem at all. At Proteus' proposal that he shall start life in the sea, where a creature can gradually—and, as Proteus realistically notes, at the expense of other life—evolve to higher forms, Homunculus immediately expresses comically incongruous olfactory delight in the smell of seaweed wafted to him by the breeze, and the group moves at Proteus' suggestion to a point by the sea where the odor will be still more pungent and from which they will have a close view of an aquatic group now floating up.

The Telchines, forgers of Neptune's trident, which they display as 8275–8312 visible proof that no storm can disturb the calm sea on which this *trionfo* is supposedly being staged, come from Rhodes, the island of the Sun, and are accordingly greeted by the Sirens as "Blessed creatures of bright day." Inasmuch as their presence represents the vicarious introduction into the mysteries of Luna of the highest symbol of life and being acknowledged by Faust, the lilting anapests of their paean to fog-dissipating Apollo nicely echo the rhythms of Faust's anthropomorphizing paean to sun-brought Spring in Outside the City Gates, and so their proud recalling of the legend that they were the first to represent gods not as monsters but simply in human shape reflects both Faust's consistent humanism and his ever-growing power to distinguish sharply between symbol and reality. The episode of the Telchines, coming so soon after that of the Cabiri, marks the rapid progression from "lower" to "higher" forms that makes the larger pattern of Classical Walpurgisnight basically identical with that of Masquerade, although its total function only becomes clear after Proteus has commented on it. For Proteus' scornful observation that "dead works" of art produced by human hands—the famous statues of ancient Rhodes—are ever impermanent, are "For the sun's all-holy rays of light / . . . a jest alone," reflects Faust's humble recognition that man, however high his place in the order of creation, is not the be-all and end-all of the cosmos. And if Faust began his dream quest under a one-sided aesthetic compulsion, in the course of it—and *before* he has found Helen— he has already repudiated that unhealthy form of aestheticism which would make art an end in itself.

8313–38   The theme of the impermanence of all human achievement is restated in general terms as Proteus, becoming a dolphin, invites Homunculus to climb on his back and let himself be wedded by him to the sea. Proteus' declaration, that "A life on earth, of whatever kind, / Is simply a perpetual grind," does not lack tragic overtones of Faustian pessimism, but it is a far cry from Faust's original expressions of suicidal despair or from the view expressed by Mephistopheles in Prologue in Heaven that things on earth are "heartily bad, as always." Thales can therefore with good conscience urge Homunculus to accept Proteus' invitation and yet also drily observe that by beginning the long evolutionary process in the sea he will put off for the maximum possible time the day when he enjoys the mixed blessing which is, as Proteus immediately states more explicitly, to be a human being with no prospect of a higher form of life. And, although Proteus may properly question the value of a human existence like Thales', the best consequence of which would seem to be an endless afterlife "amid pale hosts of ghosts," Thales' countering assertion, "It all depends; it's surely also fine / To be a worthy man in one's own time," demonstrates that Faust now fully shares the view expressed by the Player of Prelude on the Stage, that "A fine young fellow here and now / Is something worthwhile too, I think." For to be at some time "a good man" living his life in the here and now to the best of his abilities is the appropriately Faustian goal set for the little Faust who is Homunculus.

8339–78   The appearance of a ring around the moon is recognized by the Sirens as the sign that the climactic moment of the *trionfo* has come. What Nereus' "benighted traveler" called a lunar halo, he and his fellow spirits recognize as doves sent by Paphian Aphrodite to accompany his daughter on her conch-journey—a fancy of which

Thales approves because it satisfies that "something sacred" which is the "worthy" Nereus' paternal pride. Then those who draw the conch of Aphrodite that is bringing Galatea themselves arrive from Cyprus on various traditional sea monsters, their stage-direction names of Psylli and Marsi—tribes famed in antiquity for reptile lore—merely indicating that they are to pass in serpentine lines like those soon enjoined by the Sirens upon all Galatea's water-attendants. If their expression of eternal devotion to their "loveliest lady"—a devotion that has fearlessly survived the destruction Cyprus has known under such different symbols of sovereignty as Roman eagle, Crusaders' cross, Venetian lion, and Turkish crescent—recalls what Faust once called his "eternal, eternal" love for Margarete, its specific historical-temporal frame of reference also makes it Faust's final poetic profession in Classical Walpurgisnight of his faith that the best of classical antiquity is still the living heritage of modern man.

The Sirens now call upon the Dorides to bring into view their 8379–8423 blood-sister Galatea, "your mother's counterfeit, / Earnest, and of godlike air, / Deservedly immortal, yes, / But like mortal women fair / In her tempting gracefulness"—a characterization that makes Galatea the divine counterpart of the Helen of whom Faust's Chiron declared, "Grace's power there's no resisting." As they pass before Nereus, the Dorides coyly beg their father to permit them to enjoy forever the loving gratitude of shipwrecked sailors whom they have rescued. Ironically praising their ability to combine acts of mercy with sources of pleasure, Nereus reminds them not only that Zeus alone can grant immortality but also that theirs is an element—water is here a symbol of the finite, for in it Homunculus is to seek finite existence—which does not permit even love to be constant. In the saddened Dorides' graceful acceptance of the ineluctable transitoriness of the most profound of human relationships, and in their beloved Sailors' healthy willingness, untainted by any transcendental impulses, to content themselves with their present good fortune—their somewhat inelegant "We've never had it so good"—as long as it lasts, Faust finally expresses his awareness that no mortal love may properly deserve the epithet "eternal."

As the Dorides and their Youths affirm in their different ways 8424–31 the value of the fleeting moment which is all that even the longest love can be, Galatea moves in late Renaissance theatrical splendor across the scene. The program of the festival permits her and her father to glimpse each other fleetingly, and although she bids the dolphins that draw her conch to tarry, she has passed out of sight before Nereus can speak. He may grumble at his daughter's seeming indifference—justly if it be true that parental devotion can never be fully reciprocated—but his recognition that a momentary glimpse of her can sustain him for another year reaffirms once more Faust's faith that the value of the moment lies within itself and is not to be enhanced by its static perpetuation.

8432–87   Transported by "the beauty and the truth" of what he sees, Thales bursts forth in praise of Oceanus, the ultimate source of his first principle, Water, while Nereus describes how the great aquatic procession moves off into the distance with Galatea's gleaming loveliness always undiminished. Then Homunculus passes by on Proteus' dolphin-back, his voice for the first time truly resonant as he sings in duet with Proteus-Nature the beauty of the waters in which he is to gain life, and the Triumph of Galatea reaches its grand climax when, pulsating with light, he orgastically smashes his vial against her throne and merges his flame with the waves of the now suddenly luminous sea. If Nereus asks "what new mystery . . . / Is to our eyes in rite revealed," it is because Homunculus' attainment of life is theoretically the only nontraditional element in this annual celebration of the mysteries of Galatea-Aphrodite which, like all Greek mysteries, represent birth and fertility rites and are the quintessential antithesis of the Brocken cult of sterile sensuality. The self-destruction of Homunculus is a *Liebestod*, a death of self, in the sense that only by merging one's being in another's can full selfhood be gained; as such it is Faust's mature poetic affirmation of the supreme positive significance of a relationship with Margarete that at shorter view could seem only the expression of fatally destructive passion. Accordingly, the first dream play of his classical Walpurgis Night ends as the Sirens ecstatically hail in Eros the true first principle, and in Homunculus the symbolic embodiment of the now visible union of contradictories—fire and water—which is the mystery of life itself, and the curtain falls as all voices join in a paean to the four elements that symbolize physical totality.

The triumphal conclusion of Classical Walpurgisnight is the triumph of Faust's creative imagination and his unconditional profession of faith in the inexhaustible creative force which makes life and matter one. With themes and motifs furnished by the misguided Wagner and the uncreating anarch Mephistopheles, and by an interpretive poetic mirroring of his own experiences and insights, he has composed a masquerade whose rising scale of being this time expresses successfully his affirmative vision of the dignity of man and the meaningfulness of the cosmos in which man has his being. As life and light and love have triumphed over the darkness of ugliness and death that marked Erichtho's prologue, Faust has triumphantly met the challenge to demonstrate the positive significance of classical myth, while his own myth of Homunculus has shown his clear awareness that to cultivate the primitive for its own sake is tantamount to needlessly sacrificing a rich birthright of culture for the dubious privilege—this is the *reductio ad absurdum* of romantic primitivism—of beginning life again at a lowest animal level. And if it is even greater folly to attempt to revive literally a dead past—Faust's recognition that Helen must remain a symbol— than to seek to prevent necessary and healthy historical changes, which is what he had sought to do at the seat of empire, then the second dream play of Faust's classical Walpurgis Night, the drama of his connection with the ideal of womanhood that he has projected as Helen of Troy, may properly be both a repudiation of uncritical Graecophilia and the statement of his view that history, like the life of the individual, has meaning only as a process of constant change.

CHAPTER XIX

The Meaning of Human Identity

Faust's demonstration in Classical Walpurgisnight of his luminous sense of the mutability of things and of the oneness of the physical, aesthetic, and moral realms represents dramatically his clarification of the confused impulse that originally motivated his desire to possess Helen, who even before his descent to the underworld had already ceased to be the statuesque and timelessly mature beauty of the dumb show in Knights' Hall. In his first dream play he could ignore—as is proper in Aristophanic comedy, but surely only there—the fact that utopian clairvoyance and finite reality are actually incompatible. It is one thing to set up Mephistopheles as a sort of straw man and then knock him down; it is something very different and far more difficult, however, to create a dream play in which the ultimate limitations of reality and the finiteness of man are never glossed over despite its author's complete freedom to invent what he will without regard to petty realistic considerations. Yet Faust's Helen phantasmagoria is such a play, and both its hero and heroine alike act as finite, autonomous human beings. For Helen, as the poetic projection of one who has just professed to faith in the supreme worth of finite human life—hence the triumph of the humanly divine Galatea and Homunculus' heroic urge to live even at the price of ultimate mortality—can be neither the mere succubus of Faust legend nor merely an impersonal symbol of Faust's highest aesthetic ideals, but must share even his human finiteness. To the extent that she does so, and to the extent that she is, like Faust himself, an integrated personality, his dream play will show symbolically how great has become his potential ability to act on what he has learned by trial and error since leaving his prison study with Mephistopheles. And because Helen is an ideal projection of Faust's own imagination, she may also be in *Faust* the one dramatic antagonist fully his moral and intellectual equal.

Fully nine times as long as its feeble Northern counterpart, the Walpurgis Night's Dream intermezzo, and even slightly longer than Classical Walpurgisnight, Faust's *Helen* opens as its heroine, attended by a chorus of women, takes her place before the façade of a Greek palace. Whereas in the scene Pharsalian Fields Faust maintained the fiction of recreating the outward forms of classical Greek drama only during the opening monologue of Erichtho, and then permitted himself a freedom of versification and a disregard of classical formal restrictions equally appropriate to utopian comedy and his sense of utopian freedom, throughout the whole of Before Menelaus' Palace at Sparta and even into the next scene he sustains a rigidly circumscribed dramatic style, visibly inspired by the model of Attic tragedy, that represents the resolve to demonstrate the validity of his insights within a strictly delimited, symbolically finite segment of human experience. As a free adaptation of Aristophanic comedy mirroring Faust's euphoric confidence in man's oneness with nature, Classical Walpurgisnight could properly ignore Greek limitations on the number of actors and traditional unities of time, place, or theme, although its concluding *trionfo* already marked a return to a stricter dramatic form more appropriate to its theme of Faust's reawakening sense of finite realities. Now the world of his dream ceases to be one of an easy interplay of natural and human forces, and becomes one in which forms are largely predetermined and in which the only dramatic movement is that of human thought and feeling. For Faust's *Helen*, however much a phantasmagoria, is first and foremost his dramatization of the life of earthbound man.

The stately entrance of a buskined Helen—that the Greek 8488-8515 protagonists of *Helen* wear the cothurnus is evident from the final stage direction of its last scene—is an omen of tragedy appropriate to Faust's awareness that his winning of her, unless it is to be only a romantic Hellenist's dream of wish fulfillment without relevance for normal patterns of human behavior, can only end in tragic separation. And after the panoramic stage of Classical Walpurgisnight the limited perspective of Before Menelaus' Palace is also a symbolic reminder that individual finiteness is never to be entirely outweighed by even the most grandiose vision of man's godlike dignity. If Helen insistently announces that she comes from sea to land, it is because earth is in *Faust* as always (Prologue in Heaven; Pleasant Landscape) the only sphere of man's striving; the waters of the Aegean Sea may symbolize life or being or pure existence, but Sparta is the world of human realities at a highly sophisticated stage in the development of civilization. That Helen is accompanied by the Chorus of Trojan Women as she identifies herself, and that these interrupt her with dialogue-like reassurances in the course of her exposition of the circumstances of her return to Sparta, are details that suggest the older Attic tragedy of Aeschylus or Sophocles, who still allowed the chorus a dramatic function, rather than the dramatic technique of the more modern Euripides, who rarely used the chorus except for lyric interludes between the episodes of his tragedies. If these touches of archaism as it were announce a play as starkly simple, and as economical in its use of individual actors, as Aeschylus' so nearly monodramatic *Prometheus Bound*, the hardly less archaic device of expository monologue is not, as sometimes in Euripidean tragedy, simply an economical means of reaching the purely human dramatic situation as quickly as possible. For, like the scene in which Faust himself first appeared, a scene less important as identificatory or dramatic exposition than as symbolic statement of a terrible aloneness, this prologue episode is predominantly monodrama insisting by its very form that at this point Helen is in far greater measure an Aeschylean or even Sophoclean heroine of isolating mythical stature than a humanly frail woman such as Euripides—to Aristophanes' disgust—preferred to portray.

In identifying herself as "Admired much and much condemned, this Helen, I," Helen establishes herself not only as the legendary figure whose beauty is so unconditionally praised in the *Iliad* and whose character is presented in such a dubious light by Euripides, but also as the statuesque beauty whose deportment in the Rape of Helen evoked equally extravagant admiration and condemnation from those who there saw her; if her words recall, moreover, those of Aphrodite in the prologue to *Hippolytus*, it is rather because Euripides' goddess is a creature of too-human frailties than because Helen is endowed with literally divine attributes, and so they place her at once in that realm of human value judgments which is now of paramount importance. With her apostrophe to the palace before which she stands, she begins to be divested of mythological attributes, for in calling its builder "my father" she is allowed to forget, though now only fleetingly, the Jovian parentage that makes it necessary for her a moment later to describe her childhood playing with Clytemnestra—Tyndareus' daughter by Leda—as "sister-like." It is obvious dramatic irony that, at the very outset of a dream in which she is to play a new tragic-poetic role, Helen should express the hope that by passing through the doors through which Menelaus came as suitor she may end forever the vicissitudes that have made her the heroine of "myth" and (poetic) "tale." With far subtler irony it is simultaneously indicated that her "fate" is neither a divine malignance toward man (the archaic religious factor of Greek tragedy) nor a supernatural trial of her virtue (the Judaeo-Christian view most evident in medieval and post-medieval morality plays), but rather a consequence of her own character (the humanistic concept that character is fate). In recalling the circumstances which led to her seizure by Paris—it is important to remember that Faust's Helen is always the heroine of his Rape of Helen, not the crafty protagonist of Euripides' *Helen* or the *casus belli* of the *Iliad*—she avoids all mention of her fatal interest in the handsome Paris, even implying that there could have been no such interest on the part of one who visited the temple at Cythera "obeying sacred duty." Like Margarete, whose classically idealized counterpart she is, Helen is an autonomous moral agent whose beauty has had tragic consequences. She too has known the pain—to a lesser degree—of being the subject of unpleasant gossip. The very complexity of her mythological-literary past symbolizes psychological reality, the multiple dualities of finite human nature, and that personal past which no responsible man may conveniently leave behind him by saying, as she does, "may all remain behind / That up to now, fate-fraught, encompassed me with storms."

Reminded by the Chorus that hers is the fortunate possession of 8516-59 beauty able to subdue the sternest of heroes, Helen interrupts their ode at the end of the strophe—its iambic-anapestic march rhythms are those traditional in the *parodos*—because it is fitting for her alone to be concerned with what may be the consequences for herself of her return to Sparta. Uncertain whether she is to be "consort" and "queen" or to die as "victim" (*Opfer*) of Menelaus' wounded pride and as a "sacrifice" (also *Opfer*) to appease divine wrath long directed against the suffering Greeks—the fate from which one legend says she was saved only by Aphrodite's intervention, and from which she escapes in Euripides' *Trojan Women* only because her still doting husband pretends he will destroy her on their return to Sparta—she again seeks to evade personal responsibility for her ambiguous position by insisting that "the Immortals" "equivocally" allotted her notorious and fatal beauty. All that is certain so far is that Menelaus has treated her with strange detachment—as well he has had to, since his only function is, himself a shade, to have conducted the shade of Helen "in the hollow ship" which is his insubstantial (also *hohl*) vessel to a situation in which she may, to all intents and purposes an autonomous human being, meet Faust on the same dream plane of unreal reality—and that he has ordered her to inspect, while he passes his warriors in farewell review, the state of a household in which no changes will have taken place since his departure for the Trojan War.

8560–90   In their antistrophe the Chorus seek to reassure their visibly disturbed mistress by declaring that her beauty can safely challenge that of Menelaus' hoard of gold and jewels—the theme is the contrast between art and nature first introduced in the flower episode at the opening of Masquerade and since developed by Faust in other variations. As if she has been silently speculating on the significance of Menelaus' words, Helen ignores the Chorus' remarks and resumes her account of his speech, which concludes with ominous instructions that she make preparations for a sacrifice all the details of which are specified except the nature of the victim, a fact underscored by the cruel irony of Menelaus' "But then all else I leave to your providing care" after the completeness with which he has enumerated the necessary pieces of sacrificial apparatus. Rightly terming his failure to indicate a victim "suspect," Helen nevertheless declares she will not let care—the Fear of Faust's Victory allegory—paralyze her and resolves to leave the event, be it good or evil by human standards, to the gods. A heroine endowed with Faustian *amor fati*, she identifies herself with mortal men as she asserts her readiness to bear whatever fate may bring—"we mortal beings can endure it well"—and illustrates her awareness that nothing future is certain by recalling that the intervention of god or foe has often stayed the fall of sacrificial axe.

8591–8646   This reversal of the motif of Margarete's execution is mistaken by the Chorus for an expression of fear-inspired wishful thinking, and in their epode they sycophantically pervert her declaration of readiness to accept life as it comes into an affirmation of shallow optimism, reminding her that they escaped death at the fall of Troy to become "fortunate" slaves of "the fairest thing on earth." Not deigning to take issue with beings merely content to exist, Helen reaffirms her obligation to enter the royal palace. If her recollection of having run up in childhood the steps she now ascends as a stately woman is again a reminder that she is in ever greater measure a normal human being, so also is her first honest acknowledgment of human frailty—her admission that the palace she now sees again is one "Long missed and much desired and almost forfeitèd." When she has disappeared from view, the Chorus chant their first *stasimon*, an ode to the happiness of one whom the gods have permitted to return from captivity to joyous scenes of her youth. Ironically inappropriate to Helen's heavy-hearted exit, it proves to be dramatically ironic when at its conclusion she rejoins them with a countenance in which their leader Panthalis is constrained to discern repugnance, wrath and surprise.

Speaking for the first time "with animation," Helen reveals that 8647–96 she, a godlike human being—"Zeus' daughter"—superior to "common fear," has retreated from her home before Stygian horror "which . . . shaketh e'en a hero's heart." But she soon recovers her self-possession, declares she will withdraw no further and—like the Pythian Priestess on discovering the temple-defiling presence of Orestes in Aeschylus' *Eumenides*—announces that she will think of some act of consecration that will permit her and her lord to enter a purified abode. At the request of the Leader of the Chorus, who assures her that she has the support of servants who revere her, Helen declares that they too will see this monster, "Unless primordial Night has swallowed up again / *Her* shape within her magic womb's profundity," and then proceeds to give a coherent report of what has happened. In the dark interior of the strangely deserted palace she discovered but one sign of life, a great shrouded female figure seated by the dying embers of its hearth. Assuming this to be a stewardess appointed by her husband, Helen ordered her to busy herself with the work of the household but received no response except a gesture warning her to withdraw. Then—this is Gothic romance in classical costume—as she turned angrily away to hasten toward the steps that lead to nuptial couch and treasure room, the spectral figure rose and imperiously blocked her further advance. And so she has returned perforce to her attendants, who now see for themselves the indescribable form of Phorkyas-Mephistopheles, as it appears between the still open doors of the palace, a fearsome nocturnal monstrosity that Helen is nevertheless confident cannot harm herself or her women, creatures of Apollo's day and light.

In their third ode the Chorus speak as one person, first describing 8697–8753 in a double strophe the final fight at Troy and sounds of battle amid which were heard the cries of the gods and the strident voice of Eris, then in double antistrophe the city's burning and colossal

shapes of angry gods fleetingly glimpsed through smoke and flame.
These memories of past horror have been evoked by the larger-than-
life frightfulness of Phorkyas, whose presence they directly acknowledge in their mesode (fifth strophe), asking whether they actually ever
saw what they have just described—"or has my mind, / Fear-
encompassed, only imagined / All that confusion?" In doubting the
actuality of their memories the Chorus are questioning their actual
identities, their reality, but the dream-motif of the uncertainty of
what is real and what is illusion is not further developed at this point,
and they assert—like Faust declaring "Indeed I wake" at the beginning of his Classical Walpurgisnight vision of Leda and the swan—
that the horribleness now visibly confronting them would prove
tangible had they but the courage to lay hold of it. When they have
tentatively identified Phorkyas as one of the Graeae who has
ventured into the light of day, they declare, misunderstanding Helen's
defiance of the supernatural, that her "ugliness" is a "shadow" that
Apollo's eye will never see (second double strophe), although they
are "mortals" who must suffer the sight of her abominable
wretchedness (penultimate antistrophe). But when Phorkyas now
advances "boldly" toward them, their only and feeble defense is to
threaten her with the curses of "fortunate ones whom the gods
created" (final antistrophe).

8754–83   The presence of Mephistopheles-Phorkyas, the visible embodiment of error and evil, expresses Faust's awareness that in finite
reality man must always struggle against hostile forces, and the
Fate-like figure of Phorkyas, unloving, unloved, and unlovable,
symbolizes the necessary stimulus to the strivings of the good man
as Faust now conceives him. Phorkyas' first remarks are a classicizing
elaboration of the dictum that Modesty and Beauty are lifelong
enemies, together with its application by means of Homeric simile
to the Chorus, whom he calls "you bold ones come from alien land"
—he is now made to identify himself with the Greeks he purports to
scorn—and compares with croaking birds of passage whose way will
not be his. Although he addresses himself explicitly to the Trojan
Women, his assertion that Beauty remains steadfastly shameless until
it is embraced by "Orcus' empty night" or until "old age it first
subdue" is a realistic reminder of what must be the ultimate fate of a
purely human Helen. After this calm preamble follow a series of
unrestrained invectives accusing the Chorus, for whose dignified
bearing Helen will soon vouch, of behaving like drunken Maenads,
of howling like dogs (a nice touch after the earlier insinuation that
they trumpet like cranes) and of being a grasshopper-swarm of camp

followers and streetwalkers. And if Mephistopheles' discursions on modesty and shamelessness have represented a grotesque but healthily comic variation on a theme central to the tragic outcome of Faust's relationship with Margarete, his simile of the grasshoppers— symbol of man's animal limitations ever since Prologue in Heaven— is equally important as an expression of Faust's awareness that man's central concern is to demonstrate the innate dignity by which he raises himself above the mere beast of the field whose only immortality is its offspring.

In putting a stop to Mephistopheles' hyperbolic denunciations of her attendants, Helen insists both that she will not allow her authority as mistress to be usurped and that, whatever their backgrounds, the Trojan Women have demonstrated the virtue—which Faust so admired in Margarete—of selfless devotion "As we did bear our wanderings' hard vicissitudes, / In like of which men often think but of themselves." Threatened with punishment if she does not keep her proper place, Phorkyas immediately acknowledges, though again with sententious *double-entendre*, the authority "That god-blessed ruler's noble spouse deserves / By virtue of long years of wisest management," and then sows new seeds of discord by superfluously demanding protection "Against this flock which, placed beside thy beauty's swan, / Are nothing more than plainly-pinioned gaggling geese." The indirect allusion to Helen's dubiously immaculate conception is lost as individual members of the Chorus begin a stichomythic exchange of insults with Mephistopheles that rapidly progresses from sententious generalizations to classicized billingsgate and reaches its climax as Panthalis and Phorkyas threaten one another with the solution of the riddle of their respective identities. Mephistopheles' iterated insistence that the Chorus are vampiristic creatures whose closest kin dwell in Orcus recalls the Homeric picture of Odysseus in the underworld as he keeps at a distance the shades attracted to his warm-blooded presence until he can interrogate Tiresias, whom Phorkyas has also mentioned, and so the apparently gratuitous logomachy serves the purpose of at last seriously weakening Helen's self-assurance by undermining her sense of certain identity. [8784–8825]

For the first time Helen fails to meet a situation with apt sententiousness, for to speak of "discord that in secret festers" after the blunt abuse just heard is to digress, however true it may be that the master becomes "himself confused" when domestic strife prevents the execution of his orders. But then she confesses the cause of her sudden weakness, which is her feeling that she may herself belong to the underworld, her uncertainty—like that of the Chorus in their [8826–63] most recent ode—whether her past is real, and her fear lest in her present and future existence she may still be "That city-waster's horrid visionary form" which is the Helen of myth and poetry (hence the epithet "city-destroying," a pun on *Helénē* and *helépolis* which goes back to Aeschylus). In view of Mephistopheles' plain intention to hurt her, it is dramatically ironic that Helen should now turn for reassurance to Phorkyas, alone of those in attendance upon her not visibly infected with her own horror, who with character-istically cruel Mephistophelean irony asserts that a sense of dreamlike dissociation from reality is simply the normal consequence of having been favored by the gods with an extraordinary measure of good fortune and then begins to adduce in confirmation the very adventures the memory of whose fateful effects has just shaken her profoundly. How well Faust understands Mephistopheles is evident in Phorkyas' emphasis on sensuality and brutality—her suitors are "men in the heat of love," "Theseus, lustfully excited, seized you young, / A Hercules in strength"—while his own ideal of womanhood is reflected in her stichomythic countering of Phorkyas with details that emphasize her better qualities (her gratitude to Patroclus, her bearing of a legitimate daughter to Menelaus, and "that half-widowhood" of a loyal wife during a husband's absence which ended in the "disaster" of her seizure by Paris).

8864–81   When what he implies was a willing departure "for Troy's betowered town / And unexhausted joys of love" reminds Helen of "an infinitude / Of all too bitter sorrow," Mephistopheles expresses surprise, since legend and Euripides' *Helen* have it that the Helen of Troy was but a double of the true, Egyptian one. And so, admittedly more confused than ever, Helen declares, "I know not even now which one of these I am," and collapses into the arms of her attendants after Phorkyas' final blow of recalling the still more relevant legend of her marriage after death to the dead Achilles.

As shadow I, to him as shadow was I joined.
It was a dream, the words themselves say even so.
I faint away and to myself become a shade.

8882–8908   The Chorus' fourth ode, in which they enjoin to silence a monster as ugly of speech as of looks, represents not only the passage of time between two episodes—a protagonist unconscious has in a sense made an exit—but also the first stage of a transition to a less classicizing style. Although it begins with combinations of trochee and spondee as unusual in normal German as in normal English and hence more emphatically "Greek" than the iambic-anapestic or trochaic-dactylic patterns of earlier odes, it becomes trippingly dactylic in its final strophe (epode), which even fails to correspond to the first (proöde) in number of lines. If this structural irregularity provides a transition to the introduction of a new meter at the beginning of the next episode—the tetrameter catalectic, a trochaic-dactylic line used in Attic tragedy for passages of recitative and one which in German moves more rapidly than the six-beat iambic trimeter employed for dialogue until this point in *Helen*—it also indicates Faust's readiness, after what by modern feeling is a last fling of archaizing heaviness, to shift Helen from the Attic stage to a setting in which he himself can appear without incongruity. And a still more overt hint of his satiety with grecism and latinism is the deliberately grotesque apposition to Cerberus of the wolf in sheep's clothing of the Sermon on the Mount still further disguised by heavy classical periphrasis. "For the man, evil though seeming benevolent, / Lupine wrath under fleece of ovile wool, / Far is he more horrid to me than the three- / headed canine's jaws"—this is healthy comic relief and a nice reminder that Faust's quest of Helen is not to end in tragedy as stark as that of his connection with Margarete.

Endowed with Faust's own power to withstand successfully the paralyzing influence of bitter memories, Helen retains what the Chorus has called her "soul, / Already prepared to escape," and resumes her place in their midst as Phorkyas extravagantly praises the sunlike radiance of her beauty. Exhausted by her experience, she nevertheless declares, "But for queens is it befitting, it is fitting for all men, / To compose themselves with boldness, come whatever sudden threat." (This sentiment is a generalization of Faust's injunction to himself as he was about to awaken in the scene Pleasant Landscape, when the Spirit Chorus exhorted, "Although others drag and dally, / Do not hesitate to dare; / All is done by spirits lofty / Of bold actions' need aware.") No sooner, however, has she ordered Phorkyas and her attendants to hasten the sacrificial preparations which Menelaus instructed her to make, than a new blow falls—Mephistopheles' warning that she is the victim. When he tells the frightened Chorus that they too are to die—to be hanged and hang like thrushes from palace rafters is the fate meted out by Telemachus to the serving women who had intercourse with Penelope's suitors—Helen and her attendants stand petrified in a grand tableau of astonishment and fear. Again he maliciously insists that they are ghosts and removes them still further from reality by comparing to "lifeless pictures" these creatures who are "Afraid to leave a daylight that's not rightly yours," adding the Sophoclean observation, consonant with his own

8909-36

view that all transitory things are worthless (first interview with Faust), that even real people are but ghosts who never resign themselves to the inevitable necessity of death.

8937–70   After this passing expression of Faust's sense of human finiteness comes a new and unclassical bit of supernaturalism, the entrance at the clapping of Phorkyas' hands of masked dwarfs who set up the apparatus of sacrifice in accordance with a series of Mephistophelean orders vividly adumbrating Helen's bloody death and ending with the ironic reassurance that her mutilated body will receive a dignified interment. If these waddling dwarfs are the Gnomes of Masquerade in their third metamorphosis, now no longer satire-serving figures of Aristophanic comedy but Gothic-romantic monsters symbolizing sadistic cruelty, the picture of Helen's execution which they help to project is the dream counterpart of Margarete's vision of her own execution, a detail that further establishes Helen's identity with her. There is a sudden comic reversal as Panthalis now turns respectfully to Phorkyas—"Experienced and wise, you seem to wish us well"— for helpful suggestions and as the Chorus (in their strophe) beg the "most venerable of Fates" and "wisest Sibyl" to spare their pleasure-loving lives. Helen, however, has not lost her sense of human dignity and asserts that she does not share her attendants' fear, that she feels only pain at the prospect of death. Her cautiously expressed readiness to accept Phorkyas' aid is seconded by the Chorus' urgent plea (antistrophe) to be told how to escape the "nasty nooses" they imagine are already tightening about their necks and will choke them to death "if you, Rhea, all Immortals' / Lofty mother, favor us not" —a nice serio-comic variation on the motif of Mephistopheles' incongruous homage to the goddess of life at the end of Pharsalian Fields.

8971–9002   Warning Helen and a Chorus only too glad to be patient—"for listening we live"—that he must now speak at great length, Mephistopheles explains with long-winded periphrasis that he who stays home and minds his own business will not get into trouble, while he who "impiously" deserts his household will find everything changed, if not destroyed, on his return. "These well-known saws" seem pointless to Helen, who also senses a reproach implicit in the reference to impious absences from home and therefore urges Phorkyas to tell a straight story without superfluous allusions to "things unpleasant." But Phorkyas insists that he is merely being "historically factual," not blaming anyone, and goes on to explain that during *Menelaus'* protracted absence—the motif of the uncertainty of poetic time recalls the casual Homeric account of how Menelaus, though eager to return home, took a vague number of

years for the journey from Troy and arrived eight years too late to
have prevented Agamemnon's murder—things have changed in
Sparta. Again Helen thinks she hears a reproach, this time of her
husband, but Phorkyas ignores the interruption and narrates how
bold Northern invaders have occupied a valley of the Upper
Peloponnesus and from their impregnable fortress there make raids
at will upon the Lacedemonians and their land.

Although this successful barbarian invasion, by which the 9003-30
Peloponnesus came under the control of Western European feudal
lords during the Fourth Crusade, or two millennia after her own
day, at first seems impossible to Helen, as a timeless poetic figure
herself she is readily convinced that Phorkyas speaks the truth when
he declares, with considerable understatement, "They had the time;
it's been perhaps near twenty years." And as one who has always
fared well at the hands of princes, she immediately asks whether
these invaders have an overlord, or whether they simply constitute an
alliance of many bandits, and is reassuringly told that they are not
brigands and that their leader, though powerful, "was content with
a few voluntary offerings" when he visited Menelaus' palace during
Phorkyas' stewardship. Asked how this lord looks, Phorkyas gives a
picture of Faust as Faust sees himself—"a cheerful, jaunty man,
good-looking too, / Endowed with depth of mind that but few Greeks
possess," one who is both magnanimous and trustworthy. If Faust's
jauntiness and intellectual depth are attributes that Margarete told
Faust at their first rendezvous especially impressed her, the insistence
that his Barbarians are less barbaric than the Greeks before Troy is
an allusion to Achilles' cannibalistic threatening of the wounded
Hector—Voltaire had cited the relevant passage from the *Iliad* to
make the same point—equally appropriate to Mephistopheles'
avowed hostility towards things Greek and to Faust's own awareness
that not everything Greek is worthy of an enlightened man's unqualified admiration. By having Phorkyas describe his splendid castle
more at length than himself, Faust avoids self-adulation, and by
having her address the Chorus rather than Helen as she does so, he
avoids the appearance of trying to win Helen by vaunting his wealth,
the ignoble opening tactics of his campaign to seduce Margarete.
And in allowing Phorkyas to compare ancient Greek architecture
unfavorably to Gothic—the theme, deriving from the Architect's
condemnation of the Doric temple of Knights' Hall, had been
inverted by Mephistopheles-Homunculus in Laboratory—Faust
nevertheless is a humanist sufficiently classical to depreciate only
the primitive, cyclopean structures of Mycene, and sufficiently

anti-transcendental to make Phorkyas' highest expression of praise
the ironical observation that not even a thought could gain a foothold
on his castle's vertical exterior.

9030-70   The Chorus' curiosity about coats-of-arms allows Phorkyas to
contrast invidiously the "richly meaningful" ornamentation of Greek
shields with the stereotype emblems of medieval and modern
heraldry that adorn the spacious halls of Faust's castle, and to assure
the ever-hopeful Chorus that they will be able to dance there with
blond young men who emanate an aura of youth. "Paris had that
aura quite / Unique when to your queen he did draw nigh," is a
typically Mephistophelean taunting digression that permits Faust to
have Helen interrupt Phorkyas with almost the same words Mephistopheles used in Knights' Hall when he was carried away by
enthusiasm for her beauty, and she warns, "You fall / Completely
out of role; now finish your discourse!" Coming immediately to the
point, Phorkyas tells her that he will at once surround her with
"that castle" if she will utter a definitive "Yes." Although the Chorus
importunes her to save herself and them, Helen still hesitates to
believe that her husband intends her harm, but when Phorkyas
reminds her—or tells her, since the legend is post-Homeric—how
Deiphobus, whose concubine she was after Paris' death, had been
cruelly mutilated by Menelaus, she can only comment mechanically,
as if her husband's true character had been for the first time revealed
to her, "He did do that to him, did that because of me." And as
Mephistopheles, no longer promising her an honorable death,
declares that she is to share the fate of Paris' brother because he who
has possessed beauty whole cannot bear to share it with others—
this is a grotesque dream variant on Faust's vow of Knights' Hall
to die if he ever renounce Helen—trumpets are heard in the distance.
Phorkyas interprets the harsh sound as the announcement of the
jealous Menelaus' imminent arrival; the Chorus imagine that they
see the flashing of arms; and, in his role of faithful stewardess,
Mephistopheles proleptically welcomes his king and master, and tells
Helen's attendants that they see her death approaching and that their
own deaths are now inevitable.

9071-77   There is a pregnant pause, then Helen announces that she has
decided to follow Phorkyas to the castle of refuge. The Euripidean
stratagem that will bring her to Faust—one as simple as that of
Menelaus in *The Trojan Women*, of Pylades in *Iphigenia among the
Taurians*, or of the wily heroine of *Helen*—has succeeded. But Helen,
rightly distrusting the good offices of a clearly "hostile demon,"
declines to reveal what she will do after she reaches Faust's castle.

The rest I know alone; what there the queen may in
Her heart of hearts conceal in deepest secrecy,
Let that be kept from all.

More properly confident of his ability to woo Helen successfully than
he was of his prowess as a seducer on the occasion when, having
ordered Mephistopheles to procure him Margarete by nightfall, he
bragged, "Had I but seven hours clear, / I wouldn't need a devil
near, / To help seduce a thing like her," Faust endows Helen with the
right of an autonomous human being to prefer death to the alternative
of being wooed by a man who may well be less worthy than the
monstrous Phorkyas has claimed.

As the Chorus begin the *exodos*, rejoicing at their escape from 9078–9126
death and the prospective security of fortifications as strong as those
of Troy—"Which did after all / Yield to infamous guile alone"
(proöde)—fog gradually obscures the stage, and they realize that they
have seen the Eurotas and the swans upon it for the last time (strophe),
although they still hear the swans' trumpeting, which they hope may
not forebode the deaths of their swan-necked selves or the death of
their swan-conceived mistress (antistrophe). Finally in complete
darkness (epode), they momentarily remember that they are creatures
of the underworld and ask,

Does not Hermes float
There up ahead? Surely his golden staff
Summons us back and commands our return
To the joyless days of Hades' grayness, a
Realm eternally void, yet crowded,
Overcrowded, with shapes elusive?

At this identification of Mephistopheles' realm of the Mothers as
simply the shadowy underworld of the Greeks, the fog suddenly
disappears and the Chorus find themselves alone with Helen in a
medieval courtyard whose sunless gloom persuades them that they
have but left one form of captivity for another (recitative strophe).
Without interruption of its dialogue or action—the late Renaissance
theatrical technique is one of which Calderón was the supreme
master—the setting of *Helen* has become one in which modern men
have lived; hemmed in by Gothic architecture, like Faust at the
opening of his Tragedy, Helen now stands on the threshold oɪ
symbolic finiteness. Faust—or Goethe—has achieved the tour de
force of recreating the spirit and style of Euripidean tragedy in his
dramatization of Helen's return to Sparta, a subject that no ancient
or other dramatist seems ever before to have treated.

CHAPTER XX

The Winning of Helen

Although Faust's *Helen* begins like a trilogy in the Greek manner, its second and third parts cannot continue to preserve the unity of time that is a patent "classical" feature of Before Menelaus' Palace, since this would be incompatible with the reawakening sense of reality that makes Faust transport Helen from antiquity to the historical age in which he himself lives. Yet he attains a greater degree of unity of action than the Greeks themselves demanded by letting the action continue without pause from one part of his trilogy to the next, while he provides as much unity of place as there is in Aeschylus' *Oresteia*, which opens in Argos and ends at Delphi, by his fiction that Helen always remains on Greek soil. And by integrating his Chorus with the action of his trilogy to a greater degree than any Attic dramatist ever did, he—or Goethe—not only increases the effect of unity of action but also avoids separating his dramatic episodes proper from each other by static choral passages that would diminish the impression of an uninterrupted sequence of dream moments.

9127–81   The scene Inner Courtyard of a Castle ("faced with ornate and fantastic medieval buildings") opens as Panthalis sententiously condemns her fellow attendants' too feminine lack of equanimity and bids them await in silence their mistress' decrees. But Helen, emotionally and physically exhausted by what has happened, hopes only that the absent Phorkyas is announcing her arrival "to the wondrous hero-lord'—"I want an end of wandering, wish peace alone." Her lack of vitality is mirrored in the suspension of dramatic action which is Panthalis' repeating of her hope that Phorkyas may even now be wandering about "in the labyrinth / Of this strange harmony of many castles' walls" in search of its master; and if the phrase "labyrinth of this strange harmony" reveals once more that Faust is no rabid neoclassicist, it also insists that his dream castle is a setting symbolic of the finite sphere of human existence, of what in Dedication was called "The labyrinthine-errant course of life." Then the tempo of Panthalis' speech changes, and in staccato phrases she marks a great movement of people, which she interprets to mean that Helen is about to receive the noble reception that is her due. Where stood the blind façade of Menelaus' deserted palace there is now a castle stirring with life, and the Chorus, suddenly cheerful again, describe in tripping rhythms (proöde in predominantly anapestic tetrameters) the entrance of handsome young pages. Their fear that these youths might be unreal is both a reminder of their own unreality and a characteristic expression of subconscious awareness that dream experiences remain elusively incomplete—an incompleteness metrically reflected in the absence of the last stress of their proöde's final line. But when the handsomest pages have set up a canopied throne and Helen has taken her place on it at their pantomimic invitation, the Chorus arrange themselves in lines on its steps and joyously proclaim that she has been more than fittingly received (epode in choriambics except for its last two lines, whose trochaicdactylic pattern reflect the Chorus' confidence that now all is well).

Faust's dignified entrance is described by Panthalis. He lets her insist that his "pleasing presence," unless it be deceptive, reveals a man who "will succeed / In all he undertakes"—an echo of his high resolves of Pleasant Landscape—and declare, "Forsooth is he to be preferred to many men / Whom I have also seen held in high esteem," itself a nice blending of modesty and self-appreciation in the style of the once frequently cited eighteenth-century aphorism, "Je suis très peu quand je m'examine, beaucoup quand je me compare." Why Faust has not chosen to welcome Helen immediately upon her arrival becomes clear from his first speech and the episode of the negligent watchman which it introduces. The fiction that her beauty has blinded Lynceus not only permits him to pay her extravagant compliments in the Gothic-Baroque manner; it also creates a dramatic situation which immediately demonstrates her practical autonomy as the suzerain of her new environment. The shift from iambic trimeter to blank verse, used by Helen as well as Faust, continues the already inaugurated transition from neoclassical formalism to a style that can juxtapose "Greek" and more modern elements less obtrusively, since in German iambic pentameter has

9182-9212

been the verse of all important dramas on classical themes since it was first introduced in the eighteenth century. More important than the introduction of a Renaissance verse form, however, is the Renaissance preciosity which Faust's speech begins to introduce, for such touches as his description of Lynceus as one "Who, failing duty, me of duty robbed" prepare for the fact that Lynceus is about to address Helen in a rhyming verse form (redondillas) which Romantic translators and imitators of Calderón forever identified in German with "Catholic-medieval" drama and the extravagance of the Renaissance's *estilo culto*.

9213–45   A watchman's pardonable negligence is itself a typical Renaissance motif. Found, for instance, in Gascoigne's masque *The Princelye pleasures at the Courte at Kenelwoorth*, it was best known to Goethe's contemporaries from Scott's account in *Kenilworth*, and so the episode of Lynceus carries Helen beyond the Fourth Crusade, when Faust's medieval castle might have been constructed, into the High Renaissance and Faust's own time. Accepting the fiction that she has power over her subjects' life and death, although she suspects that it may only be a test of her queenly qualities, Helen bids the accused speak. In rhymed trochaics as "unnatural" in German as the unrhymed trochees that have contributed so much to the "Greek" effect of *Helen* up to this point, and with a wealth of conceits insistently emphasizing that we have reached the age of Marino, Lyly, Góngora, and Calderón, Lynceus defends himself by praising his "divinely granted mistress" as a sun that, miraculously rising in the south, momentarily placed him in a dreamlike trance (the motif is a variation on Mephistopheles' claim that Faust's physical helplessness is Helen-induced), and as a goddess whose dazzling beauty has so blinded him to all else that even now he can declare, "Boldly threaten to destroy me, / Beauty can subdue all wrath."

9246–72   Faust's tribute to Helen is simply the Italian proverb "Tutto cede alla beltà" expanded with a generous use of anaphora, word-play, antithesis, periphrasis, and hyperbole. Intended merely as a gracious compliment, unless its glib effusiveness is also Faust's atonement for the cruel threats which brought her to his castle, it nevertheless suggests the theme of fatal beauty—Margarete's "Fair was I too, and that was my undoing." And so it once again evokes in Helen memories of her mythological adventures and renewed awareness of her now ever-more-multiple identity—her original self, her double at Troy, her shade at Sparta, her real-unreal presence at Faust's castle—but that her sense of self-assurance is not seriously threatened is evident from her calm dismissal of Lynceus: "Remove this worthy

man and set him free; / May no blame smite whom gods infatuate."
Indeed, the primary function of her speech of acquittal is not
psychological, but stylistic, for, despite its classicizing tone—one
line even exemplifies iambic trimeter—her enumeration of past and
present adventures and incarnations constitutes a paradigmatic
illustration of the rhetorical device of balanced parallel series so
immoderately exploited by Renaissance manneristic poets. It is thus
natural for Faust, taking his cue from Helen's words, to offer himself and all that is his to one who "smites so surely" with the Shafts
of Love that "even loyalest vassals" are become rebellious. What the
German Emperor's plight has demonstrated to be a fiction, the
medieval theory that property and rights are only to be held in fief
from a suzerain powerful enough to guarantee their security, provides
the poetic conceit which will permit Faust to woo a theoretically
autonomous Helen, who tacitly accepts the advantages accruing to
women of sufficient beauty or social status from Christianity, Courtly
Love, and Cognate Succession.

Hardly has Faust figuratively placed himself and all he possesses 9273–9332
at his lady's feet, when Lynceus returns with dreamlike immediacy to
place before her the gift of all the treasures he has acquired over long
years of military adventure. If Lynceus, a man important enough to
have porters to do his bidding, himself carries the chest of jewels he
offers Helen, it is because his independence is a transparent fiction
only; as Faust's dream agent he is making Helen a present of the
same jewelry that Faust once, more deviously and with less honorable
intentions, had Mephistopheles leave for Margarete to find. Even as
Helen's unidealized prototype was urged then by Marthe to put on
"A necklace first, a pearl then on your ear" (The Neighbor's House),
so Lynceus now recommends that Helen wear only an emerald
pendant and pearl earrings—"Rubies hardly will avail, / Carmine
cheeks do turn them pale." The rhyming iambic couplets in which
Lynceus speaks mark the penultimate stage of the transition from
exclusively stichic and strophic verse forms to ones whose pre-
dominant formal characteristic will, as ordinarily in *Faust*, be rhyme
alone; his account of how he collected unique treasures—"But what
I ever strove to glean / Were rarest things that men have seen; /
Whatever other men had got / Was only withered grass, I thought"—
is both a new variation on the curio-motif of High-Vaulted Narrow
Gothic Room and a reminder of the centuries of warlike migrations
of Germanic tribes that intervened between the end of classical
civilization and the establishment of feudal and modern societies.

Only after he has allowed Lynceus to pay Helen for him the 9333–35 compliment that her beauty makes everything else seem worthless does Faust inform him that she is already mistress of the castle and all it contains. He himself then magniloquently orders her "unblamed but unrewarded" vassal to prepare "paradises / Of lifeless life" within so that splendor, "bedazzling all save gods"—and, by implication, not dazzling for one whose beauty makes her divine—may meet her eye when she enters. But after Lynceus' parting tribute to the sway held over all things by beauty which outshines the sun (a metaphor surpassing even the hyperbole of his original comparison of Helen to the sun), maneristic stylistic devices suddenly cease to be conspicuous. A Renaissance poetic context has been firmly established, and the moment when blank verse can be metamorphosed into pentameter couplets is at hand.

9356–84   Invited by Helen to join her on her double throne and so strengthen her position, Faust lets himself be confirmed "as co-regent of thy boundless realm" and seats himself beside her without further ado. And although Helen says she has many questions she would like to ask, her first—and only—one is how she can learn to speak with the strange but pleasant caressing effect that Lynceus' use of rhyme has produced on an ear attuned only to classical verse. This dreamlike concern with an apparently incidental acoustical phenomenon again rapidly advances the action, permitting Faust to make and have accepted his declaration of love to Helen in a brief exchange of highly stylized lyrical responses—a dramatic device, faintly recalling the liturgical origins of medieval drama, of which Calderón was the greatest master. An apt pupil, after having heard Faust match her question with a line ending in an assonance, she is able to furnish pure rhymes when she now completes his next three couplets. Although this brief introduction by the direct method to the art of modern verse begins in almost banal "Will-you-teach-me-your-language?" fashion, the ironic fact that Faust is the creator of the situation raises the exchange above the level of a conversational gambit or a showy poetical effect. He may momentarily seem to be subscribing once more to the standard romantic thesis that art is simply self-expression—his "it must issue from the heart" again echoes his advice to Wagner about effective persuasion—and to the German-romantic view that true poetry is the expression of unattainable longing (*Sehnsucht*). But he soon makes clear that he regards as happiness only longing fulfilled in the here and now: "The present moment only—is our bliss, / Is treasure, prize, possession, surety."

9385–9410   The interruption of the duet-like love scene between himself and

Helen by a highly classicistic ode is Faust's acknowledgment that lyric dream and crass reality represent two very different levels of human experience. If the Chorus profess not to blame Helen, as much a prisoner as they, for granting the castle's lord "friendly show of favor" (strophe) and observe that "women to men's love accustomed" grant their favors as circumstances dictate (antistrophe), their cynicism represents what Schiller and the German romanticists regarded as classical realism—art representing self-contained reality, as opposed to medieval-modern "romantic" art which, thanks to the Christian dualism between immanence and transcendence, is so imbued with a sense of the insufficiency of actuality that it reveals its creators' unsatisfied longings (*Sehnsucht*) and so far falls short of its ideal goal that its created illusions still convey a sense of illusion-destroying irony. Faust, then, is ironically aware of the artificiality of Helen's dream autonomy and even doubts whether a Greek-realistic Helen could love him with the Margarete-like selfless devotion with which he would like to endow her. Nevertheless, he lets himself press his suit rapidly and successfully, having the Chorus observe (epode),

Near and nearer sit they already,
Lean against each other,
Shoulder by shoulder, knee to knee,
Hand in hand, cradling themselves
On their throne's
Deeply cushioned magnificence.
Majesty can allow itself
Carefree displaying
To the eyes of its people
Of its private delights and its joys.

A dream play imposes no constraints whatever, allowing Faust 9411-18 to syncopate drastically his wooing of Helen and to disregard what the Chorus in somewhat un-Greek fashion have just defined as the normal proprieties. Yet he now demonstrates with more than sufficient artistic adequacy his awareness of the truth, posited in Dedication and Prelude on the Stage and corollary to the doctrine of the oneness of the aesthetic, moral, and physical realms of experience which he proclaimed in his Triumph of Galatea, that the work of art must always in some sense be a faithful mirroring of reality. Helen's "I feel so far away, and yet so near, / And all too gladly say, 'I'm here! I'm here!'" echoes his own characterization in Forest and Cave of the intensity of his passion for Margarete,

15—G.F.

"I'm near to her though I were far away, / And I can ne'er forget, can never lose her." And, although incidentally an expression of the dream motif of dream-within-dream, his "Breathless I seem; words tremble, die away; / It is a dream without a place or day," well recaptures the sense of the unimportance of purposeful self-interest that he had when he succumbed to "love's revery" during his first visit to Margarete's room. By introducing into his and Helen's final professions of love inner rhymes that create marked, time-taking caesuras, he represents symbolically his natural human impulse to prolong a moment of happiness beyond its natural time. Indeed, these inner rhymes, by giving the passage an emphatically lyric form—a lyric is above all a poem of emotions experienced in an immediate present—simultaneously reflect his urge to escape completely from the finite necessity which is time itself. But Faust resists the temptation to sacrifice artistic truthfulness to such impulses and, with the pretext that he is assuring Helen she need not be troubled by her sense of new identity—which is here simply the consequence of loving and being loved—declares, "Life's our allegiance, brief though it may be." And since he remains even in his dream committed to his faith that life may never properly be a static moment, these words clearly mean that he is now ready for a new dramatic development, a symbolic equivalent of life's continuing its inevitable course.

9419-41   The precipitous entrance of Phorkyas is both the visible intrusion of "reality" into a lyric dream world and a dream motif deriving from Mephistopheles' unwelcome interruption of Faust and Margarete's first intimacies. Faust reveals a healthy sense of irony by having Phorkyas formulate his reintroduction of the themes of mutilation, sacrificial death, and mass execution, his warning of Menelaus' supposed approach, with a superabundance of that very rhyme which he has so recently told Helen is the stylistic feature par excellence of the language of the heart, for a tercet with the mono-rhyme -*ibeln* and the inner rhyme -*ibelt* introduces thirteen lines with the striking rhyme scheme *abb acc add aee a*. As angry as when Mephistopheles intruded upon himself and Margarete in the scene Summerhouse—then he stamped his foot and exclaimed "A beast!"—Faust now couches his reproaches in dignified iambic trimeters and with classical sententiousness better suited to his present heroic role and to his ever greater emotional maturity. And he confidently asserts the ironic truth, "There is no danger here, / And even danger would be only empty threat."

9442-81   Signals, explosions and alarums, martial music and marching troops—the stage direction could come directly from Calderón—permit Faust to demonstrate how well protected Helen is, that "Who can protect her vigorously / Deserves alone his lady's favor," and to fulfill in dream form some of the high ambition for which he found no worthy outlet at the Emperor's court. In ballad quatrains, and in the laconic style revived by Napoleon and used in military proclamations ever since, he first reminds his troops of their ever-victorious record and bids them drive the always piratical Menelaus back on to the sea. Then, remembering to speak in the name of "Sparta's queen," he promises his generals that they shall hold in fief the territories they conquer—a reminder that duchies were originally imperial gifts—and assigns the defense of the Peloponnesus to German, Goth, Frank, Saxon, and Norman, thereby suggesting still other important historical developments that have taken place since the end of classical civilization than those mentioned in Lynceus' account of how he collected his rare treasures. And he concludes his speech from the throne on an appropriately idealistic note, and at the same time returns us to the golden Middle Ages which are the primary setting of the action of the present scene, by painting a vision of prosperous domestic tranquillity under a Spartan suzerain who will guarantee "each one of you" his every legal right.

While Faust, having left the throne, speaks with his generals, 9482–9505 the Chorus elaborate on his sentiment that the brave alone deserve the fair, adding corollaries which he could not develop himself without sacrificing his role of man of immediate action. They insist (strophe) that the price of continued possession of things worth having is perpetual reconquest. (Their "highest good" refers only to Helen, but in the waking moment which is his dying, Faust will ultimately generalize what they say, offering it as the supreme insight accessible to finite man: "He only merits freedom and his life/ Who conquers them each day anew.") Thus Faust reformulates without its original bitter overtones his Easter Eve assertion that "Whatever legacy your fathers left you, / It must be earned if you're to own it" and harmonizes it with his first challenge to Mephistopheles, "If ever I recline on bed of leisure, / Then let me cease at once to live!" If their praise of Faust's bold and wise leadership (antistrophe) is only again dream fulfillment of his still unsatisfied practical aspirations, their admiration of the mutually advantageous spirit of cooperation which his feudal military organization symbolizes—theoretically—is his reaffirmation of the insight he had first let Chiron express for him, that highest achievement cannot be the result of singlehanded effort. Only after these expressions of Faust's practical idealism do the Chorus become frankly selfish and express satisfaction that, by their mistress' having found a powerful protector, their safety is guaranteed.

9506–61   As his generals depart, Faust returns to the dais on which Helen sits and, standing beside her, announces that he and she shall remain where they are, letting her well-rewarded princes guard the circumference of the Peloponnesian "non-island" which not only geographically but also culturally—"a land to be a blessing to all peoples"—is an integral part of Europe. That Faust should make decisions without consulting Helen is inevitable, but he here restores the delicate balance between objective, psychological-dramatic verisimilitude and subjective, dream-psychological consistency by justifying his announcement with an appeal after the fact to her natural affection for the country of her birth. "Before the sphere that's your possession, / Give preference to thy native land!" Then, momentarily carried away by his enthusiasm for the timeless glory of Greece, he—or Goethe—paints the Arcadian landscape of time-honored pastoral tradition with a vivid conciseness surely unsurpassed in the history of non-Oriental descriptive poetry, evoking mountains sparsely green, descending brooks, verdant hills abounding with sheep and cattle, natural caves, Pan and nymphs, luxuriant valleys, dense forests, shaded pastures, and plains with ripening orchards and bees productive of honey, in six dynamic stanzas (the twenty-four lines contain more than that number of forms of verbs of action, while forms of the verb *to be* occur but thrice). This unspoiled Greece is Paradise itself, the supreme Golden Age of Western art and literature; Faust can rightly say in reference to the picture he has painted,

A birthright here is ease congenial,
And cheeks and smiles of cheer do tell;
Each man in his own place can be immortal,
For all are satisfied and well.

And he whose own child could hardly be said to have lived at all may well ask whether a people who always develop from a happy childhood to a normal parental maturity are gods or men. But his answer to his question remains consonant with the naturalistic humanism to which he has already given expression in his Triumph of Galatea: these Arcadians are man at his potential best and in harmony with nature, and Apollo in shepherd's guise was but the counterpart of the fairest of them—"For when the sway of Nature is not hindered, / All realms of being merge as one."

In again expressing his faith in the oneness of all realms of 9562-73
experience, Faust has reminded himself that he and Helen symbolize
the triumphant coexistence of man's dream ideal and his real present
in the timeless realm of poetry. More properly than when he sought
to comfort Margarete in her prison cell, he can urge his beloved to
let bygones be bygone.

This too have you and I achieved together;
Let what is past now ever be bygone!
O, feel that you are child of God the Father,
To primal being you belong alone.

If in Faust's system of values all perfection is of the same essence,
Helen not only may but must simultaneously represent man in
harmony with himself, with Nature—the uncorrupted primal order
of the Golden Age of myth—and with Beauty. And so, suiting his
dramatic action to his figurative words, Faust now metamorphoses
the courtyard of his castle into an Arcadian grove, and he and Helen
disappear from view as their thrones become parts of a series of leafy
bowers placed beside cavern openings in the precipitous rocks that
surround their old-new world. Through Homunculus, Faust successfully met the challenge, in Classical Walpurgisnight, of finding an
artistically adequate transition back from the eternity of myth to the
finite realm of physical existence; whether he can as successfully
return from the timeless Arcadia of poetry to normal human realities
in the final scene of his *Helen* will therefore be a central, though not
the sole, element of its dramatic interest.

CHAPTER XXI

The Limits of Art

The setting of Shaded Grove is a classicistic Garden of Eden separated from non-Arcadian reality by a natural palisade of rock that establishes a deliberate parallel between this scene and Rocky Inlets of the Aegean Sea. Although its background grottoes recall countless Renaissance paintings whose artists would have filled them with the still tame birds and beasts of a teeming Paradise, the grove's Graeco-Roman associations are effectively made paramount by the fact that it is the landscape-with-classical-figures-only which after the latter half of the seventeenth century long remained obligatory for literary and artistic re-creations of antiquity, whether pastoral in spirit or not. The Arcadia throughout which Helen's sleeping attendants lie scattered is, like its Judaeo-Christian counterpart, a world without Death or Sin or Error, and hence the symbol of a very limited aspect of reality. With the entrance of the towering figure of Phorkyas it acquires its Tempter, but since Faust has already recognized Mephistopheles' function as being in the last analysis only that of serving as a stimulus to positive action, and since there is no classical equivalent of the Tree whose fruit gives certain knowledge of good and evil, the gap between Arcadia and the finite reality of a full human life to which Faust aspires even in his dreams at first remains far greater than that between the Garden of Eden and the world after the Fall.

How Faust will realize in poetic statement the symbolic return to reality to which he has already committed himself is the crucial question posed at this point. If he does not successfully demonstrate that he is fully aware of the finiteness, not only of human life, but also of that artistic creativity of men which in his Triumph of Galatea he proclaimed to be governed by the same natural laws, then he has lost man's proper course and Mephistopheles may rightly claim that Faust, though sleeping, has forfeited life for the pleasures of the empty dream of an endlessly perpetuated moment of bliss which is Arcadia. Still more important, however, is the fact that if the gap between the timeless world of immortal poetry and that of finite human experience is not bridged convincingly, with aesthetic adequacy, the vision of life which Faust has offered in the two dream plays of his classical Walpurgis Night will be anticlimactically weakened and to all intents and purposes nullified. And with this anticlimax *Faust* itself, although it might still be read and admired because it contained effective statements of a great poet's vision of life, would cease to be an integrated work of art. For failure to integrate satisfactorily Classical Walpurgisnight and *Helen*, which together constitute a quarter of it, into the large design of the drama would mean that Goethe's *Faust, A Tragedy*, remained a dream at best only three-fourths realized and was indeed merely the literary potpourri that all hostile critics and far too many uncritical admirers have considered it. The representation of Faust's dramaturgical powers in the course of the action of Shaded Grove is thus identical with the crucial moment in the action of *Faust* as a whole. If drama and drama-within-drama become one, if all levels of experience at last merge on one poetic-symbolic level, and if Faust, the symbol of potentially infinite human creativity, can be shown to be fully identical with Faust, the symbol of human finiteness, then and then only can *Faust* be in any measure rightly called an artistic unity. For Faust himself, however, the conclusion of his dream quest for Helen is the supreme test of an artistic integrity which, given his premise that the aesthetic is one with the moral and natural realms, must meet the challenge of representing effectively the integrated totality of man's—or all "good" men's—existence.

Accordingly, Faust lets Mephistopheles announce to his dream audience—it is the masculine public of a classical Greek theater to which Phorkyas, like the Choral Leader of Old Comedy, addresses himself—that they are at last about to see the denouement of this long series of believable miracles, while by having Mephistopheles first wonder whether the Trojan Women have seen in dream what he has seen with his own eyes Faust once again indicates that this Arcadian grove is a world not of literal but of dreamlike reality. Awakened by Phorkyas, the Chorus eagerly ask what wonderful things have happened and, already bored by Arcadia, declare, "Best 9574–98 of all we like to hear of things we can no way believe in." And so, after a brief account of how he has been in constant attendance upon Faust and Helen since they first found privacy "in these caves, these grottoes, and these bowers," he tells the story of their child's birth. If the Chorus fail to show surprise when he indicates that Helen had reached an advanced stage of pregnancy but mockingly object to the account of an underground search for roots, moss, and bark that he offers in corroboration of his discreet helpfulness, it is because a pregnancy, however much syncopated, is a natural phenomenon, while a subterranean landscape duplicating that of earth is pure "fairy tale." The motif of whole underground worlds, a dream-adaptation to pastoral conditions of the Emperor's masquerade vision of his own courtly environment projected into a Plutonic underworld (report at beginning of Palace Garden), thus permits Faust to insist that the only important aspect of reality to be suspended for the present scene is time. Simultaneously, it reveals how much Faust has matured by this point in his development. The cave—on Easter Eve to "Float with spirits by a mountain cave" was dream-escape from his prison study; on the occasion of Mephistopheles' second visit to him he cursed "this cave of sorrow" which is man's corporeal being; "the safe cave" of his Forest and Cave soliloquy stood for an illusory sense of harmony with nature and self; during his classical Walpurgis Night caverns have successively represented the futility of hoarding unutilized wealth (fable of Giant Ants and Arimasps), wish-fulfillment (Faust's departure for caves beneath Olympus), chimerical unreality (abode of the "unknown" Phorcides), the realm of ugliness (Helen's defiance of Phorkyas), of death (Phorkyas' "Orcus' empty night"), and, finally, of Arcadian effortlessness (the natural cave-shelters of Faust's paean to pastoral Greece)— this symbol now represents life creating and life created.

9599-9624   "But to my great surprise there echoes laughter through the mighty caverns." With these words Mephistopheles has announced that life, even in a poetic dream-world, still continues to triumph perpetually over the spirit of annihilation which he claimed to be at his first interview with Faust. The grotesque humor of a literally bouncing boy and the comic absurdity of a child who is a miniature adult both ultimately reflect Faust's awareness that the crystallized Homunculus which Mephistopheles let float about in Wagner's laboratory was an incongruous symbol of organic life. But this child is "a wingless genius, faunlike yet in no way bestial," which means that he is not the diabolic fruit of sensual passion, as was the son of the traditional Faust and his succubus Helen, but rather a neo-mythological counterpart of his namesake, the winged Euphorion said to have been born to the shades of Helen and Achilles. Although his wild leaping recalls Mephistopheles' nimbly leaping Cupid of the end of the scene Witch's Kitchen, it is far more than a satiric motif; it is the visible evidence that he is endowed not only with Helen's beauty and grace, but also with Faust's own adventurous, active impulses. And comic though may be Phorkyas' picture of the sedate Faust and dignified Helen in their role of doting parents and his report of how he shared their parental concern when their wingless son momentarily leapt out of sight, the situation he describes is basically a normal human one, a point subtly emphasized by the "natural" simplicity of syntax, the sudden abandoning of classicizing rhetorical artifice, which gives his "Greek" trochaic tetrameters an entirely new quality in this expository passage.

That Euphorion—Phorkyas never uses the auspicious name—is born a fully developed youth is, however, dramatically ironic in a way that Faust himself does not realize, for the absurdity of childhood without infancy is also a pathetic reminder that he never saw a child by Margarete, that he can fulfill his parental instinct but imperfectly in the dream which again unites him with her in the mask of Helen. If the transformation of the naked *genius* into "a small Apollo" simply by the acquisition of the appropriate costume is an ironically imperfect representation of man's ideal normal development as Faust had evoked it in his recent paean to Arcadia, the prototype of Euphorion is the one boy of Faust's dramatic existence, his "dearly beloved son" in Masquerade. Both Euphorion and Boy-Charioteer share the same tenderly parental affection, and Euphorion's golden lyre and flaming crown—the latter corresponding to the jeweled fillet that set off Charioteer's dark eyes and black hair—and his equally ornate costume further insist that he is to be a symbolic counterpart of Masquerade's self-consuming Genius of Poetry as well as the symbol of individual development and human-Faustian aspiration.

Miraculous as are the physical attributes with which Faust endows him, Euphorion nevertheless symbolizes finite man. If Helen warns him, "free flight is not for you," and if Faust seconds her by insisting that to leap he must ever renew contact with earth, it is because Faust is acutely aware that man, though it be his proper destiny to aspire, must never forget that he is always "the son of earth." When in Pleasant Landscape Faust turned his back to the sun, symbol of the unknowable and infinite, he renounced as an aberration unworthy of one resolved ever to strive toward life's most perfect forms the escapist dream of freedom through flight that he had so frequently formulated earlier in moments of frustration and despair. Only now, however, does he make clear that highest striving need not be exclusively identified with goals successfully attainable or concretely tangible. For, if to venture above and beyond the level of what he can enduringly achieve is the right and duty of the good man, the achievement of limited flight only—the leaping of Euphorion—ceases to symbolize tragic failure because imperfect aspiration is potentially counterbalanced by actual finite achievements. To be an earth-bound Antaeus only is no more the whole destiny of man than is perpetual soaring above reality and without contact with it. But to gain "like Antaeus, son of Earth"—the incautious metaphor "I, an Antaeus in spirit," with which Faust at the opening of Classical Walpurgisnight revealed his humanistic determination to affirm the positive significance of all things Greek, has become a simile—the strength for ever-new effort from ever renewed contact with earthy reality is the only way to realize human life as a harmonious totality.

In his Triumph of Galatea Faust demonstrated his attainment of a vision of the oneness of all being fundamentally identical with that posited in the prologues to *Faust*. Now he demonstrates an understanding of man's divine dignity not only in full concord with those poetic statements but surpassing at least one of them, Prologue in Heaven, in the nonambiguity of the poetic symbols with which it is expressed. For, whereas almost all the symbols of that Prologue were borrowed from theological, mystical, and religious writings, those of Shaded Grove are exclusively ones whose value has been established in the course of the dramatic action of the Tragedy of Faust proper. And in unwittingly metamorphosing Mephistopheles' simile of the leaping grasshopper whose perpetual falling back to earth symbolizes the meaninglessness of human effort into the metaphor of a godlike youth whose very power of flight, whatever its limitations, symbolizes the obscure compulsion which gives to life its supreme value—in doing this Faust has attained by his long path of error to the supreme insight that striving can be simultaneously a means to realizable ends and an end in itself, and so he has come to share the Lord's tragic-untragic vision of man's destiny offered us in Prologue in Heaven.

9625–78   When the conditions of the continued existence of him who "even as a boy proclaims the future master of all beauty" have been stated, and when Mephistopheles has assured them that they will soon see him "with admiration most unique," the Chorus momentarily prolong the untragic atmosphere of idyllic parental joy by

matching Phorkyas' "miracle" of the modern-romantic Euphorion
with the equally implausible, Lucianic tale of Hermes' miraculous
infancy. For the last time Faust develops the comic possibilities of
Mephistopheles' protested ignorance of classical antiquity (strophe)
and once more reaffirms his humanist's faith in the enduring and still
unsurpassed glory of a civilization whose mythopoetic fancies—
"graceful invention"—are "more worthy of credence than truth"
(antistrophe). His comparison of Hermes' escape from swaddling
clothes to the slipping of a butterfly from its chrysalis adapts the
metaphor with which Mephistopheles mocked the newly-graduated
Student's changed appearance to a myth that, given the parallels
between Hermes and Euphorion, represents symbolically both man's
innate power of growth and his natural impulse to achieve autonomy
as soon as he can (second strophe). But, by interrupting their ode
so that it ends, not with a generalizing epode about Hermes' many
legendary contributions to the arts and sciences but with an antistrophe exclusively devoted to Hermes' roguish thefts—the Chorus'
enthusiasm for "the tutelary genius" of "all who seek advantage"
is of course completely in character—Faust effectively deprives the
classical prototype of Euphorion of all broader significance and as
it were artistically subordinates his Graecophilia to his more basic
concern with symbolic representation of the totality of man's life in
a here and now.

From within the cave occupied by Faust, Helen, and Euphorion 9679–86
is heard the sound of melodies for strings played by a chamber
orchestra, and the dramatic action is momentarily interrupted as the
Chorus and Phorkyas listen attentively to this music and give
pantomimic signs of being profoundly stirred by it. By constituting
the background of the spoken voice throughout the whole episode
in which Euphorion appears and until the ode that marks its termination, this musical accompaniment underscores the scene's unique
importance both in Faust's *Helen* and in *Faust* itself. The insistent
modernity of an extended passage in the style of lyric melodrama—
whole scenes accompanied by music are a development of late
Renaissance drama and were introduced into German romantic
drama by admirers of Calderón—announces an immanent return
from classical and medieval-Renaissance archaism to dramatic as
well as musical contemporaneity and so prepares for Faust's
inevitable reawakening to the very modern spiritual world which is
his Renaissance Germany. And, of greatest immediate importance,
modern-romantic—if not musicologically romantic or modern—
music marks a temporary triumph of the spirit which distinguishes

post-classical times from historical antiquity, and so permits the climactic scene which leads immediately into the denouement of *Helen* to counterbalance by virtue of its functional importance any impression of one-sided neoclassical enthusiasm that Faust's immoderate use of classicizing elements might create. But that the victory of the romantic and sentimental is not to be an unconditional defeat of a classical antiquity which can always symbolize certain eternal human experiences with unsurpassed effectiveness, is ironically evident from the glibness with which Phorkyas tells the Chorus,

Hear these loveliest of noises,
Free yourselves of myth today!
Your old hodgepodge of Immortals—
Give it up, it's quite passé.

None will understand you ever,
We exact a greater toll:
Only what the heart can offer
O'er our hearts can have control.

By once again having Mephistopheles parody the lesson in *bouts rimés* which he gave Helen, Faust effectively insists that art fundamentally emotional in inspiration need not exclude the possibility of the heart's being affected by art of another kind, that inspired emotion need not automatically produce great art, and so he demonstrates that he has attained to two more insights posited in Dedication and Prelude on the Stage.

9687-9710   As Mephistopheles, his expository function fulfilled, withdraws to the background, the Chorus so fall under the spell of modern-sentimental music—"We're brought to the verge of tears"—that they begin to speak in rhyme. The lines "Solar splendor does not matter / When suns in the soul abide, / When we in our hearts discover / What naught else can e'er provide," mark their complete conversion to romantic sentimentality and to an aesthetic subjectivism corresponding in the realm of art to the ethical subjectivism whose disastrous implications were the dominant theme of the First Part of the Tragedy, and at this moment Euphorion, the symbol par excellence of man's fatal propensity to ignore objective reality, appears with his parents. For a brief time Helen and Faust enjoy what the Chorus call "Many years of happiness" and what Helen— this is the first and only time Faust exploits the motif of a trinity seriously—describes as the "divine delight" of two become three. Then the idyll of marital and parental bliss tragically denied Faust and Margarete in their "real" existences begins to be threatened as they experience the bittersweet anguish of seeing their son start to achieve a life of his own.[1]

Although Faust, in his waking hours never a paragon of practical 9711-66 moderation, now gives himself the tragicomic role of timorous father using bodily restraints to keep his son from standing—or, more exactly, not standing—on his own feet, he is realistically aware that it is unnatural for a child to remain as closely attached to his parents as they are to him, that to perpetuate unduly the moment of familial self-sufficiency would be to kill life and to substitute inertia and the static for natural growth and development, and so he lets the Chorus warn, "Union soon ended / Is this, I fear!" Having declared "Only for your sakes / Will I forbear," Euphorion filially shifts from his own abrupt rhythms, which have temporarily infected the speech of Faust, Helen, and the Chorus, to less staccato meters. But his restlessness prevents his heeding Helen and Faust's injunction, "Let rural beauty / Quietly reign," and with his mother's approval he strikes up a tune and leads, in "Intricate dance," the Chorus, whose hearts are soon completely captivated by him. Faust, however, less confident than Helen of his son's ability to achieve mature self-restraint, wishes this moment of pastoral "frivolity" were already finished. For his heightened sense of reality enables him to regard Euphorion without Helen's sentimental leniency, to represent himself as a character moved by profound emotion but not blinded, as he was when involved in passion for Margarete, by sentimentality—something few nineteenth-century writers, even the great realists, ever did successfully.

There is a pause after the dance, by the end of which the Chorus 9767-9818 share Euphorion's elation—hence the ominous reintroduction of the short staccato line—and then he proposes that they and he shall play "a new game," tag. As he disappears in Faustianly resolute pursuit of Trojan Women only too willing to have him catch and embrace them, Helen and Faust both express their recognition that Euphorion is hopelessly incapable of moderation, while their impression of hearing "a sound like horns reëcho / Loudly through the woods and valleys" emphasizes, since the sound of hunting horns in forest depths is a patently romantic literary and musical motif, that Euphorion's immoderation is above all modern-romantic. Then the Chorus reappear one by one, reporting that Euphorion would

---

[1] From this point until Euphorion's first exit (11.9711-84) the verse of the text is continuously characterized by a highly complex blending of assonance and rhyme that confirms insistently, though without obviousness, the themes of overt and latent restlessness paramount in the episode devoted to him.

pursue only the fleetest and wildest Trojan Woman, a young girl whom he now carries in his arms. Boyhood has become adolescence, the chase has become the expression of newly gained consciousness of "new vigor and autonomy." But since the theme of awakening erotic desire is subordinate to that of increasing physical maturity, Euphorion can quickly shake off the last flames of the passion by which he has been burned and, forgetting the girl who has eluded him, turn his thoughts to the attractions of the wide world outside the "rocky confines" of Arcadia. If the motif of the girl's escape recalls with romantic-Hellenic appropriateness Greek vase paintings of Thetis freeing herself from the arms of Peleus, that of Euphorion's ability to cast off the last remainders of an unpleasant past is the counterpart of Faust's own experience of protective oblivion in Pleasant Landscape. Surely ominous, however, is the taunting "Follow me to realms aerial, / Follow me to graves funereal" with which the girl rises out of view, for it marks the realistic intrusion into Arcadia of death; nothing can ever literally escape from the underworld-realm of things past, and after every poetic dream there must come a rude awakening.

9819–50   Having bounded to the top of the precipitous palisade that surrounds the grove, Euphorion recognizes that he is in the center of the Peloponnesus, a land "Joined to both earth and sea." The sea, however, as realm of life's unhindered potentialities since Faust's Triumph of Galatea, is a symbol alien to Faust's land-bound Arcadia, which represents finite possibilities realized under optimum conditions, and so the Chorus hastily urge Euphorion to remain "in this fair land" of peace and plenty. But he, scorning "Dreams of idyllic peace," wants the victory of action even, as he reveals with youthful ardor, at the price of war. The word of doom has been spoken, and the Chorus solemnly announce, "He who in peacetime / Wishes that war come back / Ever and ever / Hope's bliss shall lack." Now completely carried away by irrational impulses, Euphorion begins to speak, as he will continue to do until his death, in sentences predominantly elliptical and interjectory—with what was once considered the Pindaric obscurity of poetic ecstasy—and counters the Chorus' view that peace is "Hope's bliss" with the words,

Those whom this land brought forth,
From danger to danger,
Free men, courageous ones,
And lavish with their blood,
Blessed with a holy zeal
Not to be daunted—

May, for these fighters all,
Hope bring reward!²

Out of sight, though visible to the Chorus as a full-grown warrior 9851-76
in shining armor, Euphorion is so transported by his vision of men's
eternal necessary fight for freedom that he calls upon every man,
woman, and child to take up arms so that they may all "live
unconquered." Although this section of *Faust* was written during
the Modern Greek war of independence, the Chorus' immediate
response to Euphorion's appeal—their "Sacred poetic word, /
May it mount heavenward! / Shine out, o fairest star, / Ever still more
afar! / Yet can we hear the voice / Always, and we rejoice / That
poets are"—makes clear that he is to be regarded as subjectively
projecting into the external world a state of crisis which will gratify
his need of activity, that the creative imagination has become
unbridled and threatens to lose all contact with the world of realities
that can alone nourish it. Like the Student recently interviewed by
Mephistopheles in Faust's study, Euphorion insists that he is no
longer a child; like him he shares the belief that what exists in the
mind necessarily exists as reality also: "But bearing arms I now
appear, / A youth who with men strong, free, daring, / In spirit now
does cast his spear."

However ironic that Euphorion should wish to quit the dream 9877-9902
Arcadia of Faust and Helen—seeking to stop him, they ask, "Is our
union fair a dream?"—for an equally unreal "realm of pain," the
"path to glory" which he elects is no symbol of delusion and error
only. Not only in naval engagement and on the battlefield, amid the
sights and sounds of combat that Euphorion claims to hear, is the
price of life "pain and suffering—and death." Arcadian immortality
and ease is no life at all, and so Euphorion's resolve to seek a heroic
death—"Death's a commandment, / That's suddenly clear"—
represents his finding of a path of error by which finite life, the
highest good granted to man, can in some sense be realized. Despite
the horror with which Helen, Faust, and the Chorus react to his
announcement, Euphorion's abortive and fatal attempt to fly from
Arcadia into a world of action and so share man's lot of "care and
distress" is the dramatic demonstration of Faust's complete understanding of the nature of man as defined in Prologue in Heaven.
Faust has at last recognized that the way of error *is* man's proper

---

² "Welche dies Land gebar / Aus Gefahr in Gefahr, / Frei, unbegrenzten Muts, /
Verschwendrisch eignen Bluts, / Mit nicht zu dämpfendem, / Heiligen Sinn, / Alle den
Kämpfenden / Bring es Gewinn!" (The reading "Mit nicht zu dämpfendem" seems to
me preferable to either of the two variants sometimes selected by editors of *Faust*.)

path, has at long last reconciled the seemingly mutually exclusive principles "Men err as long as they do strive" and "A man who's good knows well the path that's proper, / Although obscure his intuitions be." He now acknowledges as both right and necessary that where there is aspiration there may be both fulfillment and frustration, that where there is a sense of nobility and innate worth there is also consciousness of insufficiency and guilt, and that where there is a living and using up of life there must be destruction and death also. The merging of Homunculus with the waters of the Aegean Sea was his confession of faith in the value of all life and being and in the supreme value of human life; the momentary flight of the deluded Euphorion, who thinks his garments have become wings, is his unqualified affirmation of the tragic dignity which is finite man's living and dying.

9903–38   No sooner does Euphorion's body fall at his parents' feet[3]—the Phaethon motif derives from the fragmentarily preserved play by Euripides—than it disappears; his halo flies skyward, and his garments and lyre remain the only evidence of his brief meteor-like existence. The person of the poet vanishes, his powers die with him, and the symbols of his achievement alone survive; the child become a man is dead, his body returns to the elements from which it came, but the memory of him continues to be a living force—these are the themes of the choral dirge that concludes the episode of Euphorion with a return to solemn metrical regularity. Taking their cue from his cry from the depths of the underworld, "Leave me not here alone, / Mother, in darkness!," the Chorus announce that his song and his spirit have won him a permanent place in men's hearts (stanza one), although they lament the untimely death of one so highly endowed (stanza two). But if he erred in willfully ignoring his human limitations—"Yet by rushing headlong onward / You were caught in matter's snare"—and revolted against propriety and necessity, the high purpose which inspired his final heroic failure nevertheless demonstrated the basic nobility of his character (stanza three). And then, generalizing, the Chorus ask what Faust now knows to be a question that can never be answered favorably for any finite man, "Who attains his purpose?"—a question which, with heroic pessimism, he declares Fate will decline to answer even on the day when, "Bleeding, all mankind is silenced." Yet the answer does not

[3] The stage direction after 1.9902 says, "one has the impression that the body is that of a figure familiar and well-known." Both Boy-Charioteer and, to a greater degree, Euphorion are endowed with attributes and interests that to Goethe and his contemporaries seemed to be salient characteristics of Byron; the threnody which follows is thus a tribute to *a* romantic poet as well as to the Poet of romantic Hellenism.

matter if man knows that no aspiration can ever be ideally realized; of this the symbol is Euphorion, who to gain life had to lose it, and so the dirge ends as the Chorus appropriately turn their thoughts from death to life. "Sing new songs and be enlivened, / Stand no more thus deeply bowed; / Earth will always new songs send, / As she has since time allowed"—man's final hope remains only the cosmic, anti-Mephistophelean force of life indestructible.

After the Chorus' threnody there is a silence heightened by the 9939–61 cessation of the orchestral background music which has accompanied the whole Euphorion episode. Imbued with Faust's own sense of the necessary transitoriness of all human experience, Helen announces that life no longer has meaning for her, embraces Faust for the last time, and, calling upon Persephone to receive her and her son, vanishes into nothingness in his arms. The dream cycle of his life is completed, and Faust is once again without wife or child. If he has Mephistopheles now come forward and urge him to use Helen's garments to transport himself "above all vulgarity" to where he and his inseparable companion are to meet again, this is simply a dream variation on the familiar motif of departing from one realm of experience to another on Mephistopheles' cloak. But in letting the robe which Mephistopheles has told him to cling to—"Demons even now / Are tugging at its edges, seek to drag / It down to Hades"— metamorphose itself into the clouds of a secularized Baroque ascension, he also immediately insists once more that nothing finite, however "divine," can be saved from the underworld of things dead and gone when it ceases to have actual or symbolic value. And how little he now esteems fetishism is evident when Phorkyas, seizing the tangible relics of Euphorion, steps into the proscenium immediately after his departure and cynically announces that with these externals he can at least lend others the semblance of being poets. With this last echo of the curio motif so extensively developed by Mephistopheles at the nightmarish opening of Faust's dream, and with the momentary reintroduction of the irregularly rhyming four-stress lines that above all others in *Faust* represent normal reality, the dramatic action of *Helen* has ended. Where Faust is to awaken from his dream, however, can only be indefinitely "far, quite far, from here," for that depends on Mephistopheles' choice of a time and a place best suited to further implicating a heroic-minded Faust in new errors.

With Phorkyas on the other side of the proscenium from them- 9962–91 selves—in the realm of reality to which Faust is about to return— the Chorus are "No more bewitched by the antique-Thessalian hag, /

16—G.F.

No more befuddled by that frenzied tinkling's sound." As Panthalis
summons them to rejoin their queen in the underworld, the dramatic
style of *Helen* is again the archaic-Aeschylean one in which it began.
After this final reminder of the witch-infested plains of Thessaly on
which his double dream-play opened, Faust completes his tragedy
with a formal *exodos*. The self-centered Chorus decline to share
ingloriously and unamused a shadowy immortality with a Helen
always to be envied (strophe), and Panthalis, scornfully consigning
her nameless and ignoble companions to the elements—to that
matter which, in the Auerbach's Cellar apologue of anticipatory
triumph staged by Mephistopheles for a then still incomprehending
Faust, symbolized the ultimate in human degradation—leaves to join
Helen. Her "By faith as well as merit identity's preserved" is both
Faust's last insistence that the individual's worth must always remain
incommensurable with his actual achievements, and his last formulation of the theme, equally important for Classical Walurgisnight and
Helen, that the achievement of meaningful identity is the only
goal toward which the good man can successfully hope to strive.
But the Chorus, failing to share in sufficient measure with
their Leader the supreme human-divine attribute of selfless
devotion that Faust has recognized to be Margarete's all-redeeming
virtue, are content to merge with "Nature's eternal-living forms"
(antistrophe).

9992–10038   Their defection in essence like that of the self-concerned
attendants of Leda in Faust's vision of Leda and the swan, the
Chorus begin to disperse in a final series of Baroque stage effects, a
first group disappearing as dryads into trees about which Arcadian
gatherers of fallen fruit "will downward bow as if before the highest
gods," another vanishing as oreads and echo-nymphs into the
palisade that surrounds the grove, and still another leaving to become
naiads of Arcadia's meandering streams. To the three traditional
elements (earth, air, water) symbolized by these groups, the fourth
and last (fire) is added by the still remaining members of the Chorus,
who announce that they will metamorphose themselves into grape-
vines. These neomythological vineyard nymphs sing, bacchante-like,
the praises of "Helios, of all the gods the greatest," and evoke the
mysteries of Dionysus that constitute the classical counterpart of
Faust's "new mystery," the wedding of Homunculus to the sea at
the end of the Triumph of Galatea. But, whereas that mystery ended
with a paean to Eros and the eternal elements, *Helen* ends with an
Auerbach's Cellar-like picture of human, all-too-human activity in
a world of time and change.

THE REALM OF
HUMAN GREATNESS

CHAPTER XXII

The Path to Power

The opening of the curtain to reveal a desolate mountain 10039–54
landscape marks the beginning of the final section of *Faust*. Into this
setting of High Mountains floats a cloud—the Baroque theatrical
machinery establishes continuity with the end of Faust's *Helen*—and
from this cloud Faust emerges after what he believes to have been a
long trip "over land and sea," although the iambic trimeters in which
he speaks suggest that he has only recently awakened from his
Grecian dreams.[1] As at the crisis of his relationship with Margarete
(Forest and Cave) and after its denouement (Pleasant Landscape),
he has withdrawn to a place of "greatest solitude," again to Mephistopheles' obvious displeasure. How well the double-dream of the
innate artist in him has served its cathartic function is clear from
the dispassionate tone in which he compares indifferently to "Juno,
Leda, or to Helen too," the recumbent "woman's form divine"
that he sees take shape in the now distant and billowing cloud. And
so, meaningful and precious to him though his dreams may have been,
it is with minimal regret that he observes the cloud become a formless
mass, "A symbol dazzling and profound of time's swift flight"
rather than, as it might have been a few moments earlier, of beauty or
of love.

Of far greater importance to him is the wisp of vapor which now 10055–66
detaches itself from his person to assume the shape of "Aurora's

[1] Faust's use of iambic trimeter is especially emphatic because he himself only
spoke seven lines (11.9435–41) in that meter during his classical Walpurgis Night. The
great political developments that have taken place in the Empire indicate that
Mephistopheles has kept Faust in his trance-like state until a new crisis furnished a
suitable occasion to involve him in new errors.

love"—of Margarete—and which floats off into space without losing the identity he has projected into it.

Like beauty of the soul that lovely form ascends,
Remaining whole, and as it to the ether mounts
It takes along with it that part of me that's best.

As he now realizes, the core of the cloud which represented the external attributes of Helen was a love that, "Had I but held it fast, all treasures had outshone." For simple human dignity, if it be a reality, is more enduring, more lasting in its influence, than the most grandiose poetic vision. And so, through a fleeting aesthetic experience—the cloud symbolism is emphatically transparent—Faust has regained his full identity, is once more a completely integrated personality; consciousness of guilt need no longer be suppressed, and he can courageously acknowledge his profound debt to the once insufficiently appreciated victim of immoderate passion. Helen has been Margarete in a mask of unsurpassable splendor, but it is only fitting that Faust should pay his final and highest tribute not to the mask but to its wearer, not to the perfection of timeless beauty but to living beauty of soul and character which, however humanly imperfect, must always remain the higher value for the good man who knows that the supreme human-divine achievement is to make the best that he can of his life here and now.

10067-104   Mephistopheles, the temptation of purely material satisfactions, appears as Faust's thoughts have turned from the ended dream of Helen to a future inspired by the living memory of Margarete, and the return to a finite world of waking reality is completed by the reintroduction of flexible rhyming verse. His seven-league boots reëstablish Northern folklore as the poetic symbol of Faust's magical power to know within a single lifetime a totality of human experience, while his Forest and Cave-like mocking of Faust's taste in wildernesses —"Why do you land where all's grotesqueness, / 'Mid gaping, gruesome growths of stone?"—indicates that Faust is once more about to come to some momentous decision, is once more granted a critical opportunity to act in accordance with his best insights. That these are ones he has expressed in his Classical Walpurgisnight is emphasized by the elaborate myth with which Mephistopheles explains how he and his fellows—St. Paul's "rulers of the darkness of this world"—escaped from the underworld "to excess power's open air," for his myth is a taunting parody of Faust's recent mytho-poetic depreciation of rabid Vulcanism. But Faust declines to let himself be involved in fruitless philosophical speculations about First

Principles—"The mountains' mass is nobly mute to me, / I ask not how or why it came to be"—and simply reaffirms his faith that Nature represents self-contained order, although by doing so in a less obviously beautiful setting than that of Pleasant Landscape he demonstrates that his Classical Walpurgisnight recognition of the beauty of the Sublime was no transitory expression of Romantic-Hellenic enthusiasm but marked a permanent aesthetic achievement.

Mephistopheles' lengthy discourse on Satan's importance for the 10105-75 physical world—"Whatever Nature's way, / I must insist the Devil had his say! / We are the ones who do great things with gladness; / Behold the marks of tumult, force and madness!"—is only the preamble to an offer of diabolic help in carrying out a project which Faust has already conceived.

But no more double-talk! I'll speak directly.
Did nothing on earth's surface suit exactly?
You have surveyed from farthest points above them
The kingdoms of the world and all the glory of them.
Though nothing can you satisfy,
Was nothing there you'd want to try?

Yet the preferred mode of Mephistophelean action still remains indirection: when challenged to guess what Faust wants to do— Faust's "great project" is to establish a new state, one in which man's best potentialities can be better realized than in the unhealthy society represented by the Emperor's world—he first pictures the capital of such a state as a sprawling metropolis whose elegant sections fail to disguise successfully the dreary lot of its teeming masses, and then represents its ruler's residence as a grandiose retreat nicely suited to the selfish pursuit of pleasure, especially dalliance with "loveliest of women."

When Faust has made clear that he wants no part of a society in 10176-88 which even material and educational advances cannot effectively remedy the causes of discontent and potential revolution and that he scorns a Sardanapalian life of voluptuous degeneracy—"bad and modern" because his classical ideal, as expressed in Chiron's apologue of the Argonauts, is heroic and cooperative, the antipode of Mephistopheles' "a solitude with lovely company"—Mephistopheles ridicules him for thinking that power does not automatically entail corruption.

May I now guess at your ambition,
Which surely is audacious, grand?
You've soared so high in lunar region
That you would make the moon your land.

In his Classical Walpurgisnight apologue of the Pygmies and the Cranes, Faust has already expressed his conviction that power must be used justly, but he is too ardent a humanist to ignore the taunt that man can achieve nothing great on earth, and declares,

> Here in this world
> There's room enough for deeds heroic.
> What shall be done might rouse a stoic,
> For I have strength for ventures bold.

In ceasing to be dispassionate Faust lays himself open to a more direct attack from Mephistophelean cynicism—"And so your aim is to win glory?"—and in countering this he both announces what he intends to do and states the article of faith by which he justifies his intention. "I want dominion of my own, / Not glory! Deeds count alone."

10189-95   In resolving to acquire power and possessions Faust has made his most momentous waking decision since he surrendered to fatal passion in the scene Forest and Cave. For although he will succumb to the temptation to realize his new intention with the help of Mephistopheles, which means that his enterprise will only represent another imperfect human achievement, he is at last endeavoring to act in consonance with his highest human ideal of selfless devotion to others' welfare. The escape from finite care and responsibility— which he first sought through magic, which he then hoped to find through death, and which he finally seemed to gain when he left his prison study with Mephistopheles—he now begins to recognize as an illusion. Whereas on Easter Eve he bitterly complained because "alien substance" limited the human spirit's flight, because worrisome Care appeared in "masks always new"—as house and home, as wife and child, as threats to life and property—and whereas at his second interview with Mephistopheles he cursed "what flatters us because we own it," now he sees that not even disinterested activity is possible unless the human spirit risks exposing itself to the modifying influence, the counterforce, of the world of tangible objects it seeks to affect, unless man accepts the responsibility for his environment which ownership of property, "dominion," symbolizes. Whether Faust will remain immune from the corrupting influence of power is an important theme of this last section of *Faust*. Far more important is whether he will demonstrate with any measure of success that material achievement and its concomitant, the achievement of material goods, need not necessarily make men prey to petty care. That this is so is evident from Mephistopheles' almost angry insistence that Faust's intention is "folly" which will inspire foolish poets to inspire posterity to still more folly. For Mephistopheles is once again scornfully expressing the view, to which he first subscribed when he advised Faust to associate with a poet if he ever hoped to experience the lot of all mankind, that poetry merely attaches artificial values to realities actually worthless. On that occasion Faust expressed only despair. Now, himself fully aware that poetry can be a highly meaningful form of human experience, he echoes the words with which he originally challenged Mephistopheles to offer him any meaningful experience—"Was any human spirit in its upward striving / E'er understood by one like you?"—and exclaims angrily,

Such folly you will never vaunt.
What do you know of what men want?
How can you, in your acid ire,
Know aught of that which men require?

When Mephistopheles ungraciously concedes that he can have 10196–234 his way—"Your will be done! To me confiding, / Reveal entire the fancies you've been hiding"—Faust explains how his bird's-eye view of the ocean's perpetual encroachment on solid land has inspired him to claim from the sea a great new territory. Although neither his project nor his observation that each new tide brings new assault is a novel one—hence Mephistopheles' cynical comment *ad spectatores* —the high importance of Faust's new seriousness of purpose is underscored by his shift to longer, five-stress lines, for it marks his first explicit waking acknowledgment that it is never for man to live in effortless Arcadian harmony with his physical environment. By comparing the forces of the sea to lawless arrogance he at last repudiates simultaneously the facile anthropomorphic equation of man and Nature which he expressed in Outside the City Gates and in his soliloquy of Forest and Cave, and the contemplative passivity which potentially underlay his conviction, first expressed when he evoked the Earth Spirit but also evident in his Forest and Cave and Pleasant Landscape soliloquies, that natural phenomena cease to be man's concern when their workings are understood. Contemplation and the achievement of high ideals are but one part of the totality of human life; the other part is the compulsion to realize human desires and aspirations within the framework of these ideals to the best of one's ability.

And so the sea, in Faust's Triumph of Galatea the symbol of infinite being, now represents perpetual repetition, "Purposeless force of elements all unruly," the eternal constants of the realm of

Nature in which man is free to act—"Here would I fight, of this I would be master"—while land, in Shaded Grove the symbol of finite but effortless security, now represents human aspiration effectively realized through the purposeful controlling of elemental forces. If, in explaining his project, Faust repeatedly emphasizes the obvious physical principle that water only runs downhill—"The slightest mound defies these ocean forces, / The slightest depth subdues them to its might"—it is because he plans to achieve "the pleasure serious / Of keeping from the shore the sea imperious, / Of limiting the realm of haughty water / And pushing it far back within its border" without recourse to magic, not like some successful King Canute but simply by application of the natural laws of physics. No small enterprise today, in ages past the creating of new arable land was the most important engineering project that could be undertaken in peacetime—hence Caesar's plan for draining the Campagna, Probus' fatal drainage program in Pannonia, Leonardo's project for Lombardy, Frederick the Great's reclamation of land in Brandenburg and, above all, the cooperative achievements of the Dutch people—and so it is doubly ominous that, as drums and martial music are heard in the distance, Mephistopheles should assure Faust, "That will be easy!"

10235–59   Perturbed to learn that the Empire is in a state of war, Faust fails to appreciate immediately that he can exploit the situation to advance his own designs. This instinctive disinterestedness, as much a basic trait of his dramatic character as a carry-over of the ideal of selfless action from his dream-achievement of disinterested aesthetic objectivity, compels Mephistopheles to be once again as devious as he was at his original interview with Faust. Before explaining what "opportunity" the war offers Faust, he appeals to his conscience and his kindness. The "good" Emperor whom "we" entertained and spuriously enriched is in trouble because, in his inexperience, he then concluded that governing and pleasure-seeking are not incompatible. Although Faust did not intend that the paper money should remain unsecured (Palace Garden!), he ignores Mephistopheles' "we" and so tacitly acknowledges the didactic failure of his great masquerade, only to elaborate on the character of the ideal prince, who must be content to devote himself selflessly to his responsibilities. For he not only hopes, as he has openly declared, to win a new dominion, but also to give it a better government than men have known before—hence the trait of secretiveness with which he endows his perfect ruler, the execution of whose "lofty aims . . . does all the world amaze."

Skillfully treating Faust's digression simply as a statement of 10260-96
what the Emperor is not, Mephistopheles hastens on to sketch a
temporary triumph of anarchy.

Men grew far bolder than they'd been of late,
For life was self-defence. That was things' state.
. . .
To such conditions none could make objection,
For each could claim to win his own election.
The least of men had nothing to deplore,
But finally the best could stand no more.
These worthy men rebelled of one accord
And said, "Who gives us peace shall be our Lord.
The Emperor can't and won't, so let us choose us
An emperor who, by being new, renews us
And makes each man again secure.
So shall we, in a world made pure,
Wed peace and righteousness to bless us."

The Psalmist's phrase "peace and righteousness," which Faust
recognizes as "clerical," introduces a passage in which Mephistopheles, simultaneously appealing to Faust's anti-transcendental
prejudices, his feeling that order is a highest value, and his innate
human kindness, warns that "our Emperor, whom we made gay,"
now faces what may be his final battle against "sanctified rebellion."
And so, having at last won from Faust an expression of sympathy—
"I pity him; he was so kind, so candid"—he sings the new tune of
"While there's life there's hope," and proposes that he and Faust
shall rescue the Emperor from the straits in which he finds himself
literally and figuratively.

As Faust and Mephistopheles move to a lower point on the 10297-344
mountain—since the stage set is a multiple one, it would seem that
they have been gradually descending during their long conversation—
the martial music which originally emanated from behind the audience
is heard again, now from beneath the stage. Surveying the valley
below, Mephistopheles announces that he and Faust can help the
imperial forces to exploit a well-taken position victoriously, and,
although the latter has little fondness for assistance of the kind
Mephistopheles can give—"Illusion! Magic! Hollow show!"—he
authorizes him to win the battle when told that "If we preserve his
throne and lands imperial, / You can kneel down and take in fief /
Vast shores you need for raw material." Faust's role is to be that of
titular field marshal, for in his waking moments he is too honest to
pretend, as he did for Helen's benefit, that he has any understanding

of the arts of war, while Mephistopheles undertakes to be Chief of a General Staff consisting of himself and three Mighty Men—three trolls who are the quintessence of primitive violence and whose Romantic-chivalric armor only heightens the ugly fact that love of brutality (Bully), lust for gain (Grabber), and the will to maintain privilege and advantage (Holdfast) are the basic motives of aggressive militarism.

10345–422   As Faust and his companion descend out of sight, the scene of the action shifts to stage level (On a Foothill). To the sound of martial music again rising from below, the imperial tent is set up, and the Emperor and his Commanding General, the Grand-Master of earlier scenes, enter with bodyguards. The Emperor's forces have been strategically withdrawn, somewhat to his vexation, to what the Grand-Master considers an impregnable defensive position, but hardly has he expressed satisfaction with the Grand-Master's placing of his troops, and wrath as much self-righteous as righteous against "the disloyal vassals" who are advancing with their supporters to attack him, when the full precariousness of his situation is revealed. A First Scout brings the news that professedly loyal subjects decline to lend active support, and a Second describes how once undisciplined rebels are now organized under the banners of a counter-emperor. The first report only furnishes the Emperor with an occasion for inveighing—too late—against heedless selfishness, but the second releases his dangerous lust for fame, and he jubilantly announces that at last—"And had you not advised me to avoid aggression, / A hero's fame had long been my possession"—he can enjoy the merited glory of a real victory instead of the illusion of glory offered by courtly tournament or masquerade triumph.

10423–501   While the Emperor instructs his Heralds to challenge the Counter-Emperor to single combat, Faust appears, in armor, with the three Mighty Men. Since his face is concealed by the half-closed visor of his helmet, and thanks to Mephistopheles' omniscience, he can present himself to the Emperor as a stranger sent to his aid by a Sabine seer, the prescient Necromancer of Norcia whom the omni-potent Emperor's use of the right of coronation amnesty had saved from death at the stake. Faust's account of the mysterious activities and powers of crystal-gazing mountain sorcerers is typically Mephis-tophelean nonsense—and satire on romantic natural-philosophic speculation—but the ever gullible Emperor, although he impatiently interrupts to ask its relevance, finds it believable and so welcomes the timely support of one who ironically insists that what "the stupid priest condemns as sorcery" is but the working of unusual natural forces. Informed of the Emperor's hope of slaying the pretender to his titles, Faust urges him—his Mephistophelean and uncharacteristic unctiousness is motivated by the fact that the prompt realization of his ambitious plans demands the Emperor's personal survival—not to risk "the head which courage in us does inspire." Although the Emperor disregards Faust's argument that authority is best delegated to others, interpreting the end of the parable of the head and other members of the state as a formulation of his own compulsion to make his enemy a footstool, the refusal of the Counter-Emperor to acknowledge even his titular existence and the advance of the foe precipitate a large-scale military action, and he promptly delegates his authority to the Grand-Master.

With the Grand-Master's tacit consent, Faust assigns his 10502–638 aggressive Bully to the army's right wing, which is to attack the left flank of the opposing forces. The center, ordered to advance more slowly, Faust reinforces with Grabber, who, joined by the camp-follower Mistress Quickloot, declares that thirst for booty will complement courage and that he will lead these troops toward their goal, "The counter-emperor's tent and wealth." The left wing, charged with defending a narrow pass, Faust strengthens with Holdfast. Then Mephistopheles arrives, announcing that behind him can be seen a great mass of knights in armor who eagerly await the signal to move into action; if he explains in an aside that these troops are collections of armor given a semblance of life by ghosts, it is because the folklore motif had become so trite in the sensational literature of romantic supernaturalism that Goethe is careful to treat it ironically and let it serve incidentally as a repudiation of inane, costume-piece medievalism. As the battle progresses the Emperor is perturbed to observe what seem to be unnatural phenomena—Grabber many-armed, ghostly flames dancing on the spears and lances of his troops—but is reassured when Faust explains the former as a mirage, the latter as St. Elmo's fire, and does not pursue the matter further when Mephistopheles assures him that he owes this natural-supernatural assistance to the grateful Sabine necromancer, whom he admits he had rescued from the fire simply to demonstrate his new importance, a heedless act that has cost him clerical favor. Still flattering the Emperor—"Benevolent acts pay interest high"—Faust now draws his attention to the appearance in the sky of an eagle pursued by a griffon. This omen—imitated from Vergil—he pretends has been sent by the seer of Norcia, and when the heraldic monster has been defeated by what he emphasizes is a genuine bird, the Emperor rightly recognizes that this augurs the victory of the imperial eagle over an unnatural pretender.

10639–782   Mephistopheles now claims to see victory on the right flank; but the Emperor, observing that there are no signs of activity at the pass which the left wing was to hold, envisages it in the hands of the enemy and despairs of the efficacy of Faust's and Mephistopheles' unholy "tricks." Confronted with what seems imminent defeat, a prospect confirmed, according to Mephistopheles, by his ravens— Faust's reassuring explanation that these birds of Odin and the Devil are simply wartime counterparts of peaceful carrier pigeons does not conceal that "raven messages" are dark tidings—the Emperor recognizes that these two have caught him in their awesome toils. When his Grand-Master declines to continue to direct a battle in great part waged by phantom forces, he reluctantly heeds Mephistopheles' request to transfer the command to him and withdraws to his tent. The way now clear for crediting victory exclusively to himself and Faust, Mephistopheles quickly routs the enemy forces with a frightening illusion of roaring mountain floods (group hypnosis as in Auerbach's Cellar and Throne Room), with Satanic fire and lightning the more terrifying because of suddenly evoked darkness, and with the horrible rattling and clattering of the ghostly armor that finally joins the fray. As the noise of battle gives way to tuneful military airs, it is apparent that the victory has been won, and when the stage is again lighted we see the Interior of the Counter-Emperor's Tent already being despoiled by Grabber and Mistress Quickloot.

10783–870   With the return to an interior scene, the characteristic externals of Calderonian comedy—a multiple stage set representing a wild and picturesque landscape, generous use of sound and other theatrical effects—are abandoned, and the grand-historical style of pseudo-Shakespearean drama is again introduced. The brief farcical episode of the futile attempt of Grabber and Mistress Quickloot to carry off the whole payroll of the rebel army is a vivid reminder that the "honesty" of the Emperor and his supporters, however much vaunted by his supernaturally intimidated bodyguards, is seriously compromised by the dubious means that have gained his side an unearned victory—hence Grabber's cynical equation of looting and imperial levies, which echoes Phorkyas' euphemistic description to Helen of Faust as an invader who demanded no tribute but accepted voluntary offerings. Accordingly, when the Emperor enters, he at once seeks to persuade his supporters, here represented by the four Princes who attend upon him, that, "Although into the battle magic somehow juggled, / When all is said and done, 'twas for ourselves we struggled. / A happy chance will always help the man who fights." If the motif of opportunism suggests that the Emperor's explaining

away of the supernatural assistance he has received is of Mephistophelean inspiration, the verse in which he speaks reveals that he is
both deliberately dishonest and pompously pretentious. For German
writers stopped using the alexandrine couplet well before the end
of the eighteenth century, not only because its stiffness and wordiness
had become permanently associated with slavish imitation of French
literary models, but also because it was the verse form par excellence
of Baroque bombast, Baroque and Rococo servility, and Rococo
artificiality. Accordingly, the alexandrines of the Emperor and his
princes represent empty pomp and circumstance, and in addition, in
his own case, the transformation of a heedless, vainglorious youth
into a rigidly pompous man.

"We praise Thee now, our God" is sung by voices legion,
And yet for highest praise I turn my pious eyes—
A thing I've rarely done—to where my own heart lies.
A young and carefree prince may waste time pleasures gleaning,
But years will teach him well to know a moment's meaning.

The obligatory scene of grand-historical significance that failed   10871-976
to materialize on the Emperor's first appearance because of his
youthful distractibility is now at long last provided. The four
Princes are given honorific offices assigned by the Golden Bull of
Milan to the Electors of the German secular states, but—and this is
as typical of pseudo-historical drama as it is appropriate to the
Emperor's pleasure-loving character—the great political significance
of the Bull is not suggested until it has first been recalled that in the
defunct Holy Roman Empire there had once been such colorful
officials as Arch-Marshal, Arch-Chamberlain, Arch-Steward, and
Arch-Cupbearer. There is no causal connection between rewards
and merit on this occasion, as the fulsome compliments with which
the Princes accept their new offices further emphasize, although the
Chancellor-Archbishop, who is to prepare the Bull, and who is
elevated to the Arch-Chancellorship, has perhaps shown sufficient
serious concern for the welfare of the Empire (Throne Room) to
merit the rights and benefits, feudal and electoral, that the Emperor
now grants him and his fellow princes; his speeches of reply are, at
least, distinguished from those of the others by their pithiness and
by the fact that they are actually expressions of gratitude.

When the secular Electors have gone, the Chancellor in his turn   10977-11042
begins to speak with pathos. Explaining that he remains in his
capacity of bishop-confessor and that the Emperor must atone for
having restored himself to power with Satanic aid, an act which

17—G'F.

aggravates his earlier offense of having freed the Sabine sorcerer, he orders him to deed to the ecclesiastical authorities the battlefield and all the surrounding territory, so that a pilgrimage church may be built on "the desecrated place." Glad to be absolved of sin, the Emperor expresses his readiness to sign the appropriate documents, only to be informed by the departing Chancellor-Archbishop that he will also be expected to furnish money—"from your loot of war"— materials and feudal services for the church's construction. Now less joyous, the Emperor recognizes that he is paying dearly for having let himself receive supernatural assistance, and he is actually irritated when the Chancellor, again turning around in the door and bowing more deeply than before, finally reveals that he knows the Emperor has had to give his coastal territories to Faust and warns him that the part of his empire which he has given in fief to "that man most infamous" will be placed under the ban unless the Church receive not only its tithe but also those feudal payments which normally accrue to the crown. Unable to object, although "The land is not yet there, it lies out in the sea," the Emperor has learned the price of blackmail is never a fixed one and, when at last left alone, declares ruefully, "At this rate I shall soon have signed away an empire."

Coming after the dramatic climax which is Faust's double dream-play and before the denouement of *Faust* which immediately follows them, the scenes that represent his resolution to create a new society and the dubious means he exploits for this purpose may well seem the most transparently symbolic in the whole of *Faust*. Their tone is, however, deliberately light, as the many satiric and parodistic motifs which appear in them insist, for they constitute an expository curtain-raiser to final scenes of great symbolic density and high dramatic intensity. But even they reach a climax of unusual effectiveness thanks to the revelation in their very last minute of the successful result of Mephistopheles' "illusion, magic, hollow show," and the simultaneous ironic revelation that Faust's brave new world is bound to the ever-inescapable, ever-imperfect past, even before it comes into being. For all their comic overtones, therefore, these scenes are marked by a strong undertone of tragic pessimism. The man of folly who is the Emperor can, to all intents and purposes, learn nothing from experience; and even Faust, a man of highest ideals, easily succumbs once more to the temptation to follow the path of irresponsibility which magic symbolizes. The Emperor deceives himself because he wants to; Faust does so despite his newly strengthened high resolutions.

CHAPTER XXIII

The Value of Achievement

So that he may create a better world, Faust has allowed 11043-142
Mephistopheles to restore to power an emperor incapable of that
selfless devotion to a great purpose which he has recognized to be the
crowning virtue of the ideal prince, has allowed a moribund feudalism
to be perpetuated without visible improvement of its institutions,
and has allowed himself to play once more the repugnant role of
magician which was his traditional namesake's. After the Alexandrian
artificialities of the Emperor's moment of illusory triumph, the
verbal effortlessness and structural simplicity of the scene Open
Landscape combine to produce an effect of idyllic realism that places
the dramatic action of *Faust* back again in the timeless present of
Faust the representative man. A Traveler returns to the humble
cottage of a couple—their names are those of the poor but contented
Philemon and Baucis whose hospitality Zeus and Hermes enjoyed
when these gods went incognito among mortals—who sheltered him
and rescued his belongings when he was shipwrecked on nearby
dunes years before. Now very old, they explain how there has come
to be a "Paradise in counterfeit" where he expected to see "the
ocean vast"; and when he has silently partaken of their hospitality,
he goes with them to their chapel to watch the sunset and join them
in evening prayer. Such is the action of the scene which explains
that Faust has successfully created a garden state, though with the
aid of unnatural—at least superhuman and inhuman—forces, and
now imperiously asks these neighbors to exchange their land for a
plot in his new dominion.

Philemon and Baucis live in a little world of idyll—hence its primary symbols, the cottage and the grove—which is menaced by a great world of new power and prosperity. For, if the grove is Arcadia, the cottage is what Faust, comparing himself in Forest and Cave to a raging Alpine torrent, used to symbolize Margarete's threatened idyllic existence. Open Landscape thus serves to create, not, as it first seems to do, an atmosphere of poeticized reality, but one of oppressive, symbolic danger underscored by the Traveler's unbroken silence from the moment of his discovery that the sea no longer lies behind the dunes and by the uneasiness which Faust's "miracle" inspires in the observant Baucis. Yet the most important contribution to the creation of this atmosphere is made by the scene's versification. After the caesura-retarded alexandrine couplets of Interior of the Counter-Emperor's Tent, with not a single run-over line in all ninety-seven of them, the reintroduction of four-stress lines with enjambement and without couplets seems a return to the metrical flexibility which in *Faust* represents normal reality.[1] But as Open Landscape progresses the fact that its verse is anything but flexible becomes audibly evident, for it consists of twenty-five strictly regular redondillas—trochaic *abab* stanzas with the *a*-rhyme feminine, the *b*-rhyme masculine—each ending with full-stop punctuation. Since this Calderonian verse form has been identified with romantic medievalism and transparently symbolic drama in the Inner Court-yard scene of Faust's *Helen*, it subtly suggests that the world of Philemon and Baucis is also one threatened by the forces of time and change, and leaves little doubt that Baucis' distrust of the substantiality of Faust's "land on water" is justified. And so, when the scene closes with Philemon's "Let us go to where we worship, / See there the last gleams of day, / Trusting in our fathers' Godship, / Let us ring the bell and pray," the nameless Traveler and his hosts have become symbols of an ending order, and we know that the end of Faust's labyrinthine path is near at hand also.

11143–62   As in Faust's dream plays and so often in Calderón's patently symbolic dramas, there is only the briefest of intervals before a new scene begins, Palace with Formal Park and Great Rectilinear Canal. The sun that sets on the humble world of Philemon and Baucis is setting also on the great domain of Faust, now very old but still prey to discontent even though, as his Lookout declares,[2] "By fame and

---

[1] True metrical normalcy is reintroduced in the following scene, Palace (11.11143–843), 85 per cent of whose lines are iambic and in which, after an opening twenty-line carry-over of *abab*-rhymes, couplets again predominate.

[2] The name, Lynceus, seems to indicate that the role of the Lookout is to be given to the actor whose talent for delivering lyric speeches effectively had earned him the Watchman's role in the scene Inner Courtyard.

fortune you are blessed." As Lynceus describes how his "last vessels" put into port—the phrase is an ominous echo of Philemon's "last gleams of day"—Faust hears the bell ring in his neighbor's chapel and is moved to an outburst of anger quite disproportionate to its nuisance value. If he asserts, "My grand estate is not yet whole," if he exclaims, "Oh were I far away from here!," it is rather because he doubts the soundness of his apparently flourishing paradise than because the proximity of their "time-weathered cottage, their crumbling chapel," seriously impairs his enjoyment of what he has achieved. And if he thinks with extreme repugnance of resting beneath lime-trees not his own—"I am afraid of alien shade"—it is surely because he knows that his brave new world has its own disturbing shadows.

With the arrival of a richly laden barge the true source of Faust's 11163–233 dissatisfaction begins to be apparent. He owes the prosperous growth of his dominion to trickery and brutal violence—to Mephistopheles and Mephistopheles' three Violent Fellows, thanks to whom his maritime ventures bring a tenfold return—and the disgust which these new Mighty Men discern in his countenance does not, as they surmise, represent lack of appreciation of their cargo's worth but the same suppressed sense of guilty uneasiness that underlies his irritation with Philemon and Baucis. Accordingly, Mephistopheles can dismiss his helpers with the assurance that a satisfied Faust will not prove wanting in generosity toward them, personally promising that they and their fellows in the fleet will be well provided for, only to turn at once to Faust and attempt to assuage his obvious discontent. For Mephistopheles has not yet succeeded in providing that complete satisfaction which was to be Faust's undoing. He may point out the greatness of Faust's achievement and the global scope of his influence:

Admit: here, from this palace here,
Your reach encompasses our sphere.
From this spot you went on ahead,
Here stood at first one wooden shed;
A little ditch was scratched in soil
Where now the plashing oar does toil.
Your lofty mind, your workers' worth,
Have won for you both land and earth.
And right from here—.

But this is primarily an indirect attempt to make Faust identify his dissatisfaction solely with its apparent cause—the inconvenient nearness of Philemon and Baucis, the "This damnèd Here!" with which Faust interrupts these flattering reminders of greatness achieved.

11234–87   And so, although he confesses shame—the motif represents inner uncertainty—at coveting their land, Faust nevertheless persuades himself that only their presence, by preventing him from surveying "all at once / A human spirit's masterpiece," spoils his enjoyment of what he has just admitted is a "worldwide realm." If the chapel bell properly reminds him of a religion which he has consistently regarded as hostile to life itself, it is obvious inconsistency that he now condemns as tomblike the fragrance of the lime-trees in which he so recently desired to establish a belvedere. "The freedom of my mighty will / Attacks in vain this sandy hill," he cries, and Mephistopheles further feeds his rage by insidiously equating a bell rung for private devotions with the bells forever rung by a clergy scornful of this life's worth. With Faust completely prey to passion—"No longer splendid is success / When thwarted so by stubbornness / That, great though his regret, one must / At last grow tired of being just"—Mephistopheles can boldly insist that one whose manifest destiny is colonization need have no scruples about forcibly transplanting his neighbors. Since a new homestead has already been set aside for them, Faust has but to say "Then go and rid me of their presence" —the fact that this line is unrhymed emphasizes the dissonant note— and the deed is as good as done.

11288–337   While Faust and Mephistopheles talked, sunset was followed by darkening twilight, and night falls when Mephistopheles leaves with the Three Violent Fellows whom he has summoned to carry out the act of *force majeure*. Their sullenness and Mephistopheles' prophetic allusion to Naboth's vineyard forebode the brutal death of the Traveler and his hosts, but for a moment all is again well in Faust's world, as the lyric sung by his Lookout declares. Yet the moment of contemplative satisfaction is brief, and during the pause which follows it the Lookout's inward vision lingers on to insist with powerful dramatic irony that the outward prosperity of Faust's latter years does not represent the subjectively satisfying fulfillment of high human aspiration toward which he resolved to strive after Margarete's death. How far the reality falls short of the envisioned goal then becomes terribly clear as, in staccato trochaics—the redondillas are the more striking after the lilting anapestic rhythm of the song just ended—the Lookout describes the destruction by fire of the world of Philemon and Baucis and announces their certain death in the smoking flames of their moss-covered cottage. After the chapel has burned to the ground, the old and hollow lime-trees suddenly burst into flame, and Lynceus pauses in stunned silence. When he is heard again, it is only to intone the dirge-like words, "What did once the eye delight / Is now one with all that's past"—an old order has perished, what has been done can never be undone.

Faust, who had retired within his palace after giving the fatal order for Philemon and Baucis' removal, is brought to its balcony by his watchman's lament. Aware only that their buildings and trees have been destroyed, he regrets his impatience. But he consoles himself with the thought that he can replace the lime-trees with a tower and from it view both his own boundless world and the new home of a couple "Who, blessed by generous indulgence, / Will pass their last days happily." He learns the ugly truth from the report of Mephistopheles and his companions—its choral form, and the doggerel-like effect produced by its unbroken succession of couplets and by its almost complete lack of subordinate syntactic elements, emphasize its impersonal brutality—and then he curses the "heedless violent act" and the "unheeding" perpetrators of it. These may cynically justify the fatal event by asserting, "The saying's old, but it is clear: / Take Force's orders with good grace! / The bold and resolute alone / Will risk the goods—and lives—they own," but the ultimate responsibility remains Faust's, who himself heedlessly let his order be executed by a destructive Mephistopheles and by brutal men already angered because he had failed to receive them cordially. After the evil chorus depart from the yard below, Faust watches the fire by the dunes die to faint glow and then, fanned by a damp sea breeze, give off smoke and vapor that are carried in his direction; his anger is now spent, and he can at last acknowledge his own irresponsibility: "A quick command, too quickly done!—"

Again Faust knows the guilt of having destroyed an idyllic existence. Although there are mitigating circumstances, this time he does not seriously attempt to place the blame on fate, as he did anticipatorily when he foresaw in Forest and Cave Margarete's destruction, or on Mephistopheles (or some higher spirit creature that had burdened him with that companion), as he did when he actually learned of her terrible flight and capture. Nor does he now, as he did after Margarete's death, find surcease in protective oblivion. At the pause marked by the dash after "too quickly done" it begins to strike midnight, and in the courtyard below him appear the shadowy shapes of Four Gray Women, phantom projections of the four great evils that he has always sought to avoid. If Faust sees these specters—Want, Debt, Care, and Woe—float toward him from the embers of the world of Philemon and Baucis, from their ashes

11338–82

11383–97

and those of the grateful Traveler, it is solely because that property is now his; for those victims of his discontent, though perhaps not carefree, gave no evidence of being prey to these basic sources of human unhappiness. In his prosperity he has forgotten what he so bitterly acknowledged on earlier occasions, that material things are not necessarily a source of happiness, and even his more recent insight (High Mountains) that responsibility is an inevitable concomitant of effective material achievement, of dominion and ownership. He may therefore, as a man of wealth, be impregnable to all but one of these grim women, Care, behind whom follows their brother Death. Care's approach through the night is thus both a reminder of Faust's claim that the seizure of the slain couple's land would remove the last blemish from his great domain and a reminder that he is therefore precariously close to enjoyment of the "bed of idleness" he repudiated as irreconcilable with a worthwhile life when he made his great wager with Mephistopheles.

11398–420   Disturbed to see only three of the Gray Women depart, disturbed also by the thought of death, Faust steps back from the balcony on which he has been standing—once more there is a Calderonian change of scene without interruption of the dramatic action—and the interior of the room opening out on to it is revealed. The incantation-like rhythms of the phantom women give way to more normal verse patterns as Faust meditates on his disturbing vision. He may seek to persuade himself that its meaning has eluded him—"I heard them speak but did not catch the sense"—but he contradicts himself by admitting that he has caught the ominous rhyme of *Not* and *Tod* (Woe and Death), the key words of the spectral episode. The wanton sacrifice of life and property to his corrosive discontent has made it impossible for him still to maintain the fiction that his dissatisfaction springs simply from petty irritations, and he confesses to himself,

And still I have not fought my way to freedom.
Could I my path of magic disencumber,
Forget of magic charms the total number
And stand a simple man before you, Nature,
It then would be worth having human stature.

He now sees that the very compact which has enabled him to experience a more-than-normal portion of the lot of all mankind has deprived him of that full responsibility for the consequences of one's actions which he has long since recognized as man's proper burden. And so Faust, who so bitterly repudiated the magical religion of his fathers and so persuasively formulated the vision of naturalistic humanism in the dreams of his classical Walpurgis Night, finally admits the cause of his basic discontent, which is that the value of his present magnificent achievement is vitiated for him by the perpetually returning memories of past magic. "For us a given day sheds reason's light, / Yet ghastly dreams entangle us at night."

It is to a Faust haunted by the ghosts of an irresponsible past that 11421-32 Care appears in person, and her appearance symbolizes Faust's readiness to assume that personal responsibility which alone can endow his life with truly universal human significance. What the Earth Spirit was to Faust the seeker after knowledge, this is what Care is for Faust the moral agent—the symbol of an enigma to which the human spirit seeks the solution, this time perhaps with more hope of a satisfactory one. To renounce magical irresponsibility demands great courage, and even Faust hesitates—"Be on your guard, o Faust, and speak no charm"—to admit the presence of a force which he knows can make brave men into cowards paralyzed by fear; as he declared on Easter Eve, when Care is in the heart, "You wince at blows that do not fall / And feel compelled to mourn imaginary losses." But he allows Care to remain and so finally achieves the totality of experience to which he sacrificially dedicated himself at his second interview with Mephistopheles. For if Death is the ultimate symbol of human finiteness, Care is only second to it, is the embodiment of man's awareness that nothing is his forever, is the symbol of a universal sense of human limitations, whether men consciously acknowledge its existence or not—"Even though no ear perceive it, / In your hearts my voice reëchoes; / Changing shape from hour to hour, / I exert a savage power."

Having known full well what Care is, Faust can disregard the 11433-52 question—his not less than hers—"Have you never met with Care?" and seek to reconcile the heroic vision of life to which he attained through tragic experience with life as he has actually lived it. Recognizing as basic and inevitable the pattern of alternating desire, dissatisfaction, rejection, frustration, and achievement that has characterized his existence, he is content, after having lived "grandly and intensely," to live now "sagely and deliberately," for only thus can the normal cycle of a man's life be completed. Unshaken, however, is his conviction that man, while on "this earthly sphere," may not properly concern himself with any Beyond.

He is a fool who casts a sheep's eye yonder,
Invents himself a double in the heavens!
Let men stand firm and look about them here;
For worthy ones the voice of earth is clear.

With these words Faust at last completely identifies himself in a waking hour with "the good man," with "men of worth," and affirms without qualification that the world in and upon which he acts, and by which he is acted upon, speaks as eloquently of a great cosmic order as the world which he merely observes. Still firm in his faith that life must be taken as it comes, that "suffering and happiness" are the necessary price of life itself, he announces his resolution to stride on undaunted by the ghosts of Care, never satisfied with any moment as an ultimate value in itself.

11453–98   But Faust's is no foolhardy courage. What he calls Care's "litany" is his recognition that dark inner forces may be more destructive than any physical danger, is a description of that moral disintegration to which Philemon, Baucis, and their guest have been sacrificed. For Care is also apathy and paralysis of the will, the mere thought of which might, as Faust declares, "drive men most sensible to madness," and can make her victims so irresolute that, though they may for a while grope their way hesitantly through life, in the end their half-existences bog down in a living hell of helplessness. Yet, knowing all this, aware that "the human race on thousands of occasions" has succumbed to the "accursed ghosts" of intangible forces of destruction, and aware from his own experience that "the spirit bond, yet firm," of these inner demons cannot be severed, Faust defies the power of Care. "But your authority, so great yet secret, / I'll never recognize, O Care!" Faust's will to triumph over the destructive forces to which he has become vulnerable by accepting finite responsibility is no less imperious than was his selfish impulse to possess—and destroy—Margarete or his grandiose resolve to wrest a brave new world from the sea. Unlike these two intentions, which could be realized with the help of Mephistopheles, his present purpose can be realized only by himself alone and in this respect corresponds to his great dream-quest of Helen. But, whereas Faust's classical Walpurgis Night represented an inner experience the event of which could not directly affect his material existence, his vision of Care represents both an inner psychological experience—hence, until her last speech, the double-monologue form of his soliloquy counterposed against her litany—and a natural world-order from whose universal laws he ceased to claim magical exemption when he recognized her presence. And so Faust feels the power which he defies as he becomes blind—as, no longer proof against physical frailty, he feels the end of life draw near.

11499–510   At last standing in Nature's presence simply as a man, Faust might now once more say, with greater justice than during his Easter walk with Wagner, "I'm human here and that's my right!" But even now he does not identify himself completely with all men—hence the still arrogant scorn of his less heroic and less clairvoyant fellow human beings in Care's parting "Mankind is blind its whole life long. / Your life is ending, be blind too!" Despite an affliction which symbolizes both sudden physical weakness and awareness that he now needs all his inner strength to resist successfully the paralyzing forces represented by Care, he resolves to consummate the enterprise which has become his life work. The light within is not dimmed; summoning his workers from their beds to execute "what still is only plan," Faust starts to grope his way out of his room confident that "a single mind"—his own—is sufficient to guarantee completion of even the greatest undertaking.

Again the action shifts to the Great Courtyard before Faust's 11511-50 palace, now lighted by torches. Instead of the laborers whom Faust called for, Mephistopheles enters, followed by a band of Lemures, spirits of the unplacated dead as represented in Roman art—articulated skeletons held together by mortuary wrappings and mummified sinews—who wonder why they have been called to work on an engineering project.

We see that pointed poles are here
And chains to measure sections,
But why you summoned us, we fear,
Has slipped our recollections.

If their verses echo the form and substance of the gravedigger's song in *Hamlet*, it is because they are neo-folkloristic emissaries of death who appear when it is time for them to claim persons and things that are about to cease to be—hence their opening "We're always at your beck and call / And think we've comprehended: / There is some country, large withal, / That is for us intended." On the same night that has seen the destruction of the little world of Philemon and Baucis, the destruction of Faust's own great dominion is to begin with the death of the indomitable will that has created and maintained it. "No skilled techniques are needed here," Mephistopheles informs his helpers, and orders the digging of the grave which is to mark the end of Faust and of all Faust's grandiose projects. Faust may mistake the soft clattering of the Lemures' spades for the distant sound of many serfs shoveling in consequence of the order he has given, but Mephistopheles' aside makes clear that it is now only a matter of time until all that he and his workers have created is destroyed by the sea and the elements. (What has been achieved with magic must be regarded as already undone by Faust's heroic affirmation of human finiteness.)

11551-61   Faust's last common human experience is to be death; but it is still to be seen whether he remains faithful even in the final critical moment of his living to his original conviction that no moment of satisfaction may ever constitute a value worthy of eternalization. If he denies that conviction, the moment of his dying must be Mephistopheles' long and patiently awaited moment of triumph; if he abides in his faith until the very end, Mephistopheles will, as the Lord foretold in Prologue in Heaven, have exerted himself in vain. Ironically unaware that his own time has come, Faust commands his overseer to hasten the completion of the great canal that, by draining a pestilent marsh and so making the domain he has created fully colonizable, will be his crowning achievement. In his intense preoccupation with his inner vision he fails to recognize that it was Mephistopheles who answered when he called for his overseer, and fails to hear him mutter, "He seems to talk of 'great canal.' / The words should be 'a grave banal.'"

11562-86   Although Faust's physical faculties are failing, he rises once more above the petty considerations that long absorbed his emotional energies and finally brought about the senseless death of his neighbors; no belvedere or lookout tower, but "living space for many millions," is his concern now. Although his visions are grandiose, the "paradise terrestrial" which he foresees is no magical utopia offering absolute security, but a world where men will perforce always struggle against Nature, free to live and be active within the limits of human finiteness. Faust's greatest achievement is thus not his impermanent conquest of Nature, but remains still his conquest of Care. The willingness to assume responsibilities and the will to resist to the utmost of one's ability the paralyzing forces of life— these he now recognizes as the necessary price of human autonomy, of the supreme good which is life lived fully. So he declares, speaking no longer for himself alone, but for all men,

This wisdom's ultimate and true:
He only merits freedom and his life
Who conquers them each day anew.

Such is his regained clarity of insight, moreover, that he also recognizes that the land he has created and expects to make livable for centuries to come is not, as he said earlier, his personal achievement only, but the fruit of cooperative enterprise: "bold industrious people" have raised his dike, "Communal effort hastens to maintain it," and he envisions a people of individually free men long vigorously sustaining itself on this new land in the face of ever-surrounding danger. With this reëxpression of the awareness of the importance of cooperation for effective activity that he first formulated as Chiron's apologue of the Argonauts, Faust allows himself the wish that he might live to see his great undertaking completed, for then—and then only—does he conceive it possible that he might properly say to the moment, "Linger a while, thou art so fair!" Finally, carried away by his vision, which has insisted that nothing permanent can ever be achieved by man, he declares,

For aeons still my earthly days' memorial
Will never disappear from there.—
Anticipating happiness so great,
This moment as the best I predicate.

With this last grandiose dream, with this momentary release from 11587-90 the narrow prison of self-interest in which he has so long tormented himself, Faust falls back unconscious, to be placed on the ground by the Lemures; like Euphorion in his classical Walpurgis Night, he has escaped from a confining, artificial existence into life and almost simultaneous death. "Not glory!" he cried as he prepared to reveal his great project to Mephistopheles, "Deeds count alone!" The total context of his final words insists that the memorial which he thinks he leaves behind is not some monument to himself, but the legacy to others of conditions of life which can only force them to share his profound feeling that to live fully is always in some sense to live precariously and heroically and, above all, in some measure selflessly. The present moment has not become for Faust the end in itself, the delusive satiation, that he originally challenged Mephistopheles to provide, and even as he lies dying the latter is constrained to declare,

No pleasure satisfies, nor any bliss,
And so he still finds phantoms quite alluring.
And this last worthless moment's emptiness—
He would, poor fellow, 'twere enduring.

Although his actual achievement is less than he believes, he has successfully demonstrated that "A good man in his groping intuition/ Is well aware of what's his proper path," for it is the direction of man's striving that can alone matter in a finite world. Unlike the dream of a golden age that can only be hopelessly regretted or helplessly desired, the vision of a realizable better world can and does enduringly affect men's practical efforts; as Margarete could inspire Faust, though her life ended in personal disaster, so can Faust's unrealized project inspire the generations that he thinks he has materially helped.

11591–611   For the dying Faust time has stopped, as it was to do if he bade the moment tarry, but it has done so only because he has achieved complete human finiteness. Mephistopheles' cynical "it is finished" thus conveys the meaning "it is fulfilled," the value of the words when uttered by Christ on the cross, although he seeks to persuade Faust even in his last helpless moments that no achievement can in the final analysis properly be called meaningful.

It's "over"! Stupid word! Why add a name?
What's over and what isn't are the same!
What use is constantly creating!
What use is our annihilating!
"Then all is over" means, to him who's clever,
It might as well not have existed ever,
Although things act as if they were substantial.
To that I'd far prefer the void eternal.

The moment is one of profound tragedy, for a human spirit has triumphed over physical limitations in the very moment of visible defeat, as it is brought to the point when it must surrender its last hold on reality. And if the attainment of tragic-heroic stature is felt to be the supreme demonstration of human worth—and it would seem to be universally so felt, to judge from the universal popularity of tragedy in folklore and myth—then Faust's worth transcends his failures and Mephistopheles' view that an impermanent existence is worse than nothing at all is sufficiently countered. Through tragedy, then, the poet offers a widely shared vision of man's proper destiny; stated effectively and with sufficiently universal symbols, it can be immediately grasped by men of different religious and philosophic persuasions and so truly represents "a secular gospel." But if the cathartic effect of tragedy is immediate, like that of a profound religious experience, its fuller implications—like those of the religious experience—can only emerge more gradually. With a drama there is always the danger that its cathartic effect will afterward be associated with some grandiose triumph or some pathetic failure of the tragic hero, rather than with his spiritual triumph only, and so between the denouement and the end of the play there usually comes a moment of final clarification, short or long, simple or complex, according to what has gone before. In *Faust* this moment is both long and complex—necessarily so, in view of the great complexity of the dramatic action that has preceded it—and begins as Faust's body is placed in the grave the Lemures have dug (Interment).

If it be remembered that the Lord of Prologue in Heaven authorized Mephistopheles to lead Faust "gently down his path" only "As long as he does live on earth," and that Mephistopheles accepted this condition without protest, it is clear that what now follows is either, like Mephistopheles' recent remarks about the futility of ever having existed at all, a last attempt to torment a still living Faust by persuading him before he dies that his vision of human dignity is a delusion, or else—and this alone is consonant with the original premise of the action of the Tragedy proper, that the Lord would never intervene in it—the dramatic projection of Faust's dying thoughts. For he alone can expect Mephistopheles, who has so often sought to weaken his sense of moral autonomy by reminding him that he "indentured himself to the Devil," to claim his soul at this point. The skepticism which underlies Mephistopheles' doubts whether he will be cheated of Faust's "spirit," whether the soul will actually leave the body, and whether Faust is yet actually dead—this is more Faustian than Mephistophelean. Mephistopheles' conjuring up of diabolic reinforcements with "fantastic" military arm-movements is pure phantasmagoria, and there is dreamlike inconsistency in his ordering "the hell-mouth"— of medieval and Baroque drama—to be brought in when he knows that Hell has many mouths and that the Dantesque hell he describes is regarded by sinners only as an idle invention. Most ironic of all, however, is that he should be so concerned with obtaining something which he declares will be only "a nasty worm" once it is torn from the body to which it belongs.

As Mephistopheles' devils, fat and thin, crowd about his grave, the forces of ultimate good to which the dying Faust still remains loyal are introduced with a Baroque deus-ex-machina effect, and with a great burst of light a Heavenly Host appears, self-declared representatives of life's benevolent forces. The sound of their boyish soprano voices is characteristically condemned as "nasty tinkling"— Faust had let Panthalis call the modern music of his Euphorion episode "frenzied tinkling"—by Mephistopheles, whose identification of the singers as castrati indicates that Faust, and Goethe, are using Catholic symbols without attaching confessional significance to them. Although there is nothing of partisan sanctimoniousness in their words, Mephistopheles angrily exhorts his troops to rally against

11612–75

11676–843

"these foppish hypocrites," who are also experienced soul-snatchers, and when a Chorus of Angels scatter roses on Faust's grave, he orders them to destroy these flowers of love (Angels' second chorus) with their fiery breaths, only to see them routed by the flames they have created. Left to confront his enemies alone, Mephistopheles finds himself burned by the rain of roses, and although pitch and sulphur are supposed to be his native elements, he is allowed to declare, "My back, it seems, is racked with pitch and sulphur." Finally stripping Mephistopheles of the veneer of sophistication which has always cloaked his devilry, Faust now lets him forget his sworn feud with heaven and burn with lust for the boyish Angels who gradually fill the stage and push him into the proscenium (the place he occupied at the end of Faust's Helen phantasmagoria). And so, when they turn away from him indifferently, Mephistopheles is only able to save face by feebly explaining that his Job-like affliction has brought him to his senses in time to see through the skin-deep illusion of love. His would-be triumphant recovery of full clairvoyance into his true nature is a last comic defeat, and the Angels, whom he impotently curses, ascend without further ado with "the immortal part of Faust." Cheated by what he regards as deliberate angelic dalliance, Mephistopheles disappears from Faust's consciousness in the role of one who only dupes himself, who is immature despite all his shrewdness and experience, while Faust remains convinced to the very end that he has lived a sufficiently good life to call what Mephistopheles has vainly claimed—"the noble soul that pledged itself to me"—"a great and matchless treasure."

Between the first appearance of the Heavenly Host and the departure of his Devils, the comic aspects of Mephistopheles' anger so completely dominate Interment that it is hardly to be noticed that the first three angelic choruses convey only key words or phrases —"Sinners forgiven," "Traces benevolent," "Roses resplendent, / Of balsam redolent," "Let spring appear," "Heavens bring here," "Blossoms of blessedness," "Love they diffuse," "Everywhere light!" The verse form of these choruses, however, is easily recognizable as that which gave the Euphorion episode of Faust's *Helen* its peculiar nervousness, and like the climactic passages of that episode these choral passages are marked by a striking use of ellipsis and interjection. In the moment of relative quiet which follows the rout of Mephistopheles' cohorts, however, comes an angelic chorus, the total sense of which can be grasped at first hearing.

What is not rightly yours,
You must beware it;

What causes you turmoil,
You must not bear it.
If violence is done us,
We must show boldness.
Lovers by love alone
Are brought to bliss.

At this point it becomes clear that Faust's Heavenly Host are not the traditional divine messengers of morality-play tradition or of medieval and Renaissance paintings of the Last Judgment, but spokesmen for his own triumphant defiance of Care. At the same time, moreover, their insistence that love can exert its influence only on those who love—seemingly but a loose afterthought demanded by their role as emissaries of God-Love—is Faust's dying reaffirmation of the causal connection between high purpose and selfless love which has been the psychological premise of *Faust* as a whole and which he himself fleetingly recognized when he identified Margarete with Helen on waking from his classical Walpurgis Night. And so, the stage picture notwithstanding, it is clear that the heaven to which Faust imagines himself being transported is to be no more Christian and conventional than was that of Prologue in Heaven: as a place of Love, Clarity, Harmony, Life, and Spirit, however, it is of the same essence as that heaven and confirms the rightness of Faust's last insights.

SUMMATION

CHAPTER XXIV

An Epilogue on Earth

The episode of Faust's interment has been the counterpart of Prologue in Heaven, although it is not an epilogue to the Tragedy of Faust but an integral part of its dramatic action. The heaven of medieval and Baroque morality play has been economically re-introduced as the burst of light diagonally above Mephistopheles' hell-mouth, and as in a morality the symbols of good and evil have stood for the last time in sharp contrast. Yet Faust's view of man and man's world is not dualistic and theological, but monistic and humanistic; his sense of the oneness of God and Nature, of the divine and the human, is the expression of a fundamentally anti-transcendental naturalism, unobtrusively present in Prologue in Heaven, whose first clear spokesmen in *Faust* were the Poet and the Player of Prelude on the Stage. Although Interment effectively insists that Faust has defeated Mephistopheles and, simultaneously, serves to complete the cosmic framework which permitted *Faust* to be a drama of symbolic supernaturalism, its ambiguous morality-play machinery can leave uncertain—especially in the theater—whether the dying Faust believes he is about to enjoy salvation and heavenly bliss or remains a humanistic naturalist until he finally loses all consciousness. The scene Mountain Gorges: Forest, Rocks, and Hermitage, serves both to clarify this final point and, returning us once more to the realm of finite human beings in which *Faust* opened (Dedication, Prelude on the Stage), to recapitulate in the form of a dramatic epilogue all the salient features—the symbolic characters, themes, ideas, and motifs—of the complex tragedy now terminating.

The first and last scenes of *Faust* in which its protagonist is an active participant both take place at night, but even as the opening scene in Faust's study was preceded by a sunlit Prologue in Heaven, so is his interment followed by the radiant daylight of Faust's last vision. The setting of Mountain Gorges, however, is no Old Testament heaven, but a Catholicized Arcadia, for *Faust* has not been a Christian mystery play, a drama of religious edification, and Faust has not been a Christian whose good works could earn him immediate admission to the company of Saints. The placing of this epilogue to the tragedy of a humanistic naturalist in a milieu familiar from Catholic legend, painting, and drama is thus ironic, if not startling, and after the anti-clerical and anti-transcendental tones repeatedly heard in *Faust*—tones that cast subsequent light on the omission of conventional Christian elements in the not irreligious, but still only superficially traditional, Prologue in Heaven—it is evident that Catholicizing symbolism is here introduced solely in the interest of artistic economy. Anchorites, then, are still creatures of this world, however near to God their solitary devotions may succeed in bringing them, while the Church Fathers, Blessed Boys, Penitents, and Virgin Mother who utter, or share in the utterance of, over four-fifths of the lines comprising this scene, have all known mortal existence. Although its religious symbolism may thus seem to make Mountain Gorges tantamount to an Epilogue in Heaven, by virtue of its predominantly temporal components it is rather an Epilogue on Earth, a companion piece to Dedication, Prelude on the Stage, Pleasant Landscape, and the opening soliloquy of High Mountains, a scene whose desolate landscape it shares, and the counterpart of Margarete's visions of the afterlife in Cathedral and Prison. Like Prison, moreover, it too recalls Piranesi, though not a dungeon from *The Prisons*, but a wild landscape from *The Views of Rome*.

11844–53   Whereas Faust's rock-bound Arcadia was a "universal" symbol to which special and even highly individual significance was attached, the rocky hermitage of Mountain Gorges is one which, at least in terms of the symbolism of *Faust*, is totally significant—that is, it represents all the realms of experience in which Faust has moved in the course of the tragedy. Into the classical paradise of Shaded Grove are introduced the still tame beasts of the Judaeo-Christian Garden of Eden—the mute and friendly lions of the Anchorites' opening chorus—and that "natural" wildness of landscape which no Arcadia could properly possess and which to varying degrees characterized the realm of impersonal Nature whenever Faust sought refuge in it (Forest and Cave, Pleasant Landscape, High Mountains). The human or once-human figures who appear may at first sight seem mostly new, but when they speak it quickly becomes clear that they are metamorphoses of Faust and other dramatic characters from his past experiences, a fact emphasized not only by what they say, but also by the metrical and verbal echoes of earlier moments in the Tragedy of Faust which mark their speech. For this heaven-like world remains from beginning to end the projection of a Faust who can no longer experience anything new, who may only draw upon memories of what he has done, has felt, has thought, and has imagined.[1]

Although he proclaims the final Faustian insight that love is essence of God-Life, the Pater Ecstaticus is a self-tormented mystic who vacillates between earth and heaven, between a physical reality that he depreciates as transitory and a quintessential Love that he fervently prays may become his through physical suffering. His is the religious equivalent of Faust's sentimental confusion of love and self-destruction at the end of Forest and Cave, and like Faust then, the Ecstatic Father is one as yet incapable of selfless devotion— hence the emphatic repetition of "me" at the end of four successive lines in his brief speech, and hence also the motif of levitation, which recalls Euphorion's unsuccessful attempt to free himself of earthbound man's necessary limitations. More stable and less egocentric by far is the Pater Profundus, whose first two stanzas incidentally picture the larger landscape of which this mountain scene is but a part. Speaking in the verse form of the Archangels' descriptive hymn at the opening of Prologue in Heaven, he discerns, much as they did, in the workings of the physical world the evidence of God-Love's universal presence, which is represented by the same four elements that represented the cosmos at the end of both Faust's Classical Walpurgisnight and his *Helen*. Unlike the Archangels, however, but like the Faust of Pleasant Landscape and High Mountains, he delights equally in the great and small phenomena of Nature. Yet he, too, has not achieved the release from self he ardently desires and, the religious counterpart of the would-be intellectual superman who on Easter Eve felt hopelessly crushed by his inability to transcend the limits of finite-sensual knowledge, regards himself as the helpless prisoner of his merely-finite senses, so that his "Tormented by dull senses' confines" is the harsh antithesis of the Lord's benedictory "Encompass you in love's propitious bonds."

11854-89

---

[1] It is pointed out by Kurt May in *Faust II. Teil in der Sprachform gedeutet* (*Neue Forschung* 30—Berlin, 1936) that, unlike those earlier scenes of *Faust* which have represented Faust achieving new insights or entering new realms of experience, Mountain Gorges introduces no metrical elements not already used.

11890-925 More important than these two Church Fathers, who have represented both universal forms of religious experience and critical moments in Faust's religious-intellectual development, is the Pater Seraphicus, whose first speech marks an abrupt transition from contemplative and descriptive elements, largely lyrical and retrospective, to an immediate present and to dramatic action. The "median elevation" to which the stage direction assigns him indicates that he, like Faust from Pleasant Landscape on, is content to know of God only what has meaning for life on this earth—hence the Calderonian redondillas, the verse of idyllic realism in the Philemon and Baucis scene, that distinguish his speech and that of the Blessed Boys while they remain with him. Completely unconcerned with self, like Faust in his best moments, he marks the approach of the "morning cloudlet" which conceals a chorus of boys who died at birth. This bodiless "band of youthful spirits"—whose method of transportation recalls the cloud from which Faust emerged after his classical Walpurgis Night and which symbolized his recognition that Helen and Margarete, "Aurora's love," were one person—are a last memory of the child Faust never saw. Counterparts of Homunculus by virtue of their insubstantiality and power of levitation, they share with him the fact that their voice must be projected ventriloquistically, although at the moment they are content to enjoy pure—or mere—"being." Invited by the kindly Seraphic Father to see the world through his eyes, they receive a lesson in seeing which is the counterpart of the lesson in talking in rhyme that Faust gave Helen in his second great dream. But the sight of a majestic and gloomy landscape is so overpowering that they immediately beg to be released and are sent on their way to higher, less substantial spheres where they can grow as they draw strength from "God's presence." Although it will transpire in the course of the scene that this advice does not represent highest wisdom, it does reveal that, for Faust, God is, as in Prologue in Heaven, the supreme symbol of growth and development (*Werden*), and it projects into a spirit-world the same forces and patterns that Faust made basic to his triumphant vision of life in the Galatea scene of Classical Walpurgisnight.

11926-941 Accepting the Seraphic Father's words of dismissal as a promise that they shall see God—"Godly this teaching, / Be now at ease; / Whom you respect, / Him your eye sees"—the Blessed Boys move off to the highest peaks of the stage set. If the incongruity of disembodied spirits holding hands and dancing in a circle to express their joys is a variation on the motif of the still vial-confined Homunculus' power to smell the freshness of marine vegetation, the dance motif itself, like its rhythms, recalls the opening of the pastoral dance passage of the Euphorion episode. As the Blessed Boys sing "Whom you respect, / Him your eye sees," the Angels who bore away "the immortal part of Faust" in the preceding scene make a significantly timed entrance. For it is Faust, not God, whom they are to see and respect. Hovering high above the earth, these Angels— the only never-mortal figures of Mountain Gorges—announce that "a noble spirit" has been saved from evil, that is, from the annihilation for which Mephistopheles has always stood. Whereas Prologue in Heaven merely promised that Faust would ultimately find man's proper path and achieve clarity of insight as he followed the path of error which is life, Faust allows himself a last aerial translation and potential heavenly salvation. For the Angels' "Whoever strives with all his heart, / For him there is redemption," is not the fulfillment of any promise, but rather the symbolic expression of Faust's conviction that his resolution of Pleasant Landscape, "Ever to strive toward life's most perfect forms," is the best possible general formulation of the moral imperative which consciousness of man's divine dignity must predicate. This resolution was, as Faust ultimately recognized, inspired by the example of Margarete's heroic selflessness, and now he again acknowledges his profound debt to her by having the Angels immediately add,

And if a love from up on high
Has given him assistance,
The blessed creatures of the sky
Must welcome his appearance.

That the Angels' "love from up on high" is a specific reference 11942-65 to Margarete becomes clear from the Younger Angels' immediate revelation that the roses which contributed so much to Mephistopheles' final defeat and humiliation came from the fair hands of "Penitents whose love is saintly"—the only non-recapitulatory detail of the first angelic sub-chorus. That Faust's translation to heavenly choirs is only a symbolic-secular apotheosis—the non-tragic counterpart of Margarete's last moments—is next made clear by the More Perfect Angels, who express his full awareness of the all-too-human weaknesses that would long exclude him, though not perhaps eternally, from any strictly Catholic heaven. "It somewhat stirs our ire / This earth to carry, / For were it cleansed by fire, / 'Twould still be sorry." If their pharisaical tone is a nice reminder of Faust's unshakable anti-transcendentalism, even more so is their insistence that only the active intervention of God—"Eternal Love only"—

could separate a vigorous human spirit from the elements that it has tenaciously attached to itself. And if Faust's body and soul are still one, constitute a "Union of two natures / Still joined as one only," he is clinging tenaciously to that contradictory finiteness which is human identity—hence the echo of his Easter Walk observation, then the expression of helpless frustration, "Two souls, alas, do dwell within my breast . . ."

11966–88   Still another echo from Outside the City Gates, this time of Faust's paean to spring, follows as the Younger Angels propose that Faust be placed "for a start— / And continuing betterment—" in the company of the Blessed Boys, who are now individual cloudlets basking "in the new spring" of new life in a new world. The prospect of constant achievement of something more and more like perfection which Faust here suggests is, for the purely human plane of being, a counterpart of the progression from lower to higher forms of life that Homunculus was promised if he wed the sea, and it is therefore with the reintroduction of the supreme symbol of man's innate power of metamorphosis, of growth and development, that the Blessed Boys take custody of Faust's body. "Gladly we welcome / This chrysalid entity, / Pledge that we'll come / To have angels' identity. / Break the cocoon that / Covers his person! / His is already the beauty and greatness / Of life itself sacred." In the Hermes chorus of Shaded Grove the chrysalis symbolized man's divinely natural impulse to achieve freedom and autonomy and so live fully even at the necessary price of self-destruction so quickly paid by Euphorion, Hermes' mortal counterpart. In Faust's vision of an afterlife, therefore, his very imperfection, the fact he has lived a full life, endows him with attributes that beings who can hardly be said to have lived at all must perforce acknowledge as highest values, and the divine worth of mortal man remains for him inextricably one with man's inevitable shortcomings and weaknesses.

11989–12012   Faust's thoughts now turn from himself to Margarete, imagined as one of a constellation of women the central star of which is the resplendent Queen of Heaven herself. These figures are neo-Catholic counterparts of Galatea and her attendants, to whose fleeting passage this ascension of Virgo as described by the Doctor Marianus closely corresponds. As Galatea was the classical symbol of the mystery of divinely human perfection—"Earnest, and of godlike air, / Deservedly immortal, yes, / But like mortal women fair / In her tempting gracefulness"—so is the "Highest Mistress of the World" the symbol of that cosmic mystery which is man's power of selfless, "sacred love" and which the Doctor Marianus begs may be visibly revealed to

him "in the blueness / Of heaven's outstretched panoply." Yet
Faust's Mater Gloriosa also shares attributes of Margarete and
Helen; like the former she is "pure in the best sense," like both she
is to be revered in her motherhood, and like the latter she is "coequal
of the gods" (Faust's exact words to Chiron) and, as in Faust's
Helen, an "elected queen." For if this Virgin Mother is endowed with
divinity, it is because she is endowed with finest human qualities;
and if she can also inspire courage and assuage passion, it is because
she embodies values and insights the necessary corollary of which is
the responsibility to act upon them.

Even before the Mater Gloriosa has appeared the Doctor 12013-31
Marianus directs his attention to the penitent women kneeling
before her—that they are first seen as "delicate clouds" is again a
reminder of the wisp of cloud that in High Mountains represented
"Aurora's love"—and declares,

You have never been traduced,
Yet yours is the privilege here
That those easily seduced
Trustingly to you draw near.

Hard indeed it is to save
Those by weakness jaded,
Yet how can desire's slave
Burst his bonds unaided?
Feet will slip when slopes are smooth,
Girls forget what matters,
When they see a friendly look,
Hear a speech that flatters!

These rather worldly observations from one who but a moment
earlier was transported by a vision of heavenly perfection are the
explanation of why Faust the intransigent anti-transcendentalist
allows himself the use of Catholic symbolism. For mariolatry is here
simultaneously awareness of an ideal of perfection and acknowledgment that such perfection is beyond mortal strength, is a special form
of Faust's more general insight that error and aspiration are
necessarily inseparable, while the belief that divine forgiveness of sin
is always possible represents a special form of his realization in
Pleasant Landscape that no man can be said to live so long as he
remains paralyzed by a sense of guilt hopelessly unatonable.

When the Mater Gloriosa floats into view with the Chorus of 12032-68
Penitent Women, three of these join in a prayer asking her forgiveness
for one of their number. Each is a prototype of Margarete, and as

each recalls the good works that have gained her grace, some important aspect of Margarete's life or character is in turn recalled. Mary Magdalene's willing humility is thus a reminder of the humble services Margarete gladly performed for her infant sister; the Samaritan Woman's allusions to Jacob's well recall both the idyllic and patriarchal motifs which Faust chose to associate with her way of life, and the moment of her first clear consciousness of guilt (the scene At the Well); while Mary of Egypt's exclusion from church and her repentant flight to the wilderness are reminders of the ostracism which finally drove Margarete to flee her home with her newborn child and of her awareness that she could not live a life of exile. If the three Penitents insist that Margarete "Knew not that she might be sinning," this is less a statement of fact than an expression of Faust's awareness that the greater guilt by far was always his. And if they describe her as one "Who but once forgot herself," it is because Faust recognizes in purgatorial atonement, in penance achieved after death, a valid symbol of the truth that no single error, whatever it may be, can seriously diminish the worth of a good human being.

12069–75   That Faust does not regard the three Penitents' intercession as anything but an expression of his profound sense of Margarete's fundamental goodness becomes clearer when she herself now adds her prayer to theirs. For although it echoes her outpouring of grief to the Mater Dolorosa of the scene By the Ramparts, there is not the least evidence of contrition in her declaration that she wants divine pardon as a sign of approval of the happiness which Faust's return already affords her. Margarete is thus a symbol here of joyous and selfless devotion, of love so great that it is worthy of transcending death, rather than the individual who once embodied these virtues, and so the tragic form which her life finally assumed can at last be forgotten as she becomes simply a special manifestation of God-Love, that force awareness of whose existence may in some measure compensate men for life's tragic failures and life's destruction. Indeed, implicit in any concept of tragedy is the subjective feeling that no failure may be complete, that there is always some triumph of the spirit, and this Faust here projects as Margarete's sense of happiness.

12076–95   The concrete symbol of human worth is still man developing and growing, however, and this man is Faust, who is now brought to the foreground as the Blessed Boys, joining the Mater Gloriosa and her penitents, announce that he still grows apace and can, as one who has lived and learned, become their valuable teacher. For even this heaven would be only a meaningless utopian dream if its creatures could not in some way acquire knowledge of actual finite existence. Aware that he has himself learned much from the example of Margarete's selfless love and basic integrity of character, Faust now lets her beg permission to instruct him in this new and brighter world. The feeling of rejuvenation he enjoys—his reappearance as the young man who lived the first great stage of his symbolic journey through life under the star of Margarete—is both a reminder of earliest happiness and an expression of the view, which he came to share with the Player of Prelude on the Stage, that true youthfulness is to be ever young in spirit. But his feeling of release "from every earthly fetter" is, like his sense of being blinded by overwhelming radiance, also the warning that death and final release are now imminent. The text of his last dream-play becomes suddenly laconic as the Mater Gloriosa answers Margarete's prayer by completing its third quatrain: "Arise and come to spheres celestial! / If he divines you're there, he'll follow too."

When profane love has thus been unconditionally recognized as 12096-111 the supreme finite symbol of God-Love, the Queen of Heaven and her attendants rise out of sight. Faust's dream ascension, the counterpart of Margarete's earthly apotheosis, is completed as the Doctor Marianus falls prostrate in prayer and calls upon all whose hearts are softened by repentance—"Alle reuig Zarten"—to avail themselves gratefully of the power of metamorphosis that enables men to realize their innate compulsion to follow what they are obscurely aware is their proper course.

Let each better impulse be
Ready for thy service;
Maiden, Mother, Goddess, Queen,
Keep thy mercy for us!

And so, as the several persons of Margarete-Galatea-Helen are now subsumed in the one person of Mary Mother of God, all the voices that have been heard during the scene join, as once did those of the Triumph of Galatea, in a final chorus proclaiming the ultimate mystery.

Things without permanence
Are symbols only;
What man can not achieve
Here is seen acted;
What's indescribable
Here may be fact;

For womanhood's essence
Serves as our guide.

In the higher worlds of myth and of poetry, and there only, can the idea of perfection implicit in man's awareness of the finite and transitory find nearly adequate expression, and there only can Dedication's things that have ceased to be become "realities" and visible event (*Ereignis*). Not God the Father, God the Son, or God the Holy Ghost, but a human-divine embodiment of "Das Ewig-Weibliche" is, even in the moment of mystic feelings which is Faust's final relinquishment of identity, the supreme and most comprehensive symbol of all those things which men regard as evidence that life is neither Mephistopheles' "void eternal" nor the romantic's vague aspiring, but is, rather, directed striving with meaning certainly intuitable if not certainly knowable. Love as physical and spiritual escape from self, as passively confident faith and actively heroic devotion, as the never entirely unselfish impulse to realize great visions and as disinterested kindness and mercy—this is "Das Ewig-Weibliche," the ideal of eternity and perfection mystically embodied by the frailty which proverbially is woman.

Mountain Gorges, the epilogue on earth which so unqualified an affirmation of secular experience as *Faust* almost demanded, has ended with all the tragedy's highest moments once more recalled. For all its surface diversity, *Faust* has proved to be always concerned with central aspects of human experience and has, in the course of its often seemingly associative unfolding, demonstrated that in art, as in the love affair which the Player of Prelude on the Stage offered as a symbol of the poet's right and duty to use life and life's chance associations as the model of what he creates, unity may be one with most multifarious complexity. If the vision of life offered in *Faust* has been complex, it still remains an imperfect symbol of life's fullness—"Alles Vergängliche / Ist nur ein Gleichnis," or, as Faust declared in Forest and Cave, "That nothing perfect ever can be man's, / That now I feel." But since life itself is compounded of evident causes and apparent chance, of elements more and less meaningful, the very imperfection of *Faust* makes it a faithful symbol of that totality of experience which is each individual's human lot—"Das Unzulängliche, / Hier wird's Ereignis"—and it may be rightly claimed that all its scenes and even its most peripheral elements have contributed to making more nearly perfect the poet's naturalistic vision of transcendence never to be known apart from immanence. The very ambivalence of the symbols of Mountain

Gorges is thus a last insistence that neither religion nor art, Goethe's "secular gospel," can unambiguously express the essence of life, and so the very process by which Catholic symbols are made catholic, in the sense of universal, to describe the Indescribable contributes fully as much to the leaving of a final impression of incommensurability on all planes of experience as does the direct poetic statement of Faust's dying visions.

The original premises of *Faust*, the inseparability of art and life, of good and evil, of the human and the divine, of the physical and the spiritual—these ambivalences have been poetically stated as the Tragedy of Faust the representative man whose final translation to a "new" sphere has left him still finite, real, imperfect, moving unnamed but with consciousness of his finite identity into the unknown of God Unknowable. If Margarete could be granted an apotheosis, it was ultimately a sentimental and hence secular one representing an instance of pathetic fallacy justifiable artistically by its function as the climax of Faust's experience of sentimental irresponsibility. Faust himself, however, can be granted no apotheosis; for if he were merged with God Unknowable, he would cease to be Faust and man, would lose the power of growth and metamorphosis without which there could be no knowledge of God-Love and God-Life.

Since *Faust* is a self-contained poetic statement, it may, I think, be properly doubted whether its complex totality can be further illuminated by any recapitulation beyond that which Goethe himself provided in its final scenes. Individual readers will undoubtedly recall other elements of the text which seem to them no less important than those Goethe chose to emphasize in his recapitulations, but when the complexity of the work of art rivals that of life itself it is inevitable that the relative importance of its constituent parts will vary even for the same reader according to the circumstances of his contact with it. This is, indeed, surely the most important reason why *Faust* has suffered such completely contradictory interpretations, and often even self-contradictory ones, for the structural complexity which contributes so greatly to its effective mirroring of life's totality also prevents the function of some of its parts, and even the literal meaning of what it says at certain points, from being transparently obvious and immediately understandable. In consequence, for instance, critics who know perfectly well that Faust's classical Walpurgis Night is a phantasmagoria easily forget its dramatic premise and unconsciously begin to treat Helen or Phorkyas or

Euphorion as autonomous *dramatis personae*, with the result that the most important scenes of *Faust* imperceptibly cease to be parts of the Tragedy of Faust and become simply masque-like passages of allegorical-didactic poetry interspersed with disparate dramatic and lyric moments. Or, to offer one more example, the first episode of the Lemures, which helps to prepare symbolically for the quickness with which Faust's death follows upon his renunciation of magic, is often read as evidence that Faust's brave new world was created, not by ruthless exploitation of human labor, but by the use of supernatural creatures—an inevitable misunderstanding if the stage direction "Mephistopheles, preceding in the role of overseer," is taken to mean that one who a few minutes earlier was clearly Faust's first executive officer should suddenly be the head of a gang of manual laborers.[2] It is to obviate such confusion, which is actually legion, that this interpretative reading of *Faust* has been written. Much meaning can be read into *Faust*, and there is unquestionably far more meaning to it than I have been able to indicate, but I am convinced that satisfactory and satisfying insights into what it "means" are most likely to be the corollary of an understanding of what it actually says and of a recognition that it sustains its dramatic form uninterruptedly from beginning to end.

For *Faust* is, as its full title insists, basically a tragedy. Heroic tragedy in the great tradition of Aeschylus, Sophocles, Euripides, Shakespeare, and Calderón, the drama of man destroyed by the larger force than himself which is life and yet enjoying triumph in inevitable defeat, *Faust* is perhaps the last great poem of its kind in the world's literature to satisfy the Aristotelian demand that tragedy inspire not only pity but also fear and admiration (awe). That it should have been conceived when it was, is even more extraordinary than the grand but not unique scale of its execution, inasmuch as

[2] The next misreading then follows automatically: although the Lemures specifically state, "We see that pointed poles *are here* / And chains to measure sections, / *But why you summoned us*, we fear, / *Has slipped our recollections*" (italics mine), it will be assumed that "Nominally they are workmen ordered out to dig a trench in furtherance of Faust's plans" (Calvin Thomas) or even said—by R-M. S. Heffner, Helmut Rehder, and W. F. Twaddell—"No civil engineer is needed for the job in hand. The Lemurs [*sic*] had come equipped with stakes and chains." If one reads back from this misinterpretation, the Lemures' lines, "We . . . think we've comprehended: / There is some country, large withal, / That is for us intended" are explained (again Heffner, Rehder, Twaddell), not as a reference to the destruction of Faust's domain, but as follows. "The Lemurs are not intellectual giants, but they seem to remember having half-heard someone talk about Faust's reclamation project. Possibly Faust himself had once addressed the assembled workmen who were to carry out the project, and these Lemurs would then have been part of Faust's audience." Need I trace this chain reaction further?

Goethe wrote it in an age whose rationalists, under the influence of ethical deism and naturalistic philosophy, had long since degraded tragedy to a form of psychological *drame à thèse* in which tragic guilt was simply willful or, more and more often, unwitting violation of a conventional code of morality; and whose romanticists, under the spell of idealistic philosophies and transcendental impulses, either had no sense of tragic necessity or else envisioned its resolution on some "higher" plane. Like that of Oedipus or Hamlet, Faust's moral and tragic guilt is but the concomitant of finite efforts to live in an imperfect world nobly and heroically; no natural moral law of compensation metes out justice to him, no providence intervenes to reward or punish him. It may be inevitable and necessary that the most harmonious human life know some dissonance and failure, but only when these are magnified by art and represented as counter-balanced by courage and a sense of clear purpose is high tragedy achieved.

Faust, then, represents such an achievement and is in the last analysis the expression of a profoundly tragic view of life. Yet, like all great tragedy, it is at the same time an expression of man's uncrushable feeling that life is always somehow still worth living, and it satisfies in very great measure his need to believe that helpless pessimism is not the final answer to the riddle of existence—hence the high esteem in which it has been held by readers of many different kinds. The elegiac tones of Dedication; the terrible despair of Faust in the first scenes of the Tragedy; his deliberate seduction of Margarete and the suffering it leads to; the many pictures of human stupidity, folly, selfishness, self-deception, and self-degradation; the political and social corruption represented by the Emperor's court; the traits of sadistic cruelty to which Faust gives vent in Before Menelaus' Palace; the only partially concealed horrors of the war by which Faust restores a worthless prince to his throne; the ruthless-ness with which he creates his new dominion and destroys the idyllic world of his neighbors; and, above all, Mephistopheles' iterated expressions of cynical pessimism—all these things and many more make very plain that Goethe had few illusions about how difficult it is for man to attain to anything approximating a good life. And although, again and again in *Faust*, life's dissonances are momentarily resolved with the aid of satire and humor—at greatest length in the high comedy of Classical Walpurgisnight—the ultimate resolution is always on the plane of tragic irony, however strongly tinged this may be, as in the Euphorion episode or in Mountain Gorges, with comic pathos.

19—G.F.

The dignity of man, to which Margarete, the neomythological mystery of Homunculus, Helen, Euphorion, Philemon and Baucis, Faust himself, and the three thousand years of Western civilization recalled by *Faust* all bear witness, is thus no expression of mere optimism, and Goethe's well-considered naturalistic humanism is far removed from that blind arrogance which inspired Swinburne to proclaim, "Glory to man in the highest, / For man is the measure of things." As Faust is no paragon of virtue, so is *Faust*, however extraordinary it may be as a poetic achievement, the imperfect work of an imperfect man well aware of these facts. But for all his profound insight into human frailty, and because he understood men as only the greatest poets of all time have been able to understand them, Goethe still felt compelled to testify with *Faust* that he recognized in man's imperfect striving for natural truths a universally shared pattern of religious experience. And as long as it can be felt that the value attached to aspiration in *Faust* is rightly a positive one, so long also must *Faust* remain one of the greatest secular poetic statements of how man searches for the meaning of life and of God.

But *Faust* is not a great drama because it expresses Goethean wisdom, a view of life which many men have shared before and since Goethe's time. It is great because it communicates a poet's highly complex vision with an exemplary effectiveness, with an artistic economy unrivaled by any other tragedy or tragic cycle of comparable scope. For all its poetic prodigality, the multiplicity of subordinate dramatic actions and the broad variety of motifs demanded by its theme of symbolic totality, the clarity of the large design of *Faust* is effectively insured by the familiarity of the Faust legend, itself but a special form of the universal myth of the magus, from which all the salient features of its plot ultimately derive. The almost systematic exploitation of already established literary forms permits an economy of dramatic statement, occasionally bordering upon the elliptical, which neither purely naturalistic nor purely experimental writing can ever achieve. Yet artistic convention never becomes a substitute for poetic statement; every symbol is defined within the text itself, and all but the most familiar of the classical and historical allusions in which it abounds are, like the literary devices to which symbolic significance is attached, given their value by the contexts in which they stand. Although every theatrical device, from those of the most primitive to those of the most sophisticated stage, that can externalize dramatic action seems to be exploited at some point in *Faust*, careful attention to psychological verisimilitude in the delineation of all important characters endows the tragedy as a whole with biographical concreteness, with human interest in the best sense of that often misused phrase.

The first great work of Western literature since Shakespearean tragedy to speak not, like French classical tragedy or the eighteenth century's bourgeois genres, for one social class; to speak not, like the morality play or its more sophisticated counterparts, the *drame à thèse* and "philosophical" tragedy, for one religious or philosophic system—*Faust* is a dramatic action set forth, despite the theatrical machinery for which its text gives full license, almost exclusively through the spoken word, so that with a few sound effects actors in any costume can, on a bare stage, project the many settings which it seems to demand. Long though it be as a drama, *Faust* is a remarkably close-knit text which, thanks to a structural economy made possible as much by the full exploitation of parallelistic variation as by the artistic shorthand of continuous use of standard literary conventions, communicates a highly complex poetic vision without ever giving the effect of skeletal bareness. As André Gide wrote of *Faust* in his journal under the date June 26, 1940, "Everything in it is saturated with life. Thought is never presented in it in an abstract form, just as sentiment is never separated from thought, so that what is most individual is still heavy with meaning and, so to speak, exemplary." With its symbols and motifs, its themes and its characters, its forms and its actions, all reciprocally strengthening their separate contributions to the total poetic statement, *Faust* must communicate to him who temporarily suspends disbelief that unique aesthetic experience which only the greatest works of the world's literature have the power to convey.

FINIS

A Note on Texts

The standard text of *Faust* is that printed in volumes 14 and 15 (1st series) of *Goethes Werke: Herausgegeben im Auftrage der Großherzogin Sophie von Sachsen*, Weimar, 1887 and 1888. All line references in *Goethe's Faust: A Literary Analysis* correspond to the numbering of lines in this edition; the spelling, but not the punctuation, of quotations has ordinarily been modernized. Two of the best German editions of *Faust* are those of Ernst Beutler (Goethe, *Die Faustdichtungen*, Zürich, Artemis-Verlag [1950]) and Erich Trunz (Goethe, *Faust*, Hamburg, C. Wegener [1949]). R-M. S. Heffner and others have compiled *Goethe's Faust: A Complete German-English Vocabulary* (Boston, D. C. Heath and Company [1950]). There are complete English translations in the original meters by Bayard Taylor—standard, but at times inaccurate—and W. H. Van der Smissen, and in not too dissimilar verse by G. M. Priest. An unusually fine translation, although its omission of about one-third of the text gives a hopelessly distorted impression of Goethe's drama, is that by Louis MacNeice. Among noteworthy translations of the First Part only are those of Carlyle F. MacIntyre, Alice Raphael, John Shawcross, and Philip Wayne. An American school edition of the German text, prepared by Helmut Rehder and others, has been published by D. C. Heath and Company; it partially replaces this firm's earlier edition, which was prepared at the end of the nineteenth century by Calvin Thomas.

INDEX

Index

References to scenes and scenic divisions are italicized; in parentheses after them are their German equivalents, followed in italics by Bayard Taylor's translation of these and by the scene number—for *Faust II*, act and scene number—in his translation. When the German names of figures in *Faust* differ from their English equivalents, they follow in parentheses. A reference to the Preface is indicated by "p."; one followed by "n" indicates a footnote on the given page; one followed by "(n)" is a simultaneous reference to text and footnote. When appropriate, italicized page numbers are used to distinguish connected discussions of scenes and mentions of on-stage figures from other references.